Discard

STONE OF KINGS

STONE
OF
KINGS

In Search of the Lost Jade of the Maya

Gerard Helferich

LYONS PRESS
Guilford, Connecticut
An imprint of Globe Pequot Press

Lyons Press is an imprint of Globe Pequot Press.

Text design: Sheryl Kober
Layout: Justin Marciano
Project editor: Ellen Urban
Maps: Trailhead Graphics Inc. © Morris Book Publishing, LLC

Library of Congress Cataloging-in-Publication Data

Helferich, Gerard.
  Stone of kings : in search of the lost jade of the Maya / Gerard Helferich.
    p. cm.
  Includes bibliographical references and index.
  ISBN 978-0-7627-6351-1
  1. Mayas—Implements. 2. Mayas—Jewelry. 3. Mayas—Antiquities. 4. Jade implements—Central America. 5. Jade jewelry—Central America. 6. Jade art objects—Central America. 7. Central America—Antiquities. I. Title.
  F1435.3.I46H45 2012
  972.81—dc23
                                                                                2011035824

Printed in the United States of America
10 9 8 7 6 5 4 3 2 1

To Florence Hood Nicholas,
who has lived a quiet life
of great adventure

CONTENTS

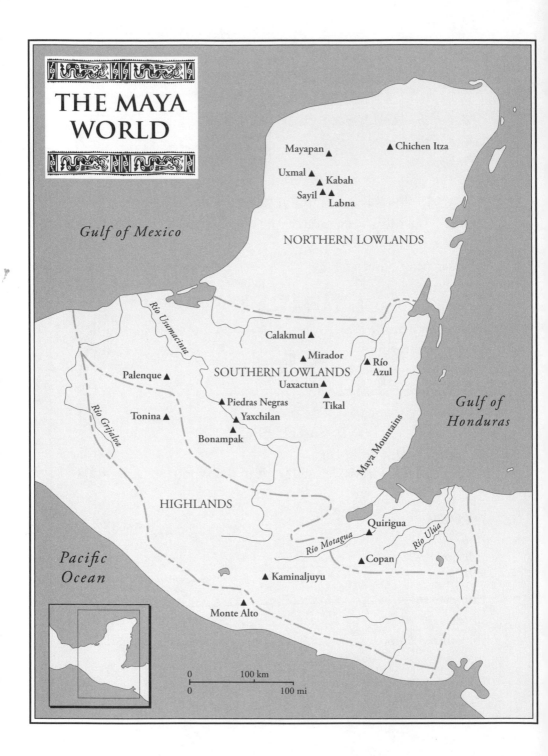

THE MAYA WORLD

Mayapan ▲   ▲ Chichen Itza

Uxmal ▲ ▲ Kabah
Sayil ▲▲
      Labna

Gulf of Mexico   NORTHERN LOWLANDS

Río Usumacinta

Calakmul ▲

▲ Mirador
SOUTHERN LOWLANDS   ▲ Río
Palenque ▲   Azul
Uaxactun ▲
Río Grijalva   ▲ Piedras Negras   ▲
Tonina ▲   ▲ Yaxchilan   Tikal
         Bonampak   *Gulf of
                          Honduras*

HIGHLANDS

Maya Mountains

Quirigua ▲
Río Motagua   *Río Ulúa*
▲ Copan

*Pacific
Ocean*   ▲ Kaminaljuyu

▲
Monte Alto

0   100 km
0   100 mi

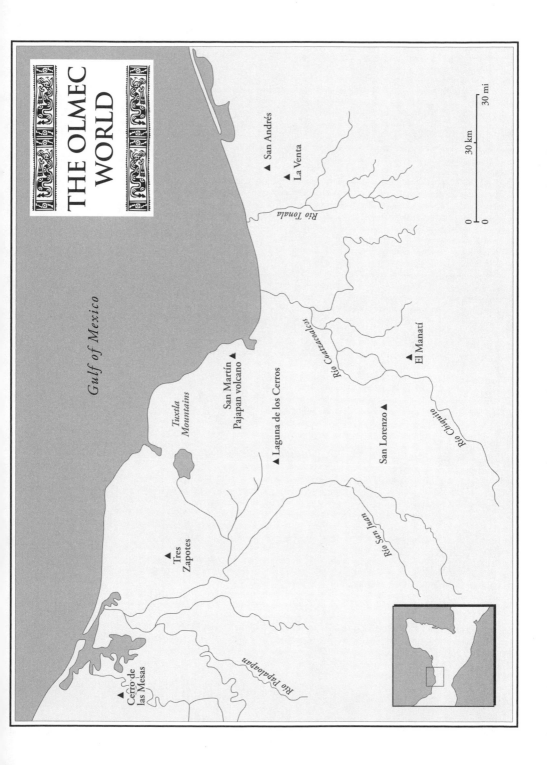

THE OLMEC
WORLD

Gulf of Mexico

Tuxtla
Mountains

San Martín
Pajapan volcano

▲ Laguna de los Cerros

San Lorenzo ▲

El Manatí ▲

Río Coatzacoalcos

Río Chiquito

Río San Juan

Tres
Zapotes

Cerro de
las Mesas

Río Papaloapan

San Andrés ▲

▲ La Venta

Río Tonalá

0   30 km

0   30 mi

PROLOGUE

I t's a warm April evening on the cusp of the rainy season. We're
seated under the long, tiled colonnade of a centuries-old house
in Antigua, in the highlands of Guatemala. My wife, Teresa, and
I have come to do some research for a travel publisher. But as the
shadows deepen and the volcanoes disappear into the darkness,
our hostess begins to spin a remarkable tale.

A tall, blonde *gringa* of a certain age, she is the sister of a friend
back in our adopted home of San Miguel de Allende, Mexico. But
you might say we were introduced by Alexander von Humboldt.
A few years ago, our hostess's husband read my *Humboldt's Cosmos*,
an account of the great German naturalist's New World odyssey.
As I relate in the book, Humboldt was born into an aristocratic
Prussian family during the Second Great Age of Discovery,
when titanic figures such as James Cook and Louis-Antoine de
Bougainville were completing their historic circumnavigations of
the earth. Though the young Alexander longed to make a grand
journey of his own, his mother pressed him into a more sensible
career as a government inspector of mines. But on coming into
his fortune after his mother's death, Humboldt persuaded King
Carlos IV to entrust him—not yet thirty, a foreigner, and a
Protestant—with the first extensive scientific exploration of Spain's
New World empire. And during five astonishing years, from 1799
to 1804, Humboldt, with his companion Aimé Bonpland, blazed
a hazardous, six-thousand-mile swath through Latin America,
from Cuba to Peru, from the Andes to the Amazon, opening the
continent to science and transforming himself into one of the
most celebrated figures of his age.

For reasons I don't fully appreciate at the time, our hostess's husband has been moved by Humboldt's story, and he has invited me to drop by if I'm ever in Antigua. When Teresa and I arrive, he's too ill to see us, but his wife graciously invites us for a drink. I expect a simple social call; then she begins her story. A story of jade. Like most people, I've never thought much about the stone— where it comes from, why it's important or interesting, even what it is. But as her voice echoes down the darkening colonnade, I feel the mounting exhilaration of a writer encountering his subject.

When I return from Antigua, I begin reading about jade and pestering archaeologists and geologists, learning everything I can about its formation, its lore, its ties to the great cultures of the past. I also discover a connection I hadn't expected. In *Humboldt's Cosmos*, I wrote about his admiration for America's native peoples

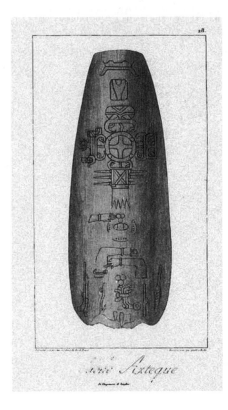

The enigmatic Humboldt Celt, as it appeared in Humboldt's Researches Concerning the Institutions and Monuments of the Ancient Inhabitants of America with Descriptions and Views of Some of the Most Striking Scenes in the Cordilleras.

and his pioneering studies of cultures such as the Aztec and the Inca. Among the tens of thousands of specimens Humboldt brought back at the end of his journey were some pre-Columbian figurines, one of which was reproduced in my book.

But this time, my thoughts turn to another of Humboldt's souvenirs. It's a celt, a polished stone shaped vaguely like the head of an axe, which was presented to the explorer by Andrés Manuel del Río, professor of mineralogy at Mexico City's national school of mining. Bluish in color, about nine inches long and a little better than three inches wide, the celt had lost its pointed end. The rest was incised with a dozen rebus-like symbols. Though a few were recognizable—a pair of crossed arms, a hand, an ornate cross, perhaps an oar and a spear thrower—their significance was long forgotten. As Humboldt realized, the celt was carved from jade.

Back in Europe, Humboldt presented the artifact, which he believed to be an Aztec hatchet, to his sovereign, Frederick Wilhelm III of Prussia, for display in the royal cabinet of curiosities, a collection of natural history and anthropological specimens. For the next century and a half, the Humboldt Celt, as it came to be known, remained in Berlin. Though the stone's message was inscribed in no known language, that didn't stop a scholar named Philipp J. J. Valentini from venturing an impressively detailed translation in 1881:

> *The man, in whose tomb the sacred stone was laid, stood high in rank and personal achievements. He never failed to appear before his gods to burn the incense on the temple's brazier. He caused his arms to bleed and sacrificed his blood by sprinkling it in the glowing embers. When he entered the* tlachco *court, his was the victory. Like darts, his balls of* hule *were flying through the ring. He had no equal in bringing to the ground his foe by* tlacoctli, *and when he seized the oar and went upon the river, he was certain to bring home the sweet turtle quivering on the barb of his harpoon. Great*

was the strength of his arms; the heavy cudgel was the toy of his
youth. There was no deer so distant nor its legs so fleet, that his eyes
could not spy or his lasso reach.

Eventually, the celt ended up in the national ethnographic museum on Stresemannstrasse. When that building was destroyed during the Second World War, the Humboldt Celt—shattered, looted, or perhaps buried in the rubble—was lost.

As I immerse myself in my new subject, the errant celt takes on a meaning for me as well, more vague but perhaps no less idiosyncratic than that suggested by Philipp Valentini: With its strange carvings and unexplained disappearance, it seems to embody the enigma of jade.

To peoples such as the Maya, jade was not only heartbreakingly beautiful but supremely powerful, and no substance was more eagerly acquired or more jealously guarded. Yet when Alexander von Humboldt arrived in Latin America, a millennium after the Maya decline and three centuries after the Spanish Conquest, no one knew where the ancients had found their jade. Humboldt searched for the source, to no avail. "Notwithstanding our long and frequent excursions in the Cordillera of both Americas," he wrote, "we were never able to discover a rock of jade; and this rock being so scarce, the more we were surprised at the immense quantity of jade hatchets, which are found on digging in plains formerly inhabited, from the Ohio to the mountains of Chile." Humboldt exaggerated the range of jade artifacts, but by the time his keepsake went missing, the mystery of the stone's origin still hadn't been solved. Like the Humboldt Celt, the Maya's jade mines had vanished.

The story that our hostess shares this evening in Antigua is of the long search for Maya jade. Part history, part science, part treasure hunt, the tale spans more than three thousand years, embracing great kings, lost civilizations, renowned archaeologists, unlettered prospectors, and hopeful entrepreneurs. It's a tale of mystery and obsession, and I can't escape its peculiar pull. Like all the others, I'm drawn into the quest for Maya jade.

PART I
THE BONEDIGGERS

ONE

"The Most Romantic of All Gems"

Yucatan, 1909. The middle-aged man was sweating inside his canvas diving suit. Peering through the helmet's tiny faceplate, he saw the tropical foliage spilling over the limestone walls of the cenote. At the other end of the pontoon, the Indian crew was working the pumps, and he felt the rhythmic puffs of oily air wafting into his helmet. He could only hope that Nicolas had trained the men well. Lumbering to the ladder, he carefully adjusted his speaking tube, lifeline, and air hose, their corked-bottle floats tied at intervals like so many crystal beads. Then, one by one, the workers approached, peered up into his clear blue eyes, and offered a solemn handshake, as though expecting never to see him again.

Chichen Itza's Sacred Well was dark and "still as an obsidian mirror." The diver released his grip on the ladder and felt cool water envelop him. Weighted down by the copper helmet, the lead bars across his chest, the iron-soled boots, he began to drop. There was a searing pain in his ears, and he reached for the valve on either side of his helmet. A hiss, and the pressure subsided. Drifting through the murk, he imagined himself as weightless as one of the silvery bubbles arcing to the surface.

Within the first ten feet, the scant sunlight faded from yellow to green to nearly black. He took out his submarine flashlight.

Edward H. Thompson in his diving gear at Chichen Itza, with his workers poised at the air pump. On his first dive into the cenote, Thompson wrote, "I felt a strange thrill when I realized that I was the only living being who had ever reached this place alive and expected to leave it again still living."

There were thirty feet of water in the Sacred Well, and beneath that an unfathomable layer of muck, masking the secrets of centuries. Not far from the cenote's sheer wall, the dredge had opened an underwater pit eighteen feet deep, its flanks studded with stone columns and blocks. As he floated past, one of the stones toppled into the darkness, loosing a shock wave that sent him tumbling; struggling to right himself, he felt as tremulous as an egg white in a glass of water. Then a strange thrill came over him when he realized that he was the only creature who had ever come here with any expectation of leaving alive.

The local people said that huge snakes and horrific monsters prowled the depths of the Sacred Well, guarding the entrance to Xibalba, the underworld that Maya kings and shamans sought to penetrate in their ecstatic trances. In 1904, when the workers were beginning to dredge, a wise man from the village had pointed to a spot beneath the water and told him, "There is where the palace of the rain god lies." Now, bounding across the mud in that direction, the diver found a deep natural depression. Through the gloom he made out a whitish smudge on the hollow's edge. Then as he drew closer, he saw that it was a collection of bones—not of jaguars or deer, but of human beings—three women, stretched out in the silt as though dozing in their hammocks. The cool, dark water had preserved fragments of their plain-woven cotton dresses, and around the neck of one were draped exquisite pendants of carved jade, their facets as crisp and lustrous as the day they were cast into the Sacred Well.

Edward Herbert Thompson had been obsessed with the ruined city of Chichen Itza for decades, ever since reading Diego de Landa's *Relación de las cosas de Yucatán* in his college days. Written around 1566 but rediscovered in a Madrid library only in 1862, the *Relación* was a veritable catalog of Maya language and culture, including their intricate, interlocking calendars. But Thompson had been especially captivated by Landa's description of Chichen Itza's Sacred Cenote and the grisly rites that supposedly had taken place there. "Into this Well," Landa had written, "they had, and still have, the custom of throwing men alive as a sacrifice to their gods in time of drought, and they believed they would not die, though they never saw them again. They also threw into it many other things like precious stones and things they prized, and so if this country had possessed gold it would be this Well that would have the greater part, so great is the devotion that the Indians show for it." It was said that sometimes during these rites, the cenote's water turned from jade green to blood red.

When it came to the religious customs of the Maya, Landa may not have been the most reliable of witnesses. Even before his promotion to bishop of the Yucatan, he had conducted a pitiless inquisition that imprisoned and tortured hundreds of people and burned most of the Maya books, or codices. Consisting of bark pages that opened like a folding screen, washed with lime, then painted with a brush, the codices were the repositories of the Maya's historical, religious, and astronomical learning. But to Landa, "they contained nothing but superstition and lies of the devil," and thanks to his implacable piety, only three examples survive, named for the European cities in which they reside—Dresden, Paris, and Madrid. (The authenticity of a fourth, fragmentary codex, the Grolier, has been debated ever since it was supposedly discovered in a cave in Chiapas, Mexico, in 1965.) For good measure, Landa forbade the Maya from writing anything else in their elegant, playful, maddeningly complex script. But he did record the words for the days and "months" of the Maya calendar, and with the help of native speakers, he compiled an exhaustive syllabary pairing each letter of the Spanish alphabet with the corresponding Maya symbol.

But was Landa's account of the rites that took place at the Sacred Well, repeated and embellished by later authors, just a sham to justify his repression—or had human sacrifices really been performed there? In 1579, Diego Sarmiento de Figueroa, mayor of nearby Valladolid, also claimed to have witnessed Maya rituals conducted at the cenote. After sixty days of abstinence and fasting, he reported, the "lords and principal personages of the land" would arrive at the Sacred Well at daybreak, "throwing into it Indian women belonging to each of these lords and personages, at the same time telling these women to ask for their masters a year favorable to his particular needs and desires."

"The women, being thrown in unbound, fell into the water with great force and noise," he went on. "At high noon those that could cried out loudly and ropes were let down to them. After the women came up, half dead, fires were built around them and copal incense was burned before them. When they recovered their senses, they said that below were many people of their nation, men and women, and that they received them . . . and when their heads were inclined downward beneath the water they seemed to see many deeps and hollows, and they, the people, responded to their queries concerning the good or bad year that was in store for their masters."

For three decades, Thompson had dreamed of exploring the Sacred Cenote and testing these rumors of human sacrifice. Like other archaeologists of his time, he had no formal training in the science. His technique was spotty, and he was often guided by intuition more than evidence. But even as a boy in Worcester, Massachusetts, he'd been captivated by the past, digging up arrowheads and other relics and donating them to the natural history society. He'd devoured John Lloyd Stephens's bestselling accounts of his travels among the Maya ruins, which had only whetted Thompson's fascination with ancient cultures.

When he was an engineering student at Worcester Polytechnic Institute, Thompson began publishing articles, including one called "Atlantis Not a Myth," which appeared in *Popular Science Monthly* in 1879, the year of his graduation. Though he'd never been within two thousand miles of Central America, Thompson confidently wrote that Maya civilization had originated on the fabled lost continent popularized by Plato. Once, he claimed, "an immense peninsula extended itself from Mexico, Central America, and New Grenada, so far into the Atlantic that Madeira, the Azores, and the West India Islands are now fragments of it. This peninsula was a fair and fertile country inhabited by rich and civilized nations, a people versed in the arts of war and civilization, a country covered with large cities and magnificent palaces, their rulers according to tradition reigning not only on the Atlantic Continent, but over islands far and near, even into Europe and Asia."

But this fabulous civilization was doomed by a colossal earthquake, which flooded Atlantis and severed its land bridge to Central America. "The earth rocks horribly, palaces, temples, all crashing down, crushing their human victims, flocked together like so many ants. Vast rents open at their very feet, licking with huge, flaming tongues the terrified people into their yawning mouths. And then the inundations. Mighty waves sweep over the land. The fierce enemies, Fire and Water, join hands to effect the destruction of a mighty nation."

Thompson later confessed his chagrin at the piece's audacity—and in his defense, the theory was only one in a rash of at-least-as-outlandish conjectures that the first American civilizations had been founded by immigrants from Egypt, Africa, Israel, and other unlikely places. But the article made an impression on two influential members of the American Antiquarian Society, Stephen Salisbury III, scion of one of Worcester's wealthiest families, and Charles P. Bowditch, noted Maya scholar and benefactor of Harvard's Peabody Museum. In 1885, when they were recruiting someone to do fieldwork at Maya sites in the Yucatan, the pair, along with U.S. senator George Frisbie Hoar of Massachusetts, invited Thompson to dinner and offered him the job. To help finance the work, Hoar had already persuaded President Grover Cleveland to appoint the twenty-five-year-old "consul-archaeologist" to the Mexican states of Yucatán and Campeche, making him the youngest member of the U.S. consular service.

Thompson spent several months poring over the Maya archives at the American Antiquarian Society and acquainting himself with Spanish and Mayan. Then he boarded a steamship for Mexico, along with his wife, Henrietta, a schoolteacher and the daughter of a whaling captain (a combination that Thompson found "cannot easily be beaten as a wife and mother"), and their two-month-old baby, Alice. Landing at Progreso, on the Yucatan's northern tip, they settled in nearby Mérida, a sleepy city of mockingbirds and church bells, where barefoot women carried their baskets to market wearing white dresses; colorful *rebozos*, big gold earrings; and gold chains around their necks. None of the city's roads was paved, not even the major thoroughfares, and after a rain, residents would pay stout, bare-legged porters to carry them across the sloppy streets.

The Thompsons began to build a bungalow in the city's cooler outskirts. The site was the raised mound of a former Maya temple, and when workers dug the foundation, Thompson made his first archaeological discoveries—ancient potsherds, shells, fragments of obsidian, even beads of jade. Feeling a "white heat" for his work, he began to explore other sites near Mérida—the cave paintings at Loltun; Uxmal, widely considered the zenith of late Maya art and architecture; and the more modest ruins at Sayil, Kabah, and Labna. But time and again, Thompson's imagination returned to the pagan rites supposedly conducted at the Sacred Cenote of Chichen Itza.

It was a blistering April day when Thompson finally saw the ancient city. Climbing a winding path, threading his way past enormous boulders and tall trees, he was reminded of forest trails he had known in New England. Then he realized that the massive blocks he passed were intricately chiseled into columns and pillars. As he began to grasp that the forest floor was actually an ancient terrace, he peered through the trees and glimpsed an ash-colored mass shimmering in the sun. He recognized it from photographs: Chichen Itza's great limestone pyramid, seventy-five feet tall, stepped and square and surmounted by a temple. In the woods beyond, verdant knobs jutted from the canopy—more decrepit temples and palaces waiting to be unearthed. The sense of antiquity was overwhelming.

The city that Thompson admired had been home to a Maya people called the Itza, who most likely migrated inland from the

El Castillo *before restoration, in a photo taken by Désiré Charnay around 1860. "Old and cold," Thompson wrote on seeing Chichen Itza's ruins for the first time, "furrowed by time, and haggard, imposing, and impassive, they rear their rugged masses above the surrounding level and are beyond description."*

Yucatan coast, perhaps around A.D. 800. It was an apocalyptic time, as the great cities that prospered in the full flush of Maya civilization—from about A.D. 250 to 900, the period archaeologists call the Classic—were tottering toward collapse. But their demise created an opportunity for the interlopers, and for the next three centuries—during the so-called Postclassic period—Chichen Itza wielded a masterful combination of conquest and trade to dominate the Yucatan like no other Maya city-state before or after. Expanding to as much as six square miles, with a population of perhaps thirty-five thousand, Chichen Itza grew into the most cosmopolitan Maya city ever built, featuring not only traditional Maya architecture but also a bold foreign style. Some of Chichen Itza's buildings so closely resemble those at Tollan, the capital of the powerful Toltecs in central Mexico, that for decades it was thought that the Toltecs had invaded the city, or at least had come to exert some powerful sway there. Now the similarities are thought more likely a reflection of Chichen Itza's sophisticated, determinedly mercantile outlook.

With its lavish temples and Sacred Cenote, and the largest ball court in Mesoamerica (a geographical and cultural area including Mexico and most of Central America), Chichen Itza also became the hub of a religious cult dedicated to the creator god, the feathered serpent Kukulkan, which had originated in central Mexico, where it was known by its Nahuatl name, Quetzalcoatl. It was in honor of Kukulkan that the Itza built their iconic pyramid, masterfully engineered so that a ribbon of sunlight slithered down the west balustrade of the main stairway on the afternoon of the spring and fall equinoxes, joining with a carved head at the bottom to form a glowing serpent. And on the pyramid's high platform, at the climax of their spectacular public ceremonies, priests would extract the beating hearts of their captives and collect their blood in shallow bowls, to sustain the god and repay him for the gift of life. Then about A.D. 1100, great Chichen Itza faltered, surpassed by its rival Mayapan, sixty miles to the west. Four centuries later, when Europeans arrived, they found only a handful of squatters at Chichen, though the cenote continued to attract pilgrims from hundreds of miles away.

Many other foreigners had passed through Chichen Itza in the centuries before Thompson. In 1531, the conquistador Francisco de Montejo had made it his headquarters, anointing the Pyramid of Kukulkan his "castle," perhaps for its appearance or perhaps to satisfy Spanish law, which mandated the establishment of a fortress with mounted cannon before the province could be considered conquered. The pyramid is still known as *El Castillo,* "the castle," but Montejo never did overcome the Maya's fierce guerilla resistance. In 1535, his army was driven from the Yucatan altogether, and it was left to his son Francisco to conquer the peninsula, which he finally achieved in 1546 after building walled strongholds at Mérida and Campeche. The last independent Maya king, an Itza named Can-Ek, didn't surrender to the Spanish until 1697.

A century and a half later, John Lloyd Stephens ("the father of Maya archaeology") reached Chichen Itza with English architect Frederick Catherwood. Others followed through the rest of the 1800s—Désiré Charnay, who recorded the ruins in moody sepia photos; the eccentric Augustus Le Plongeon, who believed that the roots of Freemasonry would be discovered in Maya culture; and Alfred Maudslay, who documented the site in his seminal, five-volume *Biologia Centrali-Americana*. But before Edward Thompson, no one had tried to plumb the Sacred Well.

⚜

In 1893, eight years after Thompson landed in the Yucatan, the spectacular World's Columbian Exhibition opened in Chicago to mark the five hundredth anniversary of Europeans' arrival in the New World. Determined to present "a perfect exhibition of the past and present peoples of America," the Peabody Museum's Frederick Ward Putnam, overseeing the fair's Department of Ethnology, commissioned Thompson to make full-size papier-mâché casts of portions of the Maya ruins at Labna and Uxmal. For nearly fourteen months, Thompson labored in the Yucatan's malarial wastelands, creating ten thousand square feet of molds—and nearly wrecking his health. As he accompanied his handiwork back to the States, he reported, his "half-conscious fever-racked body" lay in his stateroom, "tenderly cared for by [his] devoted wife."

In Chicago, the molds were filled with an artificial stone called staff, and the resulting "Mayan Village" was erected on the Midway alongside the world's first Ferris wheel, Buffalo Bill's Wild West, a Native American settlement, and a reproduction of a Cairo street populated by 175 Egyptians imported for the occasion. "Everyone who visited the Exposition will recall the weird effect produced on the imagination by these old monuments of an unknown past," said the official report of the Massachusetts Board of Managers, "standing in stately grandeur amidst all the magnificence and beauty that the landscape art and architecture of today could devise."

Allison Vincent Armour, young heir to the meat-packing fortune and a trustee of Chicago's new Field Museum, became a frequent visitor at Chichen Itza, and the year after the exposition, he donated the funds for Thompson to buy Hacienda Chichén, including the archaeological site and a hundred square miles around it; reports of the price range from seventy-five to five hundred dollars.

Thompson planned to raise cattle and timber on the hacienda, using the proceeds to finance his archaeology. But first, the sixteenth-century house, located a quarter-mile's stroll south of El Castillo, needed to be restored after its recent sacking in the great Maya rebellion known as the Caste War. Perhaps the most successful

Reproduction of a structure from the ruins of Uxmal, part of the "Mayan Village" constructed from Edward H. Thompson's molds and erected on the Midway of the 1893 World's Columbian Exposition in Chicago.

indigenous uprising ever launched in the Americas, the revolt had been sparked in 1847, when three Maya insurgents were executed at Valladolid. By the following year, federal forces had been driven from the Yucatan except for the fortresses at Mérida and Campeche, and the Maya had established independent states across the peninsula. When Thompson arrived, the war had been raging for nearly forty years, and though it would officially end in 1901 with the capture of the Maya capital of Chan Santa Cruz, it would be another fourteen years before peace was completely restored.

With his house in ruins, Thompson hung a hammock in the long eastern wing of the ancient palace known as "the Nunnery" for its supposed resemblance to a Spanish convent. An imposing, rambling structure complete with sacrificial altar in front, the Nunnery served as his home for the year that it took to make the hacienda habitable. Thompson's wife, Henrietta, had gone to work as a clerk in the consulate, and though she occasionally visited Chichen Itza, she resided in Mérida, seventy miles to the northwest, where she would give birth to seven more of Thompson's children over the next dozen years.

Even before his house was reconstructed, Thompson began digging. Hacking the growth from a forty-foot-high mound, his workers revealed a four-sided pyramid, its main stairway flanked by serpent heads more than a yard across, with gaping jaws, bared fangs, and protruding tongues. On the pyramid's upper terrace, they uncovered a heavy rectangular stone laid over a deep shaft.

Thompson ordered the men to lower him into the darkness on the end of a rope. At a depth of sixteen feet, he discovered another slab, broken and dislodged. It was the first in a fantastic series of seven graves, stacked one atop the other like dominos and littered with skeletons, clay vessels, copper bells, crystal beads, and some very fine jades, including beads, pendants, and a carved head. Nothing like the tomb had ever been seen in the Americas, and it would have been a remarkable find in itself. But below the seventh grave, some thirty feet from the pyramid's apex, Thompson's trowel again rang on stone.

Brushing away the dust, he discovered a smaller slab, which he pried loose with his hunting knife to reveal a dirt-packed cavity. Working with great difficulty in the cramped space, where the six-foot Thompson often found himself "sprawled out like a lizard," he and the workers excavated another downward-leading corridor scattered with idols, jade and crystal beads, copper bells, and charred human bones. At the end of the passageway, they found yet another great stone and, lying on the ground, a jade fish. As he freed the dirt from the slab, Thompson felt a strong draft, and when he finally pried the stone loose, he found "an opening as black as night from which poured a rush of cold air as chill as the breath of death."

"Don Eduardo," one of the workers told him, "this is surely the mouth of Hell."

"Not so," Thompson answered with characteristic aplomb. "Since when has the mouth of Hell given forth a breath as cold as this wind?"

He attached a lantern to the tip of his metal tape measure and lowered it over the edge. As he played out the tape and watched the dizzying shadows cast by the swinging light, he wondered whether it would ever strike bottom. When the lamp finally came to rest, Thompson read the depth—fifty-two feet. The next day he returned with rope and tackle, and the men winched him into the blackness, a lantern in his hand and a Bowie knife in his teeth. He touched down in a central chamber eighteen by twenty-five feet, with seven short passages radiating outward. On the floor, he spied a magnificent jade bead more than five inches in circumference. To one side of the chamber were fragments of a handsome white marble vase, as well as a jade torso that matched the head they had found earlier. Working by candlelight, Thompson retrieved a hoard of artifacts, including shattered clay vessels; shell beads;

arrowheads of obsidian and flint; tiger's teeth; a pair of pearls; mother-of-pearl plaques; and amulets, beads, and pendants of jade. It was, he decided, "not merely the tomb of a great priest, but the tomb of *the* great priest, the tomb of the great leader, the tomb of the hero god, Kukul Can, he whose symbol was the feathered serpent." He called the place the High Priest's Temple, one of the names by which it is still known (along with "the Ossario," from the Spanish *osario*, "place of bones").

Despite these discoveries, or perhaps goaded on by them, Thompson never shook his obsession with the Sacred Well, which beckoned at the end of a thousand-foot-long limestone causeway. And he never lost his keenness to prove the cenote's part in human sacrifices to the rain god Chaak. But like others before him, he had no idea how to penetrate its depths.

The word *cenote* comes from *dz'onot* in Yucatek Mayan, meaning "well." This was no well in the conventional sense, but a great oval sinkhole 170 feet wide, with sheer walls rising seventy-five feet above the surface of the water. Like all cenotes, it was created after rainwater absorbed carbon dioxide from the air and formed a weak acid. As the acidic water percolated through the ground, it gradually eroded the soft limestone, carving out a water-filled underground cavern, until the surface crust collapsed and the well was exposed. In the northern Yucatan, graced with few lakes or rivers, cenotes were vital sources of water for the ancient inhabitants. Though there are two cenotes at Chichen Itza, only the Sacred Well was said to have been used for religious rituals; most likely, it was the one that had given the city its name, translated as "Mouth of the Well of the Itza People."

When he returned to the States for a scientific conference, Thompson finally seized his opportunity. In Boston, he petitioned the Peabody and the American Antiquarian Society for a dredge, winch, tackle, ropes, steel cables, and a derrick with a thirty-foot swinging boom. He also took diving lessons. Hearing of his plan, his friends objected that no one could descend into the Sacred Well and expect to come out alive. Thompson was fit and blessed with a rugged constitution, but he was over forty years old, after all. If he wanted to commit suicide, they asked, couldn't he find a less spectacular means? But in the end, his patrons agreed to finance the scheme, dredge, diving suit, and all.

Thompson had the apparatus shipped to Progreso, where it was taken by train as far as the village of Dzitas. Since no trucks were available, the equipment had to be carted piecemeal the remaining sixteen miles to Chichen Itza, over the worst excuse for a road. After months of the hardest labor Thompson had ever known, it was all finally stacked beside the Sacred Well. Assembling the machinery was quicker but no less strenuous, and time and again Thompson expected to see the jumble clatter into the cenote or bury him and his men. He would have given years of his life, he swore, for the services of "one or two brawny, profane, and competent Yankee 'riggers.'"

For weeks, Thompson sat at the edge of the Sacred Well, musing and calculating, taking measurements and soundings. Perched on a stone ruin above the cenote's rim, he heaved in logs weighing as much as an "average native," to gauge where sacrificial victims would have landed. Christening this the "fertile zone," he resolved to start work there.

⁂

On March 5, 1904, Thompson began dredging. Standing on the planked platform in his tall rubber boots and broad-brimmed hat, he felt an inexpressible thrill as the steel jaws swung out, hung in space, then plunged into the dark water of the Sacred Well. The workers strained over the winch handles. The cable tautened. Water boiled. Then the bucket broke the surface, and dripping, rose to the cenote's edge. The workers positioned the wooden

*Edward H. Thompson with his dredge. "I doubt if anybody can realize the thrill I felt,
when, with four men at the winch handles and one at the brake, the dredge, with its steel
jaw agape, swung from the platform, hung poised for a brief moment in mid-air over the
dark pit and then, with a long swift glide downward, entered the still, dark waters and
sank smoothly on its quest."*

boom over the platform, and a carload of dark brown matter spewed out—decayed wood, leaves, and mostly, mud.

For days it was the same, the dredge working up and down, up and down, raising "muck and rocks, muck, more muck." Once its teeth gripped an entire tree trunk, which disintegrated on the platform during the next two days, leaving only a ghostly stain. Another time, the dredge raised the commingled bones of a jaguar and a deer. And there were dozens of potsherds. These tantalized Thompson, who wanted to believe them evidence of some ancient ritual, but in the end, he found them unpersuasive: Boys are boys everywhere, he figured, and a boy's instinct is to skip flat objects across smooth water.

While he waited, Thompson pondered the cenote's other legends. The water of the Sacred Well was usually turbid, ranging from jade green to rusty brown. But Thompson also saw the water turn blood red, just as the ancient sources had claimed. The green, he determined, was due to algae, the brown, to decaying leaves. And the sanguinary tint was caused by red flowers and seeds that tumbled into the water during certain seasons, lending the surface the color of dried blood.

One day, Thompson was sitting in the cenote in his scow, writing notes while a repair was made on the dredge. The boat was moored directly beneath the derrick, and when he happened to glance over the gunwale, Thompson had a revelation: Reflected in the water he could see the "many deeps and hollows" reported by the maidens who had survived their plunge into the well. Rather than the contours of a supernatural landscape, the images were simply the reflections of the cavities and striations in the cliff wall. As for the "many people of their nation" that the women had reported seeing, Thompson also glimpsed figures in the water— the reflected forms of his workmen on the bank above. And like the maidens, he heard voices—the murmurs of the laborers drifting down to him. It was, Thompson recalled, "the weirdest part of the weird undertaking. The whole episode gave me an explanation of the old tradition that developed as clearly as the details of a photographic negative."

But when no other artifacts were found, Thompson began to regret exposing his patrons in Massachusetts to such expense and himself to so much ridicule. By day, he became increasingly nervous, by night, sleepless.

One morning, he arose from yet another bout of insomnia. The day was as dark as his thoughts, and tracing the path from his house, past the great pyramid and down the processional causeway leading to the cenote, he plodded toward the staccato clicks of the dredge's brake. Taking his position under the palm-leaf lean-to, he watched the men working the winches. Slowly, the bucket emerged from the water and pivoted over the platform, as it had hundreds of times before. But as he glanced listlessly into the metal jaws, Thompson spied two yellowish, globular masses nestled in the chocolate muck.

Reaching into the bucket, he hefted the objects and saw that they seemed to be made of resin, which he confirmed by pinching off a bit and tasting it. There were some lighted embers nearby, and when he tossed a piece into them, it released a wonderful aroma; he realized he was holding globes of copal incense that had been hurled into the cenote hundreds of years before, during the rituals reported in the legends. It was just as one of the local wise men had said: "In ancient times our fathers burned the sacred resin—*pom*—and by the fragrant smoke their prayers were wafted to their god whose home was in the sun. That night for the first time in weeks, Thompson wrote, he slept "soundly and long."

He decided he would make Chichen Itza his crowning accomplishment. First, he took leave from the consulate (where his duties, as chronicled in the *New York Times*, included bailing out of prison some American fishermen accused of poaching and reporting on the exorbitant price of *chicle,* the raw material in chewing gum). Later, he retired from government service to devote all his time to the ruins. There was hardly a day when something astonishing didn't appear in the bucket of his dredge. Then, after five years, when the machine began raising just mud and sticks and slivers of rock, he started to dive. The cenote was so cold that he could work only two hours a day underwater; surfacing with his lips blue and his body prickled with gooseflesh, he'd gulp hot coffee to revive himself. Meanwhile, ensconced in Mérida, Henrietta didn't learn of her husband's submarine adventure until it was over, some two years later.

In the end, Thompson recovered nearly thirty thousand artifacts from the cenote, a fantastic haul that has been called the single most important archaeological treasure ever recovered in the Americas. There were arrowheads, flint axes, spear throwers, and a spectacular sacrificial knife with a stone blade and a wooden handle carved with entwined serpents. There were terra cotta vessels of every form and size, and earthenware figures of animals and human beings. More pieces of copal, some still mounded in their ceremonial bowls, others sculpted into fantastical creatures, including a snake grasping a man's head in its jaws. And there were incense burners, including one made from the skull of an adolescent boy. Of copper, there were chisels, bowls, and bells, pendants shaped like playful monkeys, and more skulls. Of gold, rings; bowls; cups; and basins, including one twelve inches in diameter; hammered disks, some incised with scenes of battle; realistic masks; a headband of entwined serpents; a round helmet stunning in its simplicity; ornaments in the form of human heads, deer, parrots, monkeys, frogs, turtles, crabs; and a finely wrought necklace of alternating beads and links. Dozens of skeletons of both sexes and all ages were also found, bearing out the legends of human sacrifice.

Then there were the jades. From the green waters of the cenote, Thompson raised plaques intricately worked with images of gods and kings; figurines of men and women, jaguars, and other animals; knives for extracting the living hearts of sacrificial victims; pendants of human heads, some with delicate, lifelike features, others nearly abstract; and ornaments ranging from austere rings to elaborate flower-shaped earplugs, nose rings, and necklaces, as well as hundreds of beads carved in a bewildering variety of shapes—round, flat, tubular, square, swirled. Many of the jades were of a luminous, highly prized color that has become known as Chichen green.

Numbering more than five thousand, they are still the greatest assemblage of carved jades ever recovered. Before being cast into the water, most had been broken to liberate the spirit residing within. But at the Peabody, where Thompson shipped his finds, curators were able to reconstruct many of the pieces, and from stylistic clues it was determined that most were Late Classic works from the Maya's southern range, showing that the cenote was a major destination for pilgrims from about A.D. 800 to 1534. One striking jade head was carved in A.D. 688 and portrayed Yo'nal Ahk II, king of the Maya city-state known as Piedras Negras, some three hundred miles from Chichen Itza. Other pieces were older still, apparently heirlooms that had been cherished for centuries before being offered to the Sacred Well. No other collection of jades represents such a wide time period or range of styles.

Thompson must have succeeded at Chichen Itza more spectacularly than he'd ever hoped. Perhaps anticipating trouble from the Mexican authorities, he and his benefactors kept his find secret for a decade. When the hoard from the Sacred Cenote was finally publicized in the *New York Times*, on March 2, 1923, J. C. Merriam, president of the Carnegie Institution, and Marshall H. Saville, head of the Museum of the American Indian, pronounced it "the most important source of information in unraveling the story of the Mayas now available to science." But the ensuing years weren't easy for Thompson. He'd done permanent damage to his hearing during one of his dives, when he'd become absorbed in his work, forgotten to open the valve on his helmet, and surfaced too quickly. He fell behind in his taxes, which the Carnegie Institution stepped in to pay. In 1921, during the lingering violence after the Mexican Revolution, Hacienda Chichén was looted again and burned.

Even the cenote seemed to exact its revenge. Among the artifacts lifted from the well was a four-hundred-pound statue, half jaguar, half human, which Thompson had placed in his house despite the warning of one of his workers, who had told him, "Don Eduardo had better take care. He is taking away one of the servants of the rain god." For years, the figure sat uneventfully, but when the hacienda was burned, the piece was damaged by the heat. As workers picked it up, the stone split, and the heavy base landed painfully on Thompson's toes.

"Now you see," the worker chided, "the serpent god was angry and he took this means of avenging himself on Don Eduardo."

"*Bey Ani,*" Thompson answered in Mayan. "It may be so."

In 1926, the Mexican government also vented its displeasure, seizing the hacienda and charging Thompson with the unauthorized exporting of archaeological artifacts. It would be eighteen years before the country's Supreme Court finally ruled that he had broken no laws. But Thompson had long since left Mexico, and in May 1935 had died at the home of his son Edward in Plainfield, New Jersey. Henrietta also didn't live to see her husband's vindication, having survived him by only a year. Thompson's heirs sold the hacienda, which today operates as an eco-spa hotel. In 2010, the Yucatan government bought 205 acres around the archaeological site for 17.8 million American dollars. And today, Mexico has much stricter laws regulating the collection and exportation of cultural artifacts. The Peabody began repatriating some pieces from the cenote in the 1960s, in what the museum's director called "a gesture to promote international understanding." But many works from the Sacred Well remain with the museum.

So on a warm July morning, I journey to Cambridge and stroll to the venerable brick building on Divinity Avenue. A few pieces, including the wonderfully expressive head from Piedras Negras, are displayed on the building's third level, arranged in old-fashioned cases on the creaky wooden floor, but the lion's share are not on public view.

I have an appointment to meet curator Susan Haskell and archaeologist Clemency Coggins, one of the principal cataloguers of Thompson's discoveries. After surrendering my backpack and signing a promise not to publish any photographs, I trail my hosts through corridors bristling with racks of indigenous spears, bows, and arrows. Haskell enters a code on a keypad, and we pass through a heavy metal door. Inside the vault, secreted as surely as in a royal tomb, lie some of the most thrilling treasures of Maya civilization. The smaller works recline in foam-filled boxes, while the larger ones rest incongruously on gray metal shelves. There are huge, masterfully carved, brilliant-green jade plaques; gleaming golden bells and figurines; and, on a low shelf, one of the Peabody's most famous accessions—the great, foot-long sacrificial knife, larger than I expected from its photograph and even more sinister, its dark wooden handle carved with entwined serpents and its chert blade glistening in the fluorescent light.

I've read a news story that the Peabody was negotiating with the Mexican government to return even more of the collection, but when I ask about it, Susan Haskell explains that the report was in error. Still, a century after the fact, Thompson's work at Chichen Itza remains controversial. A complex figure, he's on the one hand admired for his pioneering discoveries, his modesty, fearlessness, and sincere affection for the Maya and their culture. On the other, he's reviled, along with the institutional patrons who abetted him, for his indiscriminate methods, especially the dredging of the Sacred Cenote, which damaged some artifacts and stripped them of their archaeological context. And by packing his finds off to his patrician sponsors, he represents for some the worst of an acquisitive, imperialistic period in archaeology. Mexican historian and journalist Luís Ramírez Aznar has judged Thompson "an ambitious, clever, intelligent investigator" who "offered his virtues in service of a brutal, unbridled sacking in order to deliver into foreign hands invaluable relics that formed part of the history of the creators of the Maya-Yucatec culture."

Others are more inclined to overlook Thompson's excesses in the framework of his time and training. "He wasn't a scholar," Clemency Coggins reminds me as we stand in the vault admiring the artifacts Thompson raised. "He saw the dredging as an engineering problem." And prominent Maya and Olmec scholar Michael D. Coe, of Yale, takes an even more lenient point of view. "There are lots of villains in archaeology," he tells me, "but Thompson isn't one of them." Besides, what archaeological context was there to preserve, he asks, when the items were all just thrown into the well? "At least Thompson wrote up his findings," Coe adds. "The real sin is not writing them up."

For his part, Thompson went to his rest with his conscience unencumbered. "I should have been false to my duty as an archaeologist," he wrote, "had I, believing that the scientific treasures were at the bottom of the Sacred Well, failed to improve the opportunity and attempt to bring them to light, thus making them available for scientific study instead of remaining in the mud and useless to the world."

⁜

Of the tens of thousands of relics lifted from the Sacred Well—the gold, the copper, the human remains—Thompson was particularly fascinated by the jade, which he found "the most romantic of all gems." He wasn't alone in that assessment. For millennia in

Mesoamerica, jade had been esteemed the most precious substance on earth.

To be sure, jade was rare. And fifteen hundred years ago, carving the stone was not a casual activity. Owing to its extreme hardness and the primitive tools available (only other stones, wood, and string), its working required great skill, as well as the luxury of time—months to fashion even a small item. Doubtless, both these considerations added to jade's value.

And jade was beautiful, imbued with rich colors, subtle patterns, and a substantial, sensual feel in the hand. Along with other commodities such as cacao beans, obsidian, and sea salt, jade beads were accepted to settle debts, reward retainers, and pay tribute to royal lords. Jade has been called "the green gold of the Maya," but its value exceeded any aesthetic or commercial estimation. Not making our distinction between the living and nonliving worlds, Mesoamerican peoples believed that every object and every natural phenomenon—trees, animals, mountains, thunder, rain—was inhabited by an animating spirit with the power to intervene in human affairs. And jade's unique properties suggested that its spirit was particularly potent.

Jade was robust and immutable, impervious to fire, resistant to hammering, seemingly eternal. As Edward Thompson mused, "The years have gone, the centuries and then the cycles. . . . Even the massive pyramids have lost their outlines, but these bits of carved and polished jade are exactly as they were when fashioned. Their lines are as clear and their brightness as undimmed as when, unknown centuries ago, they left the hands of the prehistoric artists to grace the neck of a maiden or gem the regalia of a king."

Jade's green hue only added to its mystique, since green was the color of water (like the pool in the Sacred Cenote), fertility, the sacred corn plant, of life itself. In the Maya cosmos, east was symbolized by red, west by black, north by white, and south by yellow; green was reserved for the very center. It wasn't a coincidence that green was also the color of the highly prized feathers of the quetzal. With half a dozen names for various colors of jade, the Aztecs reserved *quetzalitzi* for the stone's most brilliant, luminous hue.

To the Maya, jade was also associated with wind, which brought the life-giving rains, and with breath. The stone did appear to breathe, as when water poured over sun-warmed jade rose up as vapor. And it could collect human breath, as when exhalation condensed on cold jade. No wonder lustrous, green, seemingly living jade was thought to cure all manner of physical ailments, from pain and fever to gout and head fractures, even to revive the dying. In the lovely phrase of Mayanist J. Eric Thompson (no relation to Edward Thompson), jade was "the precious stone of grace, the first infinite grace."

Arriving in the Valley of Mexico sometime between A.D. 1150 and 1300, the late-coming Aztecs generally didn't work their own jade but obtained carved pieces as tribute. That meant they didn't get the finest specimens, but it didn't diminish their lust for the stone. When the Spanish landed in Veracruz in 1519, Montezuma dispatched his ambassador Pitalpitoque to greet Hernán Cortés with an offering of jade beads. "These rich stones of *chalchihuite* [in Nahuatl, "herb-colored jewel"] should be sent to your Emperor," he told the Spaniard, "as they are of the greatest value, each one being esteemed more highly than a great load of gold."

After Cortés brushed the gift aside, Montezuma is said to have expressed relief that the benighted white men were interested only in the yellow metal that the Aztecs knew as "the excrement of the sun." Reducing jade's power to the level of parody, Spanish physician Nicolás Monardes reported in 1569 that the Aztecs used it to cure illnesses of the kidneys. Thus it was known in Spanish as *piedra de los riñones* ("stone of the kidneys") or *piedra de la ijada* ("stone of the loin"), which became *ejade* in French and *jade* in English and Spanish (where the pronunciation is HAH-day).

As Edward Thompson realized, jade had a great deal to confide about the cultures that revered it. Any ancient American city that carved jade must have had a specialized labor force, including trained artisans. It must also have had an evolved political structure, including a royal class with the authority to wear the stone of kings, as well as the need to display their rank to lesser citizens. Of course, what monarchs directed to be carved on their jades— mostly portraits of deities and their own forebears—revealed much about their history and beliefs. And the uses to which the ancient priests put their jades were crucial in understanding their rituals. Any city where jades were discovered was likely to have been part of an extensive trading network, since the stone wasn't generally found close at hand. These trade routes would have served not only as conduits for other goods but also for ideas and culture, for writing, art, and religion—for civilization.

However, for centuries no one knew where New World jade had come from, because in their mania for gold and silver, the Spanish had accomplished the unthinkable—they had made jade superfluous. Within fifty years of the Conquest, jade sources that had been worked for three millennia were abandoned and in time forgotten. American jade was "the most mysterious stone of the world," Thompson wrote, because "no modern man has yet been able to discover the deposits whence ancient man obtained it for his needs and purposes . . . no man has ever recorded the finding of American jade, except as worked pieces, amulets, votive objects, and ornaments."

In 1927, mineralogist George Kunz, of Tiffany & Co., lamented, "Jade! Why must it always present the same mystery? Plenty of jade has been found in Mexico but none in the place God put it. None. Rather it is found in wells, in graves, in other places where man has secreted it, and none of it is newly mined. Thousands of years ago it was marked by primitive man, rubbed and polished, carved and graven, all the jade that's ever been found in Mexico. No gem has ever caused the mineralogist or the archaeologist quite the heartache that jade has."

In the years after Kunz and Thompson, other spectacular carved jades were uncovered in pre-Hispanic cities in Mexico and Central America. Jade pebbles and deposits were rumored in the Mexican states of Guerrero, Coahuila, and Hidalgo, but these reports were not confirmed. And so, decades after Edward H. Thompson raised his spectacular hoard of jades from the Sacred Well at Chichen Itza, the location of the ancient mines remained one of the most tantalizing puzzles in the New World. To unravel the mystery, we need to start with the Olmecs, one of the first civilizations to prosper in the Americas.

TWO

Olmec Blue

It was January 1939, thirty years after Edward H. Thompson made his first dive into the Sacred Well at Chichen Itza. Matthew Williams Stirling was standing in the sticky Mexican sun, wearing the clipped mustache of an accountant but the high boots and slouch hat of an explorer. He was peering into the pit that his workers had opened in the heavy black soil outside the Gulf Coast village of Tres Zapotes. Staring back at him was a colossal stone face.

Rendered with boldness yet sensitivity, the huge head depicted a mature, helmeted man with oval eyes, a broad nose and mouth, and an imperious expression. The features were so lifelike that the lips seemed about to bark an order. Not the idealized image of a god, Stirling decided, but the portrait of a flesh-and-blood king who had once reigned here. The locals warned Stirling not to take a picture of the face, saying its spirit would turn away and only the back of its head would show.

Resting on stone slabs, the monument was six feet high and eighteen feet around; Stirling figured it weighed ten tons. It was carved from a solid piece of basalt—though the nearest source of that stone lay more than ten miles away, through the enveloping swamps. Who had lugged the stone all that distance? And who had sculpted it with such consummate craftsmanship? "Like a great American Sphinx," Stirling wrote in an article for *National Geographic*, "the Colossal Head, newly cleared of the imprisoning earth, still looks imperturbably toward the north across the abandoned plaza where once barbaric ceremonies were performed. Could his great mouth but speak, one of the most important chapters of American history would doubtless be revealed to us."

Stirling wasn't the first outsider to gaze at the strange monument. The gigantic head of Tres Zapotes had been discovered nearly eighty years before, when a worker clearing land for sugar cane had exposed what he thought was the bottom of an enormous black kettle. He'd sent for the hacienda owner, who'd dispatched a crew to excavate it. But frustrated that the find wasn't more transportable, or marketable, they'd left the sculpture sitting in the dirt. Though a few archaeologists and travelers had come to gawk during the next eight decades, the monument had attracted less curiosity than you might have expected for an enormous basalt head buried in the middle of nowhere. Over the years, the earth had swallowed it again, up to its enigmatic brow.

Stirling was chief of the Smithsonian Institution's Bureau of American Ethnology, where he'd gone to work seventeen years earlier, even before finishing his master's degree at George Washington University, in Washington, D.C. Before that he'd done a stint in the Navy in the First World War, then had graduated from the University of California at Berkeley, where he'd studied geology and archaeology and competed in the pole vault and triple jump. He'd conducted some digs for the Smithsonian in Florida and South Dakota, but finding that work tame, he'd resigned from the BAE and done his own exploration of the Upper Amazon. Then the Smithsonian and the Dutch colonial government had chosen him to lead an eight-hundred-person expedition to New Guinea, the largest mission of its kind ever undertaken to that point, to investigate the island's indigenous peoples, flora, and fauna. In 1928, he'd rejoined the BAE, this time as chief. He'd also met his wife, Marion, there, when she was hired as his secretary; they were married in 1933.

Stirling had been curious about the colossal head of Tres Zapotes partly because of some smaller pre-Columbian pieces that had been turning up in that part of Mexico. Carved from an exquisite jade ranging from translucent blue-green to smoky blue-gray, the pieces were executed in a strange, unclassifiable style, depicting individuals with round faces and broad noses, downward-turning mouths, and grotesque features that seemed to combine elements of human infants and jaguars. Stirling had first come across the style around 1918, while still a student, in an old picture of a small blue jade mask; then, two years later, while traveling in Europe, he'd tracked down the original in a Berlin museum. Beginning in the late 1920s, a consensus had been building—promoted by the German archaeologist Hermann Beyer along with Marshall Saville of the Museum of the American Indian and George C. Vaillant of the American Museum of Natural History—that these pieces, so different from anything Maya, had been created by a previously unknown people living along Mexico's Gulf Coast.

Stirling wondered whether the great head and the mysterious blue jades might be related. So in 1938, he'd driven down from Laredo, Texas, with the pregnant Marion and her parents. While the family toured the ruins at Monte Alban and Mitla in nearby Oaxaca, he'd doubled back to the state of Veracruz, southwest of the Yucatan, where the Mexican isthmus sucks in its belly to its narrowest girth. Arriving at Tres Zapotes after an eight-hour trek on horseback, Stirling had no time to excavate the head on that first foray. But even then, he could see that it sat in a plaza surrounded by four overgrown, obviously manmade mounds. Close by were other clusters of platforms and mounds, including one nearly 450 feet long. Apparently, there had once been a city here—some 150 miles west of the nearest known Maya site. Enlisting the patronage of the Smithsonian and the National Geographic Society, Stirling returned the following January, this time with Marion, fellow archaeologist Philip Drucker, and photographer Richard Stewart.

On this second visit, Stirling and the others journeyed by launch up the mangrove-clotted Río Papaloapan, which had first been explored by the notoriously cruel conquistador Pedro de Alvarado, who had arrived in the Yucatan with Juan de Grijalva in 1518. As the coastal sand hills gave way to broad lowlands, Stirling and the others spied the snow-dusted volcano Orizaba. Then, he wrote, "our hearts beat a little faster when we first distinguished to the eastward the hazy volcanic peaks of the Tuxtla Mountains, at the base of which lay our goal." He knew the head would still be where he'd left it, but he couldn't help wondering, "Would we find it reposing in lonely grandeur, or would we discover the remains of a great city, worthy of such an ambitious work of art?"

The next day, the launch navigated a flat, solitary landscape, streams choked with water hyacinths that clogged the propellers, channels so constricted that the passengers could touch both banks at the same time. Then, as they drew closer to the sierra, the vegetation became more lush, with parrots shrieking in the canopy and iguanas sunning themselves on shore. At dusk, the party entered Boca San Miguel, which consisted of three thatched houses. They mounted mules, and an hour and a half later, well after dark, they finally reached Tres Zapotes.

The expedition members hurriedly settled into their huts two miles outside the village. The next day, they went to work. Stirling liked to say that archaeologists often made their best discoveries soon after arriving at a site, and Tres Zapotes didn't disappoint: With local people guiding them to promising locations, the team uncovered nine other monuments in nearly as many days. Among them was a five-foot-long, broken stone box incised with mystical swirls and barely discernible, human-like figures that seemed to be engaged in battle; Stirling judged the piece "one of the finest examples of stone carving ever found in Mexico." There was also a squat, barrel-shaped basin that he believed had been used for extracting human hearts. And they uncovered a huge stela, or stone slab, more than seventeen feet long and nearly seven feet wide; broken in two and badly weathered, it was carved with the figures of three men, one of whom grasped in his hand a severed human head.

But Stirling's most exhilarating—and most controversial— discovery at Tres Zapotes was an unprepossessing fragment of another stela that he literally tripped over on the edge of a cornfield about two miles from camp. Named Stela C because it was the third they'd found, it had been broken and reused as a base for erecting another monument. On one side was the badly eroded profile of a man's face. But the back wasn't weathered at all, suggesting that the stone had rested on that side for many years before being recycled. Then, as the workers carefully cleared the mud with their hands, one called to Stirling in Spanish, "Boss, there are numbers!" And on the reverse, Stirling saw, was "the thing we had all secretly hoped might show up in the course of our work, but which not one of us had the temerity to expect," a row of elegantly carved bars and dots—figures like the ones the Maya had used to record their calendar dates.

The Maya civic calendar, or *haab*, consisted of 365 days divided into eighteen "months" of twenty days each, plus a five-day period at the end of the year, called the *Wayeb,* which was thought to be ruled by instability and peril. But for marking religious rituals and making prophecies, the Maya relied on a sacred almanac of 260 days, called the *tzolk'in*, which consisted of a series of twenty named days repeated thirteen times. (No one knows why the *tzolk'in* has this odd length; it may be derived from an astronomical cycle, such as that of the planet Venus, which appears as the morning star and the evening star for 263 days, respectively; or perhaps from the length of human gestation, which is about nine lunar months; or possibly from the multiplication of 20 by 13, the latter being a significant number to the Maya.)

The *haab* and the *tzolk'in* ran concurrently, synchronizing every fifty-two *haabs*, which is called a Calendar Round; then the cycle would start all over again. To measure more lengthy periods, the Maya used the so-called Long Count, whose start is generally traced back to the equivalent of a day in August 3114 B.C. (perhaps the putative date of creation), just as the Christian calendar begins at the birth of Christ. Using base 20, the Maya could represent any day in the Long Count by combining only three symbols—a shell (0), a dot (1), and a horizontal bar (5, with two stacked bars for 10 and three for 15). Where numbers larger than 20 were needed, zeros were used to shift the position of a digit and multiply its value, just as we do with Arabic numbers in base 10 (though the Maya didn't use decimals to record numbers smaller than 1). By comparison, it would be another fifteen hundred years before the concept of zero was used in Europe.

To record a Long Count date, a scribe would use five numbers corresponding to various units of time—the *k'in* (1 day), the *winal* (20 days), the *tun* (360 days, or 18 winals), the *k'atun* (7,200 days, or 20 tuns), and the *bak'tun* (144,000 days, or 20 *k'atuns*). There was also a great cycle of 13 *bak'tuns* (1,872,000 days, or roughly 5,128 years). This is the period ending on December 21, 2012, but contrary to the predictions of modern doomsayers, the date wouldn't have signaled apocalypse for the Maya, only the start of the next cycle in an incomprehensibly long series of cycles. As Linda Schele and David Freidel have written, for the Maya, history was not a linear progression but instead a series of "endless cycles repeating patterns already set into the fabric of time and space."

Stirling copied the date glyphs from the stela, then rushed back to camp, where Marion deciphered them using Sylvanus Morley's *An Introduction to the Study of Maya Hieroglyphics*, which the Smithsonian had published in 1915. The Maya generally wrote their dates vertically, with the *bak'tuns* on top and the *k'ins* on the bottom, but when written out in the conventional modern format, with the *bak'tuns* on the left and *k'ins* on the right, the bars and dots appeared to read 15. 6. 16. 18. (There was also a final 6, but that was assumed to designate a specific day and not to be part of the Long Count date.) The crucial first digit, counting the *bak'tuns*, was other, presumably to be found on the stela's missing piece.

Making what seemed a reasonable guess that the errant figure was a 9, Marion at first calculated the date as A.D. 478. But as Stirling examined the stone, he became convinced that he saw an additional dot above the three top bars, just at the stela's break. It was the merest suggestion of a circle, requiring an act of imagination or will to see; but if Stirling were right, it would make the *k'atun* count 16 instead of 15. More outrageously, he suggested, in light of the heavy weathering on the opposite side, that the missing number shouldn't be a 9 but a 7, yielding a date of 32 B.C.—two centuries before Maya civilization attained its zenith. It was a startling claim, and if correct, would give Stela C the oldest Long Count date ever found in the Americas to that time. (Since then, a stone panel has turned up in Chiapas with a date four years earlier.)

Before Stela C, the record holder had been a strange figurine unearthed some four decades before in a tobacco field at nearby San Andrés Tuxtla. About six inches high and carved from jade, the Tuxtla Statuette showed a fat, bald man with jolly eyes, wearing a feathered cape around his shoulders and, over his mouth, a mask in the shape of a bird's bill. Inscribed on it were glyphs that seemed to be in a language all their own—but the date, carved in a style very similar to the one on Stirling's Stela C, was also measured in the Long Count.

Like Stela C, the Tuxtla Statuette had been found well outside the known Maya range. Stirling allowed that the figurine could have been carried there—but that was less likely for the heavy stela in Tres Zapotes with its even older date. The date could have been carved later than the slab itself, as an added historical reference, though from the severe erosion, Stirling was inclined to believe that the stela was as old as the inscription seemed to

The enigmatic but seemingly jovial Tuxtla Statuette, incised with hieroglyphs and one of the oldest Long Count dates ever discovered, corresponding to A.D. 162.

indicate. But then, how had the people of Tres Zapotes come to be using the Maya calendar hundreds of years before the Maya themselves? Stirling arrived at the same conclusion that George Vaillant had suggested a decade before: There had been a civilization even older than the Maya, "a people," Stirling wrote, "whose origin is as yet very little known. Present archaeological evidence indicates that their culture, which in many respects reached a high level, is very early and may well be the basic civilization out of which developed such high art centers as those of the Maya, Zapotecs, Toltecs, and Totonacs."

The overwhelming majority of Stirling's colleagues saw things differently, and the resulting feud would occupy scholars for the better part of the next two decades. Aligning with Stirling and Vaillant were two Mexicans, archaeologist Alfonso Caso and artist/anthropologist Miguel Covarrubias. The opposition was led by the most distinguished Mayanist of his time, the brilliant, erudite J. Eric Thompson, who pronounced a date no earlier than A.D. 1200 for these contentious people, who were being called the Olmecs.

The name comes from the Nahuatl *olli*, for "rubber." Since the sixteenth century, the term had been used for people living along the southern Gulf Coast, where latex had long been collected from the rubber trees native to the area. In 1927, Hermann Beyer had applied the name to the ancient people who had carved the colossal head at Tres Zapotes. Picked up by George Vaillant and others, the term had come into general use. But it was an anachronism, since the Olmec cities were abandoned nearly two millennia before the Nahuatl-speaking Aztecs arrived in central Mexico. It seems unlikely that the Aztecs ever even heard of the Olmecs, since they didn't mention them to the Spanish. Centuries later no one could say what these people called themselves or how they named their cities. Although no complete Olmec skeletons had survived in the wet Gulf climate, the sculptures they left behind gave a tantalizing glimpse of a people who were squat and muscular, with short necks, flared noses, almond-shaped eyes, thick lips, and straight black hair. But it remained to be proven who the Olmecs were, or weren't.

In early 1942, the Japanese had American troops pinned down on Bataan, in the Philippines; in Europe, the first GIs had just landed in the United Kingdom. In Mexico, Matthew Stirling was again standing in the coastal humidity, peering into yet another hole that his workers had opened. Protruding from the pit was a bizarre, hut-like structure with rounded beams, not of wood but solid basalt. Ten feet long, a foot in diameter, and weighing two tons each, the beams had been artfully assembled like great stone Lincoln Logs. The columns forming the sides and back of the building had been set in the ground like a paleolithic palisade, then overlaid with more of the beams to form a flat roof. In front were five more of the basalt "logs," angling up to the roofline like a steep stone ramp. So tightly fitted were the huge pillars that Stirling judged it would be difficult for even a rodent to slip through. He didn't know what to make of the outlandish construction. Nothing like it had ever been seen in the Americas.

This time Stirling was at the ancient city called La Venta, in the state of Tabasco, some hundred miles southeast of Tres Zapotes and a dozen miles inland from the Gulf of Mexico. About 1925, Danish archaeologist Frans Blom and American author/anthropologist Oliver La Farge had discovered another colossal head at La Venta. But no one had come to excavate the city until now.

Dominating the horizon was a great earthen pyramid, more than a hundred feet tall, its base measuring roughly four hundred feet per side, its peak offering a view of the distant gulf. In its day, the pyramid was the largest, most sophisticated building in Mesoamerica, and it was still the most impressive manmade structure along this section of coast. More than two millennia of weather had softened the monument's outlines and lent it a fluted, conical shape, which led some to conclude it had been constructed to mimic the nearby mountains, but recent research suggests that its sides were originally square and stepped.

Around the pyramid lay a vast ruined city, with dozens of earthen platforms and mounds arrayed on a long, narrow ridge surrounded by swamps. It was on one of these platforms that Stirling uncovered his strange basalt structure. Inside, he found a raised area paved with flagstones and covered in blue clay and the reddish mineral cinnabar. Resting on this platform were the bones of two children, so badly decomposed that at first Stirling mistook them for three. It was impossible to say who they were or how they'd died, but the elaborate burial bespoke their importance—as did the rich offerings found beside them.

At Tres Zapotes, Stirling had made some astounding finds that forever changed our idea of the Olmecs. Now, at La Venta, he unearthed some of the earliest carved jades ever discovered. Carefully laid out in the children's tomb, along with other offerings, was a ransom in stone: a bright-green pendant in the shape of a jaguar tooth; sculptures of a clamshell, frog, leaf, and flower; a pair of large rectangular ear ornaments incised with eagles' heads; a long awl with a bulbous handle, used for ritual bloodletting; a bundle of stingray tails, apparently the remains of a necklace, with a central "tail" fashioned of jade; oblong beads artfully worked to resemble pieces of bamboo; a pair of hands, their wrists flexed at ninety degrees; and four green eyes, which may once have been set in wooden masks that had decayed in the tropical humidity.

There were also four standing jade figures with typical Olmec features—wide, down-turned mouth, flat nose, and an intentionally deformed head. Another statuette depicted a seated woman, so coated in red cinnabar that she didn't even resemble jade; her lips parted, her arms folded across her chest, her long hair hanging down her back, she was so delicate and expressive that Stirling considered her "the most exquisite example of jade carving known from ancient America"; others have since judged her one of the great masterpieces of Mexican art. Stirling was so captivated by the trove that he entitled his 1942 *National Geographic* article about La Venta "Finding Jewels of Jade in a Mexican Swamp."

During his seasons there, Stirling would uncover more spectacular jades, including a stone box containing three hundred artifacts—ear ornaments, a necklace with beads in the form of pumpkins and a carved turtle at either end, and dozens of jade celts. Like the Humboldt Celt, these were simple polished stones about the size and shape of an axe head (though Humboldt had called his find an Aztec hatchet, it was Olmec). Some of the jades unearthed at La Venta were in tints of green, but others were carved in the luminous tone that was being called "Olmec blue."

Then, in the mid-1950s, a decade after Stirling's last expedition there, another strange hoard was discovered at La Venta—six celts and sixteen human figurines, most carved in a ghostly sea green and all carefully buried standing upright in a circle, as if reenacting some real-life ceremony. In the coming years, archaeologists would unearth more deposits of jade celts at La Venta and other Olmec cities. Though most were plain, some were incised with fanciful figures, and a few, like the large celt known as the Kunz Axe (after George Kunz, who bought it in Oaxaca around 1890), were carved in half-human, half-jaguar forms; for more than a century, that specimen has resided at the American Museum of Natural History in New York.

The significance of the celts is still uncertain. Whereas some believe they're just what they seem—axe heads used during religious rites—others suggest they represent units of measure (like the gold bullion stacked in a modern vault) or the cobs of the sacred corn plant. Whatever else their meaning, to the Olmecs the heavy jades surely represented great wealth. Why would they bury such a fortune, where it would lie, at least to our way of thinking, useless and wasted? It's thought that sometimes the caches served as extravagant offerings to the gods, as at the dedication of a palace or temple. In the case of royal graves, it's possible they offered succor to the spirit of the deceased—or perhaps the great lords weren't considered dead at all, and so no one dared strip them of their earthly possessions.

Besides the jades, Stirling and his successors discovered dozens of stone monuments at La Venta, including a sandstone sarcophagus incised with a jaguar-like creature and seven large "altars," now thought to be thrones. The most spectacular of these shows an ornately attired man emerging from what seems to be a cave, cradling in his outstretched arms an infant with a cleft head and snarling jaws, apparently part human and part jaguar. Also uncovered were four colossal heads like the one at Tres Zapotes, each with a different-style helmet and distinctive features, supporting Stirling's theory that they were the likenesses of actual rulers.

The largest stela discovered in the city, standing fourteen feet high and weighing fifty tons, depicted two men wearing huge headdresses; the long nose and goatee of one earned him the nickname Uncle Sam, and even inspired Norwegian author and adventurer Thor Heyerdahl to suggest that Norsemen had settled La Venta. Others who couldn't fathom that the sophisticated Olmec civilization had arisen in the New World tried to trace its roots back to Atlantis, Egypt, and other improbable sources. As evidence that the founders had come from China, some pointed to similarities in the two cultures' use of jade, their calendars and astronomy, their association of the four cardinal compass points with certain colors, even the fact that both saw a rabbit instead of a man in the moon. Considering the supposed African features of the colossal heads, some speculated the Olmecs had migrated from that continent.

In 1955, three researchers from Stirling's alma mater of Berkeley, including his collaborator Philip Drucker, brought the recently

Matthew Stirling with the largest of the colossal stone heads he unearthed at La Venta, eight and a half feet high and twenty-two feet in circumference. Each of the heads was carved with distinctive features, leading Stirling to conclude they were the portraits of flesh-and-blood rulers.

perfected technology of radio-carbon dating to bear at La Venta. The technique takes advantage of the fact that, as living plants absorb carbon from the atmosphere, they also take in the naturally occurring, mildly radioactive isotope carbon-14. As animals eat the plants, the isotope enters their cells; then when those animals are consumed in turn, the carbon-14 passes to the carnivores, until every link of the food chain carries the element's mark. When the plants and animals die, they stop absorbing carbon-14, and since the isotope decays at a known rate over millennia, investigators can measure the amount remaining in a specimen to determine how many years have passed since its death.

Testing bits of charcoal from La Venta, Drucker and the others were able to show that the city was already well established by 800 B.C.—a thousand years before the Maya reached the height of their civilization. For four centuries, La Venta was the great capital of the Olmecs, its center occupying some five hundred acres, its surrounding population reaching perhaps twenty thousand souls. Then, about 400 B.C., the city was abandoned; though the causes are murky, it's thought that environmental factors, such as a change in course of the Río Palma, may have played a role.

Finally, in 1969, a farmer working near Tres Zapotes uncovered the errant top of Stela C. The missing number was 7, just as Stirling had predicted. There was no longer room for argument: At least one other great culture had existed in Mesoamerica before the Maya, and Matthew Stirling was credited as its discoverer. Today, the unprepossessing bottom half of Stela C sits in the Museo Nacional de Antropología in Mexico City, where its terse label gives no hint of its seminal role in shaping our understanding of pre-Hispanic civilization.

Even while Stirling was conducting his digs at La Venta, Petróleos Mexicanos, Mexico's state-owned oil monopoly, had begun tapping the site's oil-rich salt dome. Today, it's not archaeologists' huts that stand in the shadow of the great pyramid but wells and derricks, and the jades and monumental heads and thrones have been relocated to museums, including a spectacular sculpture garden in the state capital of Villahermosa.

※

Matthew and Marion Stirling worked in Mexico for the Smithsonian and *National Geographic* from 1939 to 1946. Marion had taken graduate courses in archaeology at George Washington University, and she helped Matthew write his articles and typed all his correspondence. ("How unfortunate," a Maya lady once confided to her, "that your husband never learned to read or write!") Besides his pioneering digs at Tres Zapotes and La Venta, Stirling was first to excavate the smaller, later site of Cerro de las Mesas, where he unearthed a fabulous cache of 782 jades, including a miniature moon-faced mask; bright-green ear ornaments mottled like lichen; human figures; long, hollow pieces resembling canoes; a pendant in the form of a macaw; and a carved infant that Stirling considered "one of the finest jades ever found in Mexico."

In 1945, after a hunter was startled by a great stone eye peering up from a forest path, Stirling discovered another Olmec site, San Lorenzo, which had risen to prominence at least three centuries earlier than La Venta, giving it pride of place as the first great capital of the Olmecs. Straddling a 150-foot-high, largely manmade ridge surrounded by marshes, San Lorenzo claimed what scholar Richard A. Diehl has called "one of the best pieces of real estate in the Olmec world"—easily defended, dry even during times of flood, convenient to sources of freshwater and food, with plenty of fertile land and easy river transportation. At its height, between 1200 and 1100 B.C., San Lorenzo counted a population of perhaps ten thousand, more than any other city in Mesoamerica at the time.

Although they boasted no great pyramid like the later La Venta, the people of San Lorenzo built hundreds of mounds and platforms, some supporting simple houses, others defining public plazas and ceremonial courts. Then, sometime around 900 B.C., as La Venta was expanding its influence, San Lorenzo was largely abandoned. It used to be believed that the cause was revolution or conquest, but now factors such as economic failure or environmental catastrophe are thought to have played a role. Though people continued to occupy the site until about 400 B.C., the same time that La Venta was abandoned, San Lorenzo never regained its former stature.

Over the decades, San Lorenzo has given up more than a hundred sculptures, including magnificent carved thrones and colossal stone heads—but strangely little jade. It's been suggested that at the time, fine pottery was still the ultimate status symbol, and that only after luxury ceramics became so readily available that they lost their cachet, did the Olmec elites turn to jade, which was more exotic, more difficult and costly to work, and imbued with supernatural powers besides. On the other hand, archaeologist Michael Coe believes that there is jade at San Lorenzo, but it just hasn't been discovered yet. It seems a plausible assumption, especially since the even earlier site of El Manatí, less than ten miles away, has yielded offerings of handsome jade celts. But for the moment, it's not San Lorenzo but the later La Venta that marks the pinnacle of Olmec jade.

Matthew Stirling led the Smithsonian's Bureau of American Ethnology for nearly three decades, until 1957. Then, even after retiring, he continued his fieldwork in places such as Panama, Ecuador, and Costa Rica. In the last, he hoped to find the mines where the Olmec had procured their jade; though he was unsuccessful, he did discover more jade artifacts there. In his final years, Stirling was honored as an elder statesmen among American archaeologists, revered not only for his contributions to the science but also for his generosity toward younger colleagues.

Half a century later, Michael Coe, Matthew Stirling's successor at San Lorenzo, sits in the spacious upstairs studio in his New

Haven, Connecticut, home and shares with me his fond memories of his mentor, who always seemed to have a cigar and glass of whisky in hand while recounting a droll anecdote or a suspenseful story. To Coe, Stirling was "a prince among archaeologists." Though his techniques may not have been superscientific, Stirling "knew how to smell out real finds" and "had the archaeological equivalent of a gardener's green thumb." He also had an abiding affection for the peasant farmers of Veracruz, which was reciprocated. When, in later years, the Stirlings paid a visit to San Lorenzo, dozens of locals came to pay their respects. And Coe confesses that when he went to work there, he passed himself off as Stirling's nephew, to trade on his predecessor's popularity.

Looking back over his discoveries in the land of the Olmecs, Stirling expressed "the satisfaction of doing a job which far exceeds the pleasure of mere travel, and the hope that we have added a little bit to human knowledge in revealing for the first time an interesting chapter of New World history." Matthew Williams Stirling died of cancer in 1975, at the age of seventy-eight.

Despite all the expeditions that followed, to Marion Stirling their early work at Tres Zapotes was the most exciting. "Everything was new to us," she wrote; "not only the archaeology, but the manner of living in palm-thatched houses which the natives built for us, as well as making friends with the villagers and learning their customs." After Matthew's death, Marion married a U.S. Army general; she died in 2001, aged ninety.

✦

Richard A. Diehl has noted that even today, "Olmec history resembles a story for which we have only a few chapter headings and text fragments." Many Olmec cities, spread over six thousand square miles in the Mexican states of Tabasco and southern Veracruz, have yet to be excavated, and the others have been explored incompletely.

Their writing survives only in fragments, as on the Humboldt Celt. But thanks to the work of Matthew Stirling and his colleagues, we know something of these shadow people.

We know that the Olmecs helped to spread the roots of Mesoamerican civilization, not through conquest but through trade, to the other cultures that rose and fell in the region over the next two thousand years, from the Maya to the Teotihuacanos and from the Toltecs to the Aztecs. We know that Olmec society was complex, governed by rulers and priests who mediated between mortals and a bewildering pantheon of deities, including those who presided over the rain and the all-important corn crop, and many who combined the features of various animals and even humans, especially the ubiquitous half man, half jaguar. We know that the Olmecs erected temples on earthen platforms and conducted public ceremonies that featured bloodletting, human sacrifice, and a sacred ballgame. They pioneered writing in the Americas, via their little-understood hieroglyphs, perhaps invented to identify the images on their monuments.

As archaeologists came to a better understanding of Olmec history, they made a new realization about Stirling's Stela C from Tres Zapotes: Though the stela had helped to prove that a sophisticated civilization existed before the Maya, it turns out that the monument is three centuries too late to be considered Olmec (as is the even more recent Tuxtla Statuette). So, though it's widely assumed that the Olmecs employed a complex calendar and were among the first in the world to use the concept of zero, there's no hard evidence for either of these accomplishments.

But there's no doubt that the Olmecs stand at the first flush of jade culture in the New World, trading the stone and creating some of the most sophisticated and beautiful carvings ever produced in this hemisphere. In fact, our knowledge of them comes mainly from these objects. Though they are the "rubber people," perhaps they should have been called the Tetlecs, from the Nahuatl for "stone." And even more than the Maya, the Olmecs excelled at carving in the round, with a unique style—simple, sensual, vigorous, naturalistic, and surprisingly modern in feel. They were as adept at creating colossal, expressive portraits in basalt as at shaping sensitive figurines in jade—all without wheeled vehicles or draft animals to transport the raw material and with no more than stone tools to work it. As Matthew Stirling put it, "La Venta people," the Olmecs, "were America's great artists. They erected huge basaltic monuments in the form of stelae, altars, and colossal heads, marked by artistic realism and simple artistic restraint."

Though they were so different, both types of Olmec sculpture—the monumental basalt portraits and the diminutive jade ornaments, figurines, and celts—served the same purpose: to display the wealth and bolster the authority of the rulers who commissioned them. The quarries where they dug their basalt were discovered at the Cerro Cintepec volcano, and it is supposed that the great stones were moved to San Lorenzo and La Venta by floating them on rafts where possible and manhandling them over dry land where necessary. Yet even as troves of Olmec jades continued to be unearthed, the location of the raw material remained a puzzle. As Matthew Stirling lamented, echoing Edward H. Thompson, "The source of the jade used in ancient Mesoamerica has always been a mystery. No mines are known where the material exists *in situ*. Apparently it was found in the form of pebbles or boulders in stream beds." But what stream beds, where?

In the late 1960s, Michael Coe suggested that the Olmecs' jade had originated on the Nicoya Peninsula of northwest Costa Rica, where blue jades had been found as grave offerings. He even speculated that the Olmecs had established military posts along the Pacific Coast in present-day Mexico, Guatemala, and El Salvador in order to secure a steady supply of the stone. But unless the quarries were discovered, such ideas would remain conjecture.

Coe wasn't the first to surmise. Ever since Alexander von Humboldt had brought his eponymous celt back to Europe in 1804, people had speculated on where the raw jade had come from. Was it, as Edward H. Thompson suggested, excavated on the lost continent of Atlantis? Or could the first settlers in the New World have migrated from the Far East, somehow bringing stores of stone? More than a few, including nineteenth-century explorer John Lloyd Stephens, believed that the jade had come, via some prehistoric overseas trade route, from China.

✢

The supposed Chinese connection did enjoy a certain logic. Jade had been carved in China since at least 2000 B.C., and there were striking similarities in Chinese and Mesoamerican attitudes toward the stone and the uses to which it was put.

In China, as in Mesoamerica, ornaments fashioned from *yu* (literally "precious stone") were worn by nobles as a badge of rank. The association between jade and royalty was so strong, in fact, that the stone's Chinese character is the same as that for "king," with the addition of a single extra dot, sometimes said to represent a piece of jade nestled in the monarch's pocket. Just as the emperor was "the son of heaven," jade was "the stone of heaven."

For the Chinese, jade was the bridge to immortality. The emperor communicated with heaven by speaking through an exquisitely carved jade disk called a *bi*, and his body might be put to rest in a spectacular armor-like suit of carved jade plaques. After death, a bit of jade would also be placed in his mouth. "He who swallows jade," it was said, "will exist as long as jade," which is to say forever.

In China, it was jade that was awarded to champion athletes, while gold was relegated to runners-up (a tradition honored at the Beijing Olympics in 2008, where first-place medals were plated with gold, as International Olympic Committee rules dictate, but their reverse was inlaid with white jade).

The stone was considered nothing less than virtue incarnate. As Confucius wrote around 500 B.C., jade's "polish and brilliancy represent the whole of purity; its perfect compactness and extreme hardness represent the sureness of intelligence; its angles, which do not cut, although they seem sharp, represent justice; the pure and prolonged sound, which it gives forth when one strikes it, represents music. Its color represents loyalty; its interior flaws, always showing themselves through the transparency, call to mind sincerity; its iridescent brightness represents heaven; its admirable substance, born of mountain and of water, represents the earth. Used alone without ornamentation it represents chastity. The price that the entire world attaches to it represents the truth. . . . *The Book of Verse* says: 'When I think of a wise man, his merits appear to be like jade.'"

In Europe, black jade hatchets were used two thousand years before Christ, when they were prized for their hardness and ability to hold an edge. But from the start, Europeans didn't understand decorative jade. Marco Polo had come across the stone in China in 1272; however, he mistook it for a type of quartz and didn't pack any among the treasures he brought back at the end of his travels. The first Europeans to see American jade were Spaniards exploring the Gulf Coast of present-day Mexico with Juan de Grijalva in 1518, but they confused it with emeralds or turquoise and failed to grasp its value to the indigenous people.

Bernal Díaz del Castillo, chronicler of the conquest of Mexico, tells how Grijalva's men were approached near the mouth of the Río Tonalá by some local people offering to trade copper hatchets, which the Spanish thought were made of low-grade gold. In exchange, the Indians craved the Europeans' green glass beads, which they apparently believed to be jade. Acquiring six hundred of the hatchets, the Spaniards congratulated themselves on their shrewdness, while the Indians celebrated their own windfall.

When the two groups later learned the reality of their bargain, they were doubtless disappointed. But, as Díaz says, "In the end it turned out to be an even deal. Both sides were equally cheated and wound up with nothing of value."

The jade that the conquistadors later shipped from the New World was the first of its kind to be seen on the Continent. It was Walter Raleigh who brought American jade to England, along with tobacco and potatoes. In his 1596 *Discoverie of the Large, Rich, and Bewtiful Empyre of Guiana,* he wrote: "These Amazones have likewise great store of these plates of golde, which they recover by exchange chiefly for a kinde of greene stones which the Spaniards call Piedras Hijadas, and we use for spleene stones, and for the disease of the stone we also esteeme them: of these I saw divers in Guiana, and commonly every King or Casique hath one, which theire wives for the most part weare, and they esteeme them as great jewels."

When Chinese *yu* was finally imported to Europe in the early seventeenth century, it was called *jade* because of its similarity to the American *piedra de la ijada*. But the stone that Marco Polo had seen in China was not the same as the one that Raleigh and the conquistadors sent back from the New World. In fact, the term *jade* refers to two different stones with unique chemical compositions.

Chinese jade is technically known as *nephrite*, a name coined in 1780 by the German Abraham Gottlob Werner, the preeminent geologist of his day (and mentor to Alexander von Humboldt). A silicate of calcium and magnesium, nephrite has crystals woven into a tight fiber, making it uncommonly dense and tough. On the standard Mohs scale of mineral hardness, where talc is 1.0 and diamond 10.0, nephrite rates about a 6.0 to 6.5. Besides China, the largest deposits of nephrite are found in British Columbia and Australia, with other sources in New Zealand, Russia, South Korea, Taiwan, Switzerland, Italy, Poland, Alaska, California, and Wyoming. Because Chinese nephrite has been mined continuously, its historic source was never lost; for centuries, the emperor's jade came from the Kunlun Mountains in western China, on the edge of the Tibetan plateau.

The other mineral known as jade is *jadeite,* a name conferred by French mineralogist Alexis Damour in 1863, after he peered into a microscope at a piece of jade from Burma and saw that it was different from the Chinese type. A silicate of sodium and aluminum, jadeite has a more crystalline, less fibrous structure than the other kind of jade. This makes it slightly harder than nephrite (about 6.5 to 7.0 on the Mohs scale) but also not quite as tough, which means that a thin slab of jadeite will shatter more easily when dropped. Like nephrite, pure jadeite is white; however, it almost always incorporates trace amounts of other minerals, which lend it its various colors—a bit of iron, green; a little chromium, brilliant green. (The chromium replaces some of the aluminum in the stone—the same substitution that transforms the mineral beryl into emerald.) Jadeite is found in a wider spectrum of colors than nephrite, including red, yellow, lavender, and even so-called rainbow jade, which combines several different hues in one stone. Jadeite also holds a higher luster due to its crystalline structure.

Since jadeite and nephrite require different geologic conditions to form, they are not found together. Jadeite is the rarer of the two, having been discovered in only a few places around the world, with the largest source being Myanmar (formerly Burma). Today, only jadeite is considered of jewel quality, and after the first jadeite was imported to China in 1784, from Burma, it quickly replaced nephrite as the carving stone of choice, a distinction it holds even today. Jadeite's most desirable color, a brilliant, translucent shade called "imperial green," is the most expensive gem in the world, valued more highly than diamonds. In November 1997, a necklace of twenty-seven imperial-green jade beads sold at Christie's Hong Kong for 9.3 million U.S. dollars, prompting the quip that some people must still believe in jade's power to confer immortality.

By the time Matthew Stirling arrived at Tres Zapotes, then, it was understood that not only did Mesoamerican jade not come from China, but also that the two weren't even the same stone. Could the Olmecs' jade have come from Burma?

※

"The Olmecs move like shadows across the pages of Mexican history," George Vaillant wrote in 1932; only "a handful of sculptures out of the known artistic traditions comprise the testimony of their existence." And their spectacular carvings, which seemed to spring fully formed from the Gulf Coast swamps, only enhanced their creators' sense of mystery. How did they develop their technical mastery and their unique style? Where did they find their precious jade? And what means—prospecting or trade or military force—did they use to procure it? Clearly, our understanding of the Olmecs—their history, alliances, economy, technology—wouldn't be complete until the jade's source was discovered. By pushing back the chronology, by showing that reverence for the stone had blossomed in a time and place even more remote than had been thought, Matthew Stirling hadn't solved the enigma of New World jade; he had only deepened it.

"There are people who know where precious stones grow," an Aztec man told the Spanish priest Bernardino de Sahagún. "Any precious stone, wherever it is, gives off a vapor or breath like a delicate smoke. This smoke appears at dawn, and those who search for such stones position themselves in a likely place and look toward the rising sun, and when they see the delicate smoke ascending, then they know that there are precious stones, which have been born there or were hidden there." Sometimes, in the years following Stirling's spectacular discoveries, it seemed that our knowledge of American jade hadn't advanced during the past five centuries, that the stone's source had evanesced like ancient smoke.

THREE

Maya Green

In Mexico City, ensconced in the cavernous Museo Nacional de Antropología, hangs a cultural icon. Created more than a millennium ago, it was fashioned from over two hundred pieces of jade and other stone, painstakingly fitted into a mosaic mask. The

The iconic funeral mask of Pakal the Great.
COURTESY OF HERBERT EISENGRUBER/FOTOLIA

cheeks shimmer with shades of green so intense they don't seem to have come from nature. The nose is long and hooked, the slender lips slightly parted. But it's the eyes that draw my attention— narrow, faintly crossed, stark-white ovals with round brown irises and pupils of obsidian. Peering into those eyes, I can almost see back to the day in A.D. 683 when the mask was laid over the lifeless features of K'inich Janaab' Pakal I, "Lord Sun Shield," Pakal the Great, the most celebrated of all Maya kings.

Though the Olmecs witnessed the birth of Mesoamerican civilization, it was their successors the Maya who traced its apogee. But these Maya were not the founders of Chichen Itza, who would begin to construct their capital only about A.D. 800. These Maya had started transforming their settlements into real cities some fifteen hundred years earlier, as the Olmec capitals to the west were prospering. Then, from A.D. 250 to 900 (more or less corresponding to the Dark Ages in Europe), they presided over the greatest cultural flowering ever seen in Mesoamerica. Constructing great urban centers such as Palenque, Tikal, Calakmul, Copan, and Tonina, they spread their civilization over more than 125,000 square miles, reaching from present-day Mexico to current El Salvador. It's not for nothing that archaeologists call this golden age the Classic period.

Unlike the Aztecs to the north and the Incas to the south, the Maya never united in a single empire but remained a mosaic of more than fifty city-states, jostling for territory, wealth, labor, and prestige. Sprawled over a wide area, the cities formed complex trade networks to obtain items they couldn't find locally, including goods such as hematite (a form of iron), obsidian, and jade. So vital was this commerce that it was entrusted to high government officials, who grew wealthy in its practice.

The Maya's population swelled, until some of their cities boasted more than a hundred thousand people. This meant more farmers and artisans, more laborers to construct their temples and palaces. But it also heightened competition among the city-states for access to the all-important trade routes and increasingly scarce cropland. Inevitably, greater tension led to more wars.

The Maya lived in a perilous, punitive world. To sustain their huge populations, they stretched agriculture to unheard-of limits, breeding more-productive varieties of corn, beans, squash, and other crops. But there was little margin for error, and a single failed harvest could spell starvation and civil upheaval. In fact, every aspect of the Maya's being, from the most exalted to the most mundane, was governed by an intimidating array of deities. If supplicated and sustained, the gods would mete out good fortune and the essentials of life—bountiful crops, prosperity through trade, victory in battle—but if offended, they could dispense hardship and death.

Guiding the Maya through this grueling existence were their kings and priests, who mediated between the mortal and supernatural realms and sought to gain the favor of gods and spirits. To aid in their divinations, the holy men recorded the movements of the planets Mars, Jupiter, Saturn, and especially Venus (sometimes known as *Xux Ek'*, the "Wasp Star"), a malicious deity invoked in warfare. To fix the days of their religious ceremonies, they predicted solar and lunar eclipses and seasonal equinoxes and solstices, and they kept an intricate calendar reflecting their appreciation of time as both cyclical (as in the Calendar Round) and linear (as in the Long Count). It's even been suggested that, to the Maya, time was a living being, like everything else in their animistic world, and that each day was imbued with its own personality, its own strengths and weaknesses, apt purposes and hazards. The priests' "awesome knowledge of the movements of the heavenly bodies must have been a source of tremendous power to them," as the great American Mayanist Sylvanus Morley wrote. "It proved to the ignorant masses that the priesthood held close and intimate communion with their greatest deities and it must be obeyed."

The supreme ruler was the king, the *k'uhul ajaw*, or "holy lord." Though the king's right to rule derived from his divine ancestors, his tenure hung on his ability to provide for his people and to defend them from threats both supernatural and temporal. For this, he needed not only force of personality, diplomatic skill, and military prowess, but the ability to sway the spirit world to his cause. In the words of scholars Linda Schele and Mary Ellen Miller, "The king was not only a religious authority, but also the manifestation of the divine in human space. . . . Through his ritual actions, the fruits of the earth grew, mankind on earth could contact and speak with the gods and the ancestral dead. The existence of the king demonstrated the supernatural order of all things within the Universe."

To nourish and placate the gods, the king conducted public rituals with music, dancing, and feasting. During these rites, he would also take a stingray spine or a needle of jade, pierce his penis, spatter strips of paper with his blood, and burn them in offering to the gods. Particularly important occasions, such as the accession of a new monarch, would be marked by the torture and sacrifice of a noble taken captive in war, his still-beating heart carved from his chest with a stone knife.

To prove their legitimacy and buttress their authority, Classic Maya kings, like the Olmec rulers before them, erected monuments to commemorate their forebears and to advertise their own triumphs. It has even been suggested that the Maya's elaborate writing was invented to broadcast their rulers' worthiness. And to display their supremacy, kings surrounded themselves with headdresses of bright feathers, mirrors made of hematite, and other items that were, said German scholar Nikolai Grube, "of great material and symbolic value, often inherited and passed down through generations, and . . . laden with spiritual energy that gave the wearer special powers."

But no substance was more awe-inspiring, more potent, or more coveted by these monarchs than jade. As American scholar Karl A.

Taube points out, "In Classic Maya art, jade is so inextricably linked to images of Maya rulers that it is difficult to conceive of them without this precious stone. In fact, one of the more common ways of portraying the abject and pathetic state of captive elites is to have them stripped of their jade finery." The ruler wore jade pendants, collars, necklaces, ear ornaments, chest plates, even nuggets of jade implanted in his teeth. When he died, a bit of jade was placed in his mouth, and his jade figures, masks, plaques, and other artifacts were sealed in his tomb. A jade headband and belt were essential badges of his office; indeed, it was impossible to crown a monarch without them. To quote Linda Schele and David Freidel, "These kingly jewels assert[ed] the inherent superiority of their wearer within the community of human beings, transforming a person of merely noble rank into a being who can test and control the divine forces of the world." Jade was the stone of kings.

Although they created other works of high art—architecture, ceramics, paintings—the Maya lavished perhaps their greatest talent on jade, shaping the obdurate stone into every conceivable ornament—jewelry, masks, headdresses, belts, chest plates, figurines. Whereas the Olmecs preferred bluish jade, the Maya favored brilliant shades of green. Though the people differentiated between the two colors, their language didn't: In Mayan, what we call "blue" and "green" have only one equivalent: *yax*.

As explorers and archaeologists excavated royal Maya tombs in the nineteenth and twentieth centuries, their spades seemed to strike jade wherever they touched ground. But perhaps the most startling discovery of all was made in the modern Mexican state of Chiapas, on the western fringe of Maya civilization. The city had been called Lakamha' ("Great Water") by its ancient inhabitants, for the ample creeks running through it. Centuries later, it was known as Otolum, Mayan for "Strong Houses." In 1567, priest Pedro Lorenzo de la Nada freely translated the word into the Spanish for "stockade," giving the place the name by which we know it today: Palenque.

✦

It was May 1949, forty years since Edward H. Thompson first descended into the Sacred Cenote at Chichen Itza and a decade since Matthew Stirling spied the colossal stone head at Tres Zapotes. At Palenque, a slender man was crouching atop a high, stepped pyramid, inside an elegant building graced with five doorways and a mansard roof. It was known as the Temple of the Inscriptions, after the great carved tablets discovered there. Taking up three of the inner walls, the inscriptions comprised one of the longest Maya texts ever found—though no one had the slightest idea what they said.

For nearly two hundred years, foreigners had been arriving at Palenque—an international who's who of artists, explorers, and archaeologists including Antonio del Río, John Lloyd Stephens, Frederick Catherwood, Désiré Charnay, Alfred Maudslay, and Frans Blom. Drawing, photographing, mapping, making plaster casts, they had transformed the city into the most studied of all Maya ruins.

You could say this latest arrival was a foreigner, too. Alberto Ruz Lhuillier had been born in Paris, in 1906, to a French mother and a Cuban father. (Alberto's first cousin on his father's side was a young man about to become famous in his own right, Fidel Castro Ruz.) Graduating from the University of Havana, Ruz had studied at Mexico City's prestigious Universidad Nacional Autónoma de México, where he'd been drawn into archaeology by the great Alfonso Caso, Matthew Stirling's ally in the argument over the age of Olmec civilization. After earning his master's degree, Ruz had gone to work at the Instituto Nacional de Antropología e Historia and become a Mexican citizen. In 1949, at the age of forty-three, he'd been placed in charge of the work at Palenque.

Tall, with dark good looks and gentle blue eyes, Ruz was known to his friends as a joker and an addict of that Maya delicacy, chocolate. He was also known for his affable chats with his workers and his outrage over the discrimination suffered by the present-day Maya. And Ruz shared the inveterate optimism of the archaeologist. Though Palenque had been studied for nearly two hundred years, only a tiny percentage of the ruins had been unearthed, so he was confident he could still find something of value amid the rubble. Ruz knew that Maya pyramids were often constructed one atop another, perhaps as a way of concentrating supernatural energy in a sacred place. The Temple of the Inscription's carvings, size, and location all bespoke the building's importance. Yet it had never been excavated. He began to wonder whether another pyramid might lie beneath.

The floor of the pyramid's crowning temple was unlike any other at Palenque, constructed not of stucco but of carefully fitted flagstones. Now, as Ruz prowled the building's central chamber, he noticed a paving stone drilled with a row of perforations. Crouching for a closer look, he noted a detail that all the others had missed: The temple's walls, instead of ending at the floor, seemed to extend beneath. The next day, May 20, 1949, he had his men lift the perforated slab, and after some probing they uncovered a flat, narrow stone, the kind the Maya had used to close a vaulted ceiling. A few days later, they found one step, then another—a stairway.

The steps had been filled with stones and clay. So the crew began to dig, hauling out the debris in buckets fixed to ropes and pulleys. Troweling downward, they found a strange, square stone tube running along one of the stairway's walls. Then, at the bottom of the forty-fifth step, the floor became wider, and they discovered an offering of two jade ear ornaments. But it wasn't the end of the stairway, only a landing where the steps made a U-turn.

Ruz worked as weather and funding allowed. After another twenty-one steps, the stairs dead-ended at a wall, more than seventy feet below the temple floor and about level with the plaza outside. Fixed to the barrier was a masonry box with another offering—three pieces of pottery, seven jade beads, another pair of circular jade ear ornaments, two shells filled with cinnabar, and a tear-shaped pearl more than half an inch long. Ruz sensed they were getting close.

Breaking through the thick stone-and-lime wall, they discovered a triangular slab nearly seven feet high, apparently sealing another entrance. At its foot, in a rough stone box, lay a mass of human bones. Ruz believed they were six sacrificed youths, though the skeletons were so mixed and in such bad condition that he couldn't be sure of the count. At least one of the victims was female, and all were nobles, judging from their flattened skulls and their jade-encrusted teeth. Ruz knew that something important must lie beyond.

Finally, on Sunday, June 15, 1952—three years after they'd begun—the crew heaved the triangular slab aside and Ruz slipped through, the first person in centuries to step into the heart of the pyramid. Consumed with emotion, he struggled to recoup his scientific detachment. He was standing in a large crypt nearly thirty feet long by thirteen feet wide, the vaulted ceiling soaring nearly twenty-three feet above the floor. But as he trained his flashlight through the ancient gloom, its rays seemed not to illuminate earth or stone, but ice. Stalactites hung from the vault like slender icicles, and the walls reflected a frosty sheen, both the result of centuries of water seepage.

The high vault was supported by black stone beams, and the stone walls and ceiling had been fitted with such care that not one piece had shifted during a millennium. Standing sentinel on the walls were nine larger-than-life stucco figures, each with a headdress of quetzal feathers; a feathered cape; and jade plaques, ear ornaments, necklace, chest plate, bracelets, scepter, and a round shield in the image of the sun god. Ruz took them to be the lords of darkness, guardians of the nine levels of the Maya underworld.

On the floor rested two exquisite stucco heads, one of a youth, the other of a gaunt-cheeked old man; both had been stripped from larger statues and left in the tomb as a kind of bloodless sacrifice. The finest of their kind ever found at Palenque, the heads were exceptionally realistic, obviously portraits of actual persons. Fixing his flashlight on them, Ruz felt moved by the "austerity, inner power, and spirit of the priestly cast."

At the threshold of the chamber, the square stone tube that they had followed down the stairway morphed into a stucco serpent, apparently forming a spiritual conduit to the pyramid's summit and the world of the living. Tracing the serpent with his beam of light, Ruz saw that it rose from an enormous limestone monument in the center of the crypt. Some thirteen feet long and seven feet wide, the monument had a stone base and sides, all worked with intricate images of richly attired figures, along with thirteen bar-and-dot dates from the early seventh century.

On the base rested a huge stone slab carved with bas-reliefs on all four sides and top, which even in the dimness, Ruz recognized as a masterpiece of Maya art. The slab's central image was a phantasmagorical figure surrounded by astronomical signs, representing, Ruz mused, "heaven—the spatial limit of man's earth, and the home of the gods, in which the unchanging course of the stars marks the implacable rhythm of time." A decade later, Swiss author Erich von Däniken would take the heavenly theme a precarious step further, suggesting that the carving depicted an extraterrestrial astronaut come to Earth to sow civilization among humankind. But there was no misconstruing what lay on top of the slab—a belt studded with jade ornaments, a jade mosaic scepter depicting the rain god, and a jade mosaic shield in the form of the sun deity. Ruz thought the monument might be an altar for subterranean rituals. Then another idea took shape: Could the huge base be a sarcophagus?

But the rainy season had already begun, and Ruz's funds were exhausted. It would be November, an excruciating five months later, before he was able to test his theory.

By then he had a plan. When they finally reopened the chamber, Ruz instructed his men to drill a hole in the monument's base, in an area without carving. The bore met with nothing but solid stone. A second attempt found a hollow core, however, and when an exploratory wire was inserted, it emerged with traces of red pigment—the color often found in Maya royal graves, signifying the east, resurrection, immortality. Now Ruz was certain: He'd discovered the largest Maya sarcophagus ever found, and a tomb of consummate importance. The realization affected him almost as powerfully as the discovery of the crypt itself.

Ruz had a delicate decision to make. Should he risk damaging the fantastically carved lid, one of the artistic glories of Maya civilization, in order to see what lay inside? He didn't hesitate for long. Since the tomb was too cramped for heavy equipment, he ordered a tree felled and its trunk cut into lengths of various sizes. The logs were then trucked to the pyramid, hauled up the seven stories to the temple, lowered with cables down the sixty-six steps of the interior staircase, and finally maneuvered into the tomb. After two days of feverish tension, the men placed at each corner of the sarcophagus an upright log with a hydraulic truck jack set on top.

On November 27, at dusk, they began to raise the jacks millimeter by millimeter. As the lid edged upward, they slipped stone slabs underneath, in case the jacks should lose their purchase. And when the devices had reached their limit, other logs were balanced on the originals and the process continued. For twenty-four "soul-shaking" hours, Ruz didn't permit himself to leave the chamber.

Gradually, a hollow came into view beneath the lid—long, vaguely fish-shaped, and sealed by another highly polished, perfectly fitted stone. This second slab had been drilled with four holes, now filled with stone plugs, which had apparently been used to lower it into place. As soon as space allowed, Ruz slipped under the five-ton lid and worked out two of the plugs. Setting his flashlight against one of the openings, he peered through the other. Inside the sarcophagus, just inches from his eye, was a human skull covered with jade.

The men slipped cords through the four holes and raised the interior slab. What followed was one of the great moments in archaeology. As the sarcophagus was opened, the cinnabar-dusted interior came into view. In the center of the fish-shaped hollow lay a skeleton. Badly deteriorated, he was resting on his back, his arms at his sides, his legs extended. And everywhere, glimmering against the reddish background, were bright green jades. In his mouth, a jade bead. On his forehead, a band of jade disks. On his ears, fantastic jade ornaments like the flowers of the sacred ceiba tree. His hair had been dressed with diminutive tubes of

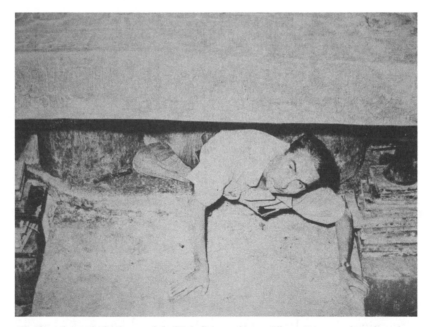

Climbing beneath the five-ton lid of Pakal's sarcophagus, Alberto Ruz peered inside and discovered a human skull covered with jade.

jade, and around his neck were draped jade necklaces of different shapes—spheres, cylinders, flowers, pumpkins, melons, even the head of a snake. Over his chest lay nine enormous strands, each with twenty-nine tubular jade beads. Both wrists were wrapped in a bracelet of two hundred jade beads, and all ten fingers wore a thick jade ring, some square, others round. His right hand grasped a jade cube, his left a jade sphere. Next to each foot lay another large jade bead and a figurine of the sun god. Over his loins lay a brilliant green figure with an oversized head and a tiny body, perhaps representing the corn god. And placed on his face was the fabulous mosaic mask of more than two hundred perfectly fitted pieces of jade and other stone. Apparently the mask had shifted during burial, and over the centuries its plaster backing had disintegrated, spilling fragments down the left side of the head.

Ruz's discovery caused an international sensation. For one thing, it was the first Mesoamerican temple pyramid found to conceal a sepulcher, calling to mind the fabulous tombs of the Egyptian pharaohs. Then there was the great artistry of the grave's contents—the lifelike stucco heads and reliefs and the enormous, finely worked sarcophagus. And not least, there were all those carved jades, one of the most spectacular caches of the stone ever found. To Ruz it was "the most extraordinary tomb so far discovered in this continent of America"; to scholars Linda Schele and Peter Mathews, the temple and tomb were "one of the greatest historical legacies of the Americas." But whose body did it shelter? No one could say, because no one knew how to read the carvings on Ruz's sarcophagus.

Beginning in the late 1800s, working from Diego de Landa's "alphabet," experts had begun to decipher some of the Mayan characters found in codices and on monuments, including words for colors and the cardinal compass points and the names of various gods. But Landa's translations seemed so rife with inconsistencies and duplications that by Ruz's time, most experts had decided that Maya writing, like Chinese characters, didn't record individual sounds but words or parts of words. And judging from the relatively few symbols used—about eight hundred, compared to twelve thousand in Chinese—they concluded that the Maya works must deal with only the limited subjects of astronomy and the calendar.

Then in the late 1950s, a few years after Ruz's discovery at Palenque, German archaeologist Heinrich Berlin noticed that certain symbols tended to appear only at given cities, leading him to suppose that they recorded either the names of the places or perhaps those of patron deities or ruling dynasties there. And so came the first tantalizing clue that the Maya's words might relate not to the movements of the heavens but to events here on earth. Later that decade, working with texts from Piedras Negras, the Peabody's Russian-born, American-educated Tatiana Proskouriakoff had a brilliant insight. Though she still couldn't translate them, she saw that the inscriptions on certain monuments combined words and dates in patterns that seemed to commemorate the anniversaries of rulers' births and accessions.

Meanwhile, the young Russian linguist Yuri Valentinovich Knorozov had made another startling claim: Since the individual Mayan characters were too numerous to be letters of an alphabet and too few to be Chinese-style characters, they must be hieroglyphs, which, like those of ancient Egypt, could stand for either a sound or a word. Though the idea was embraced by some scholars (including the young Michael Coe), it was generally met with scorn, particularly from the preeminent J. Eric Thompson, who as late as 1972, flatly stated, "Maya writing is not syllabic or alphabetic in part or in whole."

But in 1973, a team of scholars including Linda Schele and Peter Mathews met at Palenque, put Knorozov's principles to work—and over the course of a single astonishing evening managed to translate the engravings on the side of Ruz's sarcophagus. Finally, it was revealed whose remains were inside. Because his name included the glyphs for "sun" and "shield," Schele and Mathews called him Lord Sun Shield and later Pakal, the Mayan word for "shield." Rather than the visitation of an extraterrestrial astronaut, as Erich von Däniken had suggested, we now know that his sarcophagus lid depicts the apotheosis of the jewel-bedecked Pakal, triumphantly emerging from the underworld and taking his place with other deities, including the sun, the moon, and the planet Venus. The exquisite stucco heads we recognize as portraits of Pakal himself, one as a youth, the other in old age—giving us not one but two glimpses of a genuine Maya king.

Schele, Mathews, and their collaborators went much further, accomplishing something that had never been done for any Maya city: They traced four centuries of Palenque's royal dynasty back to A.D. 397, including the rulers' names and the dates of their birth, accession, and death. And as engravings from the Temple of the Inscriptions and other monuments yielded to translation, more pieces of Palenque's history fell into place. In 615, when twelve-year-old Pakal assumed the throne, the city found itself at its nadir following a pair of military defeats by superpower Calakmul and its allies. After some initial setbacks, including another loss to rival Piedras Negras, Pakal transformed Palenque into a major power and remade his capital with some of the most elegant buildings in the Maya world. After his death in 683, he was succeeded by his sons, first Kan Balam II then Kan Joy Chitam II, who perpetuated the golden age inaugurated by their father. Then in 711, the city's fortunes turned again, when it was defeated by nearby Tonina, and by the end of the century, it was languishing. The final date recorded there was 799, incised not on a great stela but on a sherd of pottery marking the accession of Janaab' Pakal III, the last king of Palenque. Not long after, the once-great capital was abandoned, eventually returning to jungle.

The same fate would befall the mightiest Maya cities over the following century. Though it's often viewed as a sudden, mystifying "collapse," it was really a gradual decay, taking place during a hundred years or longer and involving factors such as deforestation, drought, overpopulation, warfare, and ultimately, a loss of faith in the royal dynasties that were supposed to ward off these catastrophes. Through the ninth century, as people drifted out of the cities and returned to subsistence farming, construction halted and the carving of jade all but disappeared. By 909, the Maya Classic had run its course, its final gasp recorded in the last Long Count date ever discovered, on a monument at Palenque's nemesis Tonina.

But even this "collapse" didn't spell the end of Maya culture, just its shift to safer havens, where other, so-called Postclassic cities were built—in the northern Yucatan, the highlands of Guatemala, and along the Pacific Coast. And so, in places such as Coba, Uxmal, Mayapan, and Chichen Itza, branches of the Maya family tree would flourish again, with an even greater emphasis on trade and a continued reliance on military solutions to their many differences. In these new locations, as the price for keeping their thrones, rulers now shared authority with their nobles, who organized themselves into influential councils. The days of the all-powerful, divine monarch were done. And one of the prerogatives claimed by the ascendant nobility was the right to own and display jade, the erstwhile stone of kings.

Ruz continued his work at Palenque until 1958. By then, friends were calling him "*el Hitchcock de la arqueología*," for the way he teased out the suspense when recounting his exploits, especially the discovery of the tomb of Pakal the Great. In 1970, Ruz founded El Centro de Estudios Mayas, and two years later, he became director of Mexico City's Museo Nacional de Antropología, where Pakal's bones and death mask are displayed along with a reproduction of his tomb. Though Ruz was known as a joker and bon vivant in his earlier years, in later life, he showed a more somber and embittered aspect, especially toward Americans. This resentment may have stemmed partly from his leftist political leanings and partly from a feeling that foreigners had overrun his beloved Palenque and usurped his work there. In particular, Ruz despised the epigraphers, including Schele and Mathews, who, by going directly to the source, the words of the ancient Maya themselves, had overturned many of his own, more speculative theories. And so, branding the newcomers "fantasists," he persisted in his own misguided reading of the sarcophagus lid—claiming, for instance, that the king whose grave he'd discovered had died at age fifty, not at eighty as the glyphs had shown, and that his name wasn't Pakal at all.

On August 25, 1979, at the age of seventy-three, Alberto Ruz died of a heart attack while attending a scientific conference in Montreal. Despite all the accomplishments and acclaim, he'd considered his work far from finished: Among his effects, his wife, Celia, found in his wallet a little pack of cards where he'd jotted notes for four more books he'd planned to write about the Maya. Like Pakal, Ruz was buried at Palenque, his marker's stone top tracing the same gentle curve as the mansard roof on the Temple of the Inscriptions.

Today, the great majority of Palenque still waits to be excavated, meaning that most of what we know of the city comes from deciphered texts, not physical evidence. Pakal's sarcophagus still rests under the Temple of the Inscriptions; though the tomb was once open to tourists, it's been resealed for its own protection. No longer the most studied of Maya sites, Palenque continues to be one of the most popular, drawing millions of visitors each year with its elegant architecture and lush hillside setting.

Alberto Ruz cleans one of the exquisite stucco heads he discovered in Pakal's tomb.

As for the children of Pakal, resisting the carnage and cultural annihilation of the Spanish Conquest, they were still contesting their subjugation centuries later, when Edward H. Thompson arrived in the Yucatan. And even in the late 1900s, they continued to challenge the heirs of Spanish authority, with an uprising in the Mexican state of Chiapas and a brutal civil war in neighboring Guatemala. Today, the Maya number in the several millions, speaking nearly thirty languages, still occupying the land of their ancestors.

Before their writing was decoded, the prevailing view of the ancient Maya, advanced by scholars such as J. Eric Thompson, was of a preternaturally peace-loving, docile people content to spend their time gazing at the heavens. It was only after we could read their own words that the Maya were revealed in all their complexity, including their penchant for torturing and sacrificing captives taken in warfare. And so, over the course of just a few decades, a people emerged from the shadows and into the glare of history.

In the years after Alberto Ruz left Palenque, archaeologists continued to find other astounding Maya burials—and more fantastic jades. In 1962, at Tikal, Aubrey Trik of the University of Pennsylvania discovered the tomb of Jasaw Chan K'awiil I, who had been laid to rest in A.D. 734 with an astonishing hoard of jades and other stones, including a headband of emerald-green squares, an exquisite cylindrical mosaic jar with his likeness carved on the lid, a fierce life-size mosaic mask surmounted by a cross-shaped headdress, and the same enormous jade necklace seen in portraits of the ruler, some of the beads the size of small apples. Displayed in the Museo Nacional de Arqueología y Etnología in Guatemala City, the hoard is enough to make a visitor gasp.

In 1965, Nicholas Hellmuth, aged just twenty and still an undergraduate at Harvard, discovered the Tomb of the Jade Jaguar, also at Tikal. Richer with jade than any other Maya burial site except for those of Pakal or Jasaw Chan K'awiil I, the grave included a carved jaguar, another mosaic-covered jar with the king's portrait on the lid, and a treasure in jade jewelry, including a headband, necklace, pendant, bracelets, and ear ornaments. It is still not certain whose body lay in the tomb, but it's been suggested that it was Yik'in Chan K'awiil, son of Jasaw Chan K'awiil I.

In 1994, at Palenque, Arnoldo González Cruz uncovered the Tomb of the Red Queen, so-called for the rich dusting of cinnabar both outside and inside the sarcophagus. Located beside the tomb of Pakal, the burial was the most lavish at Palenque except for that of Pakal himself—with more than a thousand carvings of jade, other stone, and shell, including necklaces; ear ornaments; bracelets; anklets;

The grave of Jasaw Chan K'awiil I, as reproduced in the Museo Nacional de Arqueología y Etnología in Guatemala City.
PHOTOGRAPH BY THE AUTHOR

a headdress of flat, circular stones; and a mask carved from the green mineral malachite. It remains unknown who the Red Queen was, but it's been suggested that she may have been Pakal's wife.

And in 1995, a team of archaeologists from the University of Pennsylvania, led by Robert Sharer and David Sedat, discovered at Copan the tomb of Yax K'uk' Mo, the founder of that city's royal dynasty, who died about A.D. 435. The king's teeth had been inlaid with jade, a jade carved to resemble a woven mat had been placed in his mouth, and arrayed about him was a treasure in stone, including a large chest plate, shell-and-jade ear ornaments, and the headdress of a warrior king.

Yet, even as the discoveries continued, crucial gaps remained in the Maya narrative. From the goods found in their rulers' graves, it was clear that they relied on extensive trade routes to secure exotic commodities such as jade. And given jade's preeminent financial and spiritual value, any city that could control the stone's mining or dominate its trade would exert significant advantage over its contentious neighbors.

Indeed, it seemed plausible that some of the Maya's many wars were waged over competition for this commerce. But until the source of the jade could be discovered, it was impossible to trace those channels back to their origin, and archaeologists and historians were forced to speculate. Was a particular city located to guard a strategic jade route? Was such-and-such an alliance formed to exchange jade or to end a rival's hegemony in the stone? Could the endemic wars that played a role in the downfall of the Maya Classic cities have been fought at least in part over access to jade?

It was as if, a thousand years from now, the sources of the world's oil were lost to history. From the detritus we'd left behind, archaeologists would quickly conclude that petroleum was essential to our economy. Surely, it was a commodity for which states would pay dearly, perhaps go to war to protect. But with no knowledge of where it had been drilled, how would they explain the superpowers' intense interest in the Middle East in the twentieth and twenty-first centuries, or the support that democratic nations lent to right-wing dictators in that region? Only when the area's oil reserves were revealed would the picture snap into focus for these future scientists. That was the position of Alberto Ruz and other Mayanists when Pakal's tomb was uncovered at Palenque: Clearly, jade was a strategic resource for the Maya, one they would go to great, perhaps violent, means to procure. But the missing piece—where it had come from—had yet to fall into place. And until it did, there were many aspects of Maya history that would remain unknowable.

❖

About the time that Alberto Ruz was making his spectacular find at Palenque, an American was probing the volcanic highlands a few hundred miles to the southeast, in Guatemala. Like Ruz and his colleagues, he was tantalized by the prospect of finding jade. But he wasn't an archaeologist, and the jade he was searching for hadn't been worked into images of gods or inlaid in funeral masks. It hadn't even been dug out of the ground.

William Frederick Foshag had been a geologist at the Smithsonian Institution, in Washington, D.C., since 1919. Born in Sag Harbor, on Long Island, he'd become fascinated by geology after a neighbor had given him the run of his mineralogy library. Later, after his family had moved to California, he'd earned a Ph.D. in chemistry at the University of California at Berkeley. At the Smithsonian, he was known for opening his office one afternoon a week, so Boy Scouts and other rock hounds could lug in their mineral collections for his expert opinion.

In the 1920s, Foshag undertook a mineralogical study for the Mexican government, co-sponsored by the Smithsonian and Harvard. He spent much of the next three decades traveling that country, and in 1943, in a cornfield in the state of Michoacán,

William Foshag in Mexico in the 1940s, when he was studying the eruption of the volcano Paricutín.

he witnessed the spectacular birth of Paricutín, the only volcano whose formation was observed by scientists from conception. Starting as an opening in the earth, the volcano rose fifty feet in the first week and more than eleven hundred feet over the next year, swallowing two villages in black lava. The eruption didn't quit until 1952, and even after that, Foshag continued to study the volcano, hiring locals to take detailed readings of its activity.

Matthew Stirling, Foshag's crosstown colleague at the National Geographic Society, would call on him for mineralogical analyses of pieces he'd uncovered on digs, and out of that exposure and his own extensive work in Mexico, Foshag developed a curiosity about pre-Columbian peoples. Besides his mineral specimens, he'd bring back archaeological artifacts to add to the Smithsonian's collection. And his interest was especially keen in the nexus where geology met archaeology—in a word, jade. In 1949, the Guatemalan Instituto de Antropología e Historia commissioned him to do a mineralogical survey of pre-Columbian jades, which was published in 1954. In the monograph, Foshag recapped the history of the stone, from its ancient carving in China, to the various names the Aztecs gave it, to the techniques that the pre-Hispanic carvers had used to work it.

As you'd expect from someone of his training, Foshag also summarized everything known on the geology of jadeite. The mineral is a silicate, meaning that each molecule becomes a silicate ion—an atom of silicon bonded to four of oxygen. Silicon is among the most abundant elements on earth, and silicates make up the majority of the planet's crust. The most common silicate—and the most common mineral in the world—is quartz, which, though not as dense as jadeite, is at least as hard; some of quartz's colored forms, such as amethyst, are also used as gemstones. All silicate ions are pyramid shaped, with four triangular faces (including the base), but they come in many different varieties, according to how the individual ions are joined together. Quartz is a tectosilicate, which means its ions bond in a structure resembling the skeleton of a skyscraper. Other silicates form rings, sheets, and hourglasses; garnet and topaz are island silicates, meaning their ions don't bond at all.

In jadeite, the silicate ions join together in long chains. Besides silicon and oxygen, the molecule contains sodium and aluminum, yielding a chemical formula of $NaAlSi_2O_6$. As Foshag pointed out, jadeite is not often found in its pure form but usually incorporates other minerals such as diopside and acmite. And many minerals and rocks resemble it—actinolite, albite, beryl, chlorite, glaucophane, jasper, metadiorite, amazon stone, muscovite, soapstone, turquoise, and a fellow silicate called serpentine. This last was of particular interest to Foshag. Like jadeite, serpentine is found in a wide range of colors, from black to yellow to green, though it isn't nearly as hard as jadeite, measuring just 2.5 to 5.0 on the Mohs scale (as opposed to jadeite's 6.5 to 7.0).

In the paper, Foshag also reviewed some tantalizing discoveries of ancient workshops where jade had once been fashioned into items such as beads, pendants, ear ornaments, and mosaics. Found in the 1940s, the sites ranged from the ruins at Uaxactun, in northern Guatemala; to the village of San Augustín Acasaguastlán in the Motagua Valley, northeast of Guatemala City; to the great city-state of Kaminaljuyu, in the western part of the present-day capital. At this last location, a jadeite boulder was also found bearing ancient saw cuts and weighing more than two hundred pounds. But, like so many before him, Foshag lamented, "Jadeite has not been found in place in Guatemala or in other parts of Mesoamerica."

Poring over geological surveys, Foshag noticed that in Burma, the world's principal source of jadeite, it was always found with serpentinite, presumably because the rocks were formed together. "Any Mesoamerican location of serpentinite," he concluded, "is a possible source of jadeite." (*Serpentine* is the name of a mineral, which is a solid formed through geological activity that has a particular chemical composition and structure; *serpentinite* is the name of a rock, that is, an amalgam of more than one mineral that contains almost exclusively serpentine. By the same token, *jadeite* is the name of the mineral, whereas a jadeite rock, that is, one consisting almost exclusively of jadeite, is technically a jadeitite; in this book, I'll generally refer to jadeitites as either jadeite rocks or just jade. Except in technical discussions, I'll use *rock* and *stone* as synonyms.)

If jade were found with serpentinite in Asia, Foshag figured, it should be found with serpentinite in the Americas as well. When he investigated a small area of serpentinite in the Mexican state of Puebla, he found no jade. But in the 1930s, a German naturalist named Karl Sapper had reported large deposits of serpentinite in central Guatemala, northeast of Guatemala City, in the Sierra de las Minas, the mountains forming the northern border of the Motagua River Valley. And jade boulders and pebbles had been found nearby in the ancient Maya city of Quirigua. The Sierra de las Minas, Foshag concluded, was the place to hunt for jade.

By the 1950s, Foshag was head curator of geology at the Smithsonian and one of the country's foremost gem experts. In Guatemala, he befriended American archaeologist Edwin Shook, director of the excavations at Tikal (and codiscoverer of the jadeite boulder at Kaminaljuyu), who had also been searching for deposits of jade. Shook introduced Foshag to a young American named Robert Leslie, an organic chemist who was running an agricultural project in the Motagua Valley. A self-described rock hound, Leslie liked to spend his free time scouting the foothills of the Sierra de las Minas for specimens to add to his collection.

One day in 1952, Leslie was working at Finca Trujillo, on the north bank of the Motagua between the towns of San Cristóbal Acasaguas and Cuijo, about sixty miles northeast of Guatemala City. He was riding his tractor through a tomato field, when a boulder became caught in the cultivator he was towing. Climbing down from his seat, he saw that the dirt-encrusted stone was nearly a foot across. He worked it free and tossed it out of the way, then climbed on his tractor and went back to work.

But later that night, lying in bed, he thought about the boulder again, how exceptionally heavy it seemed for its size. The next morning, he returned to the tomato field and found it. When he washed off the dirt, he could see that the stone had been fractured around the edges a long time before, as though pieces had been deliberately chipped off. The color, grain, and texture seemed familiar—like the jade boulder from Kaminaljuyu, which he'd seen in the archaeological museum in Guatemala City. He was certain the rock was jade. True, it was a relatively small specimen and could have been carried from anywhere—perhaps even over that putative overseas trade route from Asia. But encouraged, Leslie kept looking.

Not long afterward, a little more than a mile west of Finca Trujillo, on a natural terrace above the Motagua River, Leslie came across a site with a small mound, which had previously been reported by the prominent American archaeologist A. V. Kidder. In the space of just a few minutes, Leslie picked up more than thirty chips of jade and quartz, along with an unfinished jade bead. Intriguing, but not the first such workshop to be discovered in Guatemala—and hardly anything that would qualify as the lost jade mines of the Maya.

Leslie gave some of the fragments to Kidder, who passed them to Foshag at the Smithsonian. Foshag tested the samples and found that some were similar to ancient carved jades from Guatemala. He wrote to Leslie, encouraging him to keep searching. "The usual occurrence of jadeite with veins of albite suggests that you obtained these specimens from an area very likely to contain larger and purer masses of jade," he told him. "I would guess that within a few feet or yards of where you collected your specimens there are richer masses of jade. . . . I am at present occupied on a report on the archeological jades of Guatemala and would be interested in learning more about the occurrence that you have found. While it is, perhaps, not of great mineralogical importance, it is extremely interesting from an archeological point of view, since the source of the archeological jades is unknown."

Leslie didn't discover any "purer" or "richer" jade at the site, but eventually, his search brought him to the nearby village of Manzanal. He followed the main trail north out of town. Then, half a mile into the dry hills, he stopped. On the right side of the path was a four-hundred-square-foot exposed rock formation, or outcrop, of "jadelike material." On the ground was a deeply weathered rock about the size of a fist, with angular cuts on all sides, as well as fragments of stone of a "pleasing but not very rich" green. Leslie sent them to Kidder, and Kidder forwarded them to Foshag, who pronounced the samples "entirely similar" to jades found in the archaeological sites of the Maya and other ancient Mesoamericans. From the shapes of the fragments, Foshag guessed they were scraps from the manufacture of ear ornaments, beads, and statuettes.

Foshag coached Leslie to look for serpentinite and sent him a geological map showing deposits of that rock in Guatemala. "I would be very much interested in seeing anything that resembles jade that you might find in your field trips," he wrote. "It would certainly be quite a discovery if you would find the green jade in its natural habitat."

The next month, Leslie sent off to the Smithsonian two pieces he'd dug from the outcrop itself. One was albitite, Foshag determined, but the other was almost pure jadeite. "It looks like you have one of the original sources of Mayan jade and the information should be recorded" in a scientific journal, he wrote. "If you should return to the locality sometime it would be important to search for further evidence of work by the early people."

In July 1954, Leslie left Guatemala to take a job with Eastman Kodak in Rochester, New York. The following year, Foshag prepared a letter announcing the discovery in the journal *American Antiquity* and listing Leslie as coauthor. The brief report was a watershed in American geology and archaeology. After nearly five hundred years, jade had been rediscovered in Mesoamerica—not carved into ornaments for kings, not as boulders stranded in riverbeds and fields, not as detritus abandoned in ancient workshops, but in the ground in the foothills of Guatemala.

Leslie and Foshag's find put to rest any residual speculation that pre-Columbian jades had been carved from Asian stone. And yet. . . . The thousands of pre-Hispanic jades, ranging from translucent blue to jet black, certainly hadn't all come from this one outcrop above the town of Manzanal. Where were the rest of the mines? In Guatemala? Or as far away as Costa Rica and Guerrero, Mexico, as Michael Coe had suggested? Had the Olmecs and the Maya gotten their jade from the same sources or from different ones? How did they procure the stone, and how did they transport it without wheeled vehicles or draft animals? By resolving one central issue, Foshag and Leslie had opened the door to a host of others.

The following May, William Foshag died of a heart attack at his Maryland home, aged just sixty-two. In 1957, the Smithsonian posthumously published his monograph *Mineralogical Studies on Guatemalan Jade,* and through the 1960s and 1970s, a handful of researchers continued the hunt for other sources of Mesoamerican jade. In 1967, a large boulder of jadeite similar to the stone in Foshag and Leslie's outcrop was discovered along the Atlantic Highway just east of Manzanal. "In view of the size of the boulder [more than sixty pounds] and the abundance of similar material in the immediate vicinity," wrote the discoverers, a team led by geologist Alexander McBirney, "the bedrock sources of jade must be nearby." Yet those sources were proving devilishly difficult to pin down.

Had Foshag lived, his stature in the field may have attracted the attention of a newspaper editor. But the popular press hadn't reported on his and Leslie's discovery or on the ensuing search by others. Focusing on his studies of Paricutín, Foshag's obituary in the *New York Times* didn't even mention jade or Guatemala. And so, in the coming years, the hunt for New World jade remained the province of a few specialists publishing papers in a handful of academic journals. The general public, and even researchers in related fields, were unaware not only of the discovery of jade deposits in Central America but also of the ongoing effort to find the sources where the pre-Columbian peoples had obtained the stone. To the world at large, it was as if jade still didn't exist in Guatemala.

PART II

THE ENTREPRENEURS

FOUR

Serpentine

In February 1973, a road-dusty Dodge Travco rolled into the Mexican hill town of San Miguel de Allende. Picking its way down the Ancha de San Antonio, the twenty-eight-foot motor home turned toward the Parque Juárez, a large, lush refuge with walking paths, fountains, bandstand, basketball court, and high trees where egrets raucously took their roosts at sunset. On the park's south side, the Travco's white, streamlined curves came to rest before the seventeenth-century façade of the Villa Santa Monica.

It was the dry season in San Miguel. The days would break clear, and as the clock beside the Parroquia chimed each hour in its turn, scarcely a cloud passed to mar the cerulean perfection. Then in late afternoon, as the sun would arc toward the Sierra de Guanajuato, its rays illumined the rustic buildings, until the ocher and rose walls seemed to incandesce. The first, tentative rains were still months away.

The town had been founded in 1542, as a mission to convert the Otomi and the less-compliant Chichimecas. When silver and gold were discovered to the north a few years later, San Miguel el Grande became a way station for caravans shuttling between the mines in Zacatecas and the mint in Mexico City. Then, in 1810, it played a seminal role in the War of Independence, when the region's wealthy creoles plotted to overthrow their

Spanish governors. After issuing his celebrated cry to arms in the neighboring town of Dolores, parish priest Miguel Hidalgo and his tattered army marched on San Miguel, which became the first city to fall to the rebels. Later, the town changed its name to San Miguel de Allende, lest anyone forget that its native son Ignacio Allende had been Hidalgo's general and one of the architects of independence. But Allende never lived to see the honor; he was executed in 1811 and his head hung in a cage from a prominent building in nearby Guanajuato, along with those of Hidalgo and two other conspirators, until the Treaty of Córdova, giving Mexico its sovereignty, was finally signed in 1821.

By 1900, the silver and gold had petered out and San Miguel had entered a decades-long decline. But in 1937, the town was transformed again, when Peruvian art lover and political exile Felipe Cossío del Pomar persuaded Mexican president Lázaro Cárdenas to let him convert an old convent into an art school, which he called Escuela Universitaria de Bellas Artes. An acquaintance of Cossío, American expatriate Stirling Dickinson, was named director.

Then, after the Second World War, Bellas Artes was certified under the GI Bill, and in 1948 a three-page spread in *Life* magazine trumpeted San Miguel as a paradise where "veterans go to Mexico to study art, live cheaply and have a good time. . . . They find it very pleasant in the quiet little town of San Miguel de Allende, up in the mountains north of Mexico City." San Miguel may have no restaurants and no indoor plumbing, the article continued, but "the air is crisp, the flowers are bright, the sun is warm, apartments are $10 a month, servants are $8 a month, good rum or brandy 65 cents a quart, cigarettes are 10 cents a package." After the piece was published, Dickinson received six thousand applications for his 140 places. Among the new students were a few apparently attracted more by the cheap rum than by the curriculum; locals occasionally showed their displeasure by throwing stones at the rowdy interlopers.

Despite the influx, San Miguel retained its small-town essence, as American art patron and author MacKinley Helm described in 1948. "San Miguel de Allende is not a place to be seen and enjoyed in a day," he explained to the would-be visitor. "Yet I have known certain hard-working tourists who were unable to spend a whole day there and feel fully employed. I remember being addressed, when I lived there, by a woman who said, 'What in God's name do you people who live here *do* with your time? I've been here for four hours and I've walked from one end of town to the other, examining churches. What shall I do next?'"

"This is a place," Helm explained, "where, if it hits you just right, you want to buy a house right away and stay a long time. If it doesn't so hit you, you may find it dull. It has so few 'sights.' Its charm really consists in its hillside setting and views, its well-watered gardens, in the dependable sun, and the slow seeping of time in its plazas."

Cossío and Dickinson went on to found a second art school in San Miguel, the Instituto Allende, and by the late 1960s, the town was still attracting North Americans looking for clear light, cheap living, and a frisson of escape they couldn't get in Boise or Newark. But burros and horse-drawn carriages were still plentiful in the cobblestone streets, and electrical service was intermittent; in the unlikely event that you received a call, the telephone company would dispatch a boy to your house to let you know. If you wanted to invite someone to dinner, you sent a note.

Just down the hill from the city center was the park named for nineteenth-century Mexican president Benito Juárez. In 1967, an American named Betty Kempe had bought a Colonial house on the park, once the home of Mexican opera singer and movie star José Mojica, and converted it into one of the city's few hotels.

Tall and athletic with wavy blonde hair, Betty Kempe (then Betty Johnson) had arrived in San Miguel in the late 1950s, from Fort Worth, Texas. A widow with three daughters, aged eight, twelve, and fourteen, she rented a house on Calle Barranca, with a fountain on the corner and a view of the valley, and like so many before and since, she was enchanted. For the daughters, the first six months in primitive San Miguel were torture, devoid of everything they considered necessary to sustain life. But by the end of the first year, the girls had also come to relish the high adventure, the feeling that every day was unpredictable and tinged with magic.

Just eighteen months after their arrival, the family moved again, to Europe, where Betty's third husband, an American expatriate named Gordon Kempe, was hoping to find work as a travel writer. Betty and the girls embraced the change, which seemed just the next step on the audacious trajectory they'd taken since leaving Fort Worth. Then in 1967, eight years after leaving, Betty Kempe returned to San Miguel, without the husband or the now-grown daughters, and bought José Mojica's house on the Parque Juárez.

The next year was spent restoring the four-century-old building, from the tile-roofed patio to the stone-walled reception area, to the generous guest rooms and extensive gardens, realizing her vision of a tasteful, tranquil oasis decorated in earth tones and pastels. Mojica was an amateur artist, and he'd left behind one of his own paintings, a Virgin and Child painted directly on the wall above a fireplace. Not wanting to obliterate the picture but finding that its vivid hues clashed with the softer palette she was planning, one afternoon Betty decided to mute it with an antique finish. As she was balanced on a ladder dabbing the painting, one of her workers announced a visitor—Mojica himself, who had come to see how the renovation was getting on.

Caught with her hand in the paint pot, Betty gave her most winning smile. "Sr. Mojica, I'm so glad you've come. I was thinking of toning down your painting a bit, and perhaps you can advise me on the best way to proceed."

Mojica considered the half-stained picture. "It is a bit bright, isn't it?" he finally said, then took the rest of the afternoon helping in the desecration of his own art.

By December 1968, the hotel was ready, and Betty opened it as the Villa Santa Monica, the name Mojica had given his house in honor of the patron saint of mothers.

⁜

It was early afternoon on this February day in 1973 when the Dodge Travco came to rest in front of the Villa Santa Monica. Inside the motor home was an American family—mother, father, and three girls ranging in age from ten to sixteen. They had been nearly two months on the road from Chicago, partly because they'd done some sightseeing en route and partly because Jay Ridinger refused to drive more than four hours a day. Friends in Chicago owned a home in San Miguel, and the Ridingers had arranged to rent it, but even with their dawdling they'd arrived too early: The house wasn't ready. The friends had told them to look up Betty Kempe, and though the Ridingers arrived at lunchtime, interrupting the principal meal of the day, she received them cordially.

"Tell me, pretty lady," Jay Ridinger asked, "where can a family go to amuse themselves while their house is being readied?" Betty was charmed by the six-foot visitor, bearded and sandy-haired, ten years her junior. Over time, as she learned more about him, she would be impressed.

At the age of thirty-nine, Jay Ridinger (the *g* is hard, as in *gold*) had already reinvented himself several times. He'd been born in East Chicago, Indiana, on Lake Michigan, twenty miles southeast of the other Chicago. His early years had been nomadic. Beginning when he was four, he ran away from home so many times to stay with his grandparents that his mother and father finally gave in and let him live there. At the age of seven, he returned to his parents' house, but the family moved so often in the coming years, as his mother strove to trade up to better and better neighborhoods, that he never formed close friendships. Though he played clarinet in the high school band, he wasn't particularly adept at either music or sports. But he loved the outdoors and found his niche in Scouting, where he went on to earn the rank of Eagle. When he was a child, his mother had sent him to a therapist to correct a speech impediment, and he'd developed a sonorous voice that helped him to win the presidency of his class in high school (his slogan: "Ride with Ridinger") and to earn debate scholarships in college. At Indiana University, he majored in business, though he liked to say he lettered in poker. Sociable, competitive, psychologically savvy, cool under pressure, Jay Ridinger was a very good poker player.

He stayed on at Indiana to earn an M.B.A., but as graduation approached, he felt a sense of dread, because he feared that all his education hadn't taught him to do anything. Both his father and grandfather were managers at Inland Steel Company, headquartered in downtown Chicago, and young Ridinger accepted a job with the corporation. Inland sent him to some engineering courses at Purdue, but his focus at the company was on the business of steelmaking, not on the technical side. His first turning point came when he was just twenty-five, after another junior executive commented off-handedly that neither of them would be allowed to make any significant decisions before the age of forty. Ridinger realized his companion was right; he resigned the following day.

By then he had a wife, Marilyn, and two young daughters, Robin and Renée. To support them, he and a couple of friends founded their own real estate development company. Every morning, Ridinger would get up at four o'clock to be at the local coffee shop by five, when the *Tribune* arrived. Then he'd scour the classifieds for marginal buildings that the partners could renovate and resell. The concept of condominiums was new in those days; Ridinger claimed that the first time he used the word with his lawyer he had to spell it. Before he'd reached thirty, Ridinger had taken his profits and retired to the affluent North Shore suburb of Lake Forest, buying a grand Victorian house once owned by Abraham Lincoln's brother-in-law. Ridinger dedicated a guest room to Lincoln, decorating it with flocked red wallpaper and pictures of the president; in the attic was his collection of John Wilkes Booth "wanted" posters.

Ridinger had always loved old and beautiful things, and to occupy himself he opened an antiques store. But he was restless in Lake Forest, a place, his daughter Renée says, "without sufficient oxygen for his spirit." So he moved the family, now including a third daughter, Angela, back into the city, to an apartment building he owned on Barry Avenue, an area in the process of gentrification. Though he continued to invest in property, he also turned his real estate acumen toward nonprofit ventures, working with organizations such as the Chicago Missionary Society and Jane Addams Hull House to mount demonstrations against slumlords, press the city to expand low-income housing, and help people of modest means to get mortgages.

Then Marilyn contracted breast cancer, the disease that had taken her mother at forty-one and her grandmother at forty-three. After Marilyn's surgery and radiation in November 1972, the Ridingers made plans to leave the city. Though he knew it was irrational, Jay blamed Chicago's pollution and harsh climate for her illness, and he resolved to make a new start somewhere warm and untainted. The former Eagle Scout had always been fascinated with Central America, which he imagined as a wild, exhilarating place, and he'd long thumbed through catalogs of expedition gear, picturing himself wearing the rugged clothing, hacking a trail through virgin jungle. And so, at the age of thirty-nine, as he planned his third retirement, Jay Ridinger began to look southward. In January 1973, he and Marilyn took the girls out of school, climbed into the swivel seats of their Dodge Travco, and steered for Mexico.

In San Miguel, Ridinger was eager to meet Betty Kempe not just because she was one of the few names he knew, but because she had also resettled in Latin America with three young girls. The middle daughter, Mary Lou, was now in her early twenties, blonde, nearly six feet tall, with blue-green eyes. She had majored in Latin American Studies at the University of Colorado at Boulder. Married at nineteen, she'd quickly divorced. Then, after working for a year as a social worker in Colorado, she'd come back to Mexico and enrolled in the graduate program at La Universidad de las Américas, at that time located outside Mexico City on the highway to Toluca.

Her two interests were anthropology and archaeology. One of her professors, William Swezey, liked to call archaeology "the bookkeeping of the earth," and Mary Lou Johnson liked the sound of that. When she considered the fantastic richness of Mexico's ancient cultures, the choice became clear. The year after she enrolled in the archaeology program, the university moved to Cholula, near Puebla. But the new location wasn't to her liking, and Johnson began spending weekends with her mother in San Miguel. She also volunteered for archaeological digs in Mexico City, where excavations for the new Metro were turning up Aztec sites, and at Cañada de Alfaro, in Silao, Guanajuato, since paved over to build Del Bajío International Airport. By February 1973, she'd completed the coursework for her master's degree and was working on her thesis, on ceramics from the Cañada.

Mary Lou Johnson wasn't in San Miguel when the Ridingers arrived. The previous October she'd gone to Stanford University in California, to analyze the ceramics from her dig. But in March, her research completed, she returned to San Miguel while the Chicagoans were still in town. Archaeology was another of Jay Ridinger's interests, and he persuaded Mary Lou to escort him to every site in that part of Mexico, including private pre-Hispanic collections and a local pyramid at La Cañada de la Virgen. There were also family picnics in the *campo* and frequent lunches at the Ridingers' rented house on Calle Santo Domingo, where one of their neighbors was Stirling Dickinson.

Apparently in denial about the state of his wife's health, one day Ridinger announced to Mary Lou Johnson that the family would resettle in Central America. He asked her opinion on various locations, and she immediately recommended the Colonial town of Antigua, Guatemala, which when she'd visited the year before, had struck her as "the most beautiful city in the most beautiful country in the world." Antigua, she told him, was the only place she really wanted to live.

But the Ridingers never made it to Central America that year. After just a couple of months, they cut short their stay in Mexico and flew back to Chicago, when Marilyn became too weak to continue. Her cancer had metastasized to her lungs. Two weeks after their return to the States, on July 9, Marilyn Ridinger died. Neither Jay nor the girls wanted to stay in Chicago after that. By August 15, they'd rented a house in Antigua.

Founded in 1543 as Santiago de los Caballeros, Antigua occupies a flat bowl, surrounded by three volcanoes and rugged, forested hills that extend to the edge of town. The city was once the Colonial capital of Guatemala, which at the time included not only the present-day country of that name but also current Belize, Costa Rica, El Salvador, Honduras, Nicaragua, and the Mexican state of Chiapas. With a population of more than sixty thousand, Santiago was considered one of the loveliest towns in the New World, renowned for its churches and monasteries. But after devastating earthquakes in 1717 and 1773, the government relocated to present-day Guatemala City, some twenty miles away (not far enough, it turned out, since the new site was also devastated by temblors). The old capital was largely evacuated, and known as La Antigua Guatemala, it settled into gentle neglect. By 1973, when the Ridingers' Dodge Travco turned into town, exactly two centuries after the fateful earthquake, the city claimed less than half the population of its glory years.

Antigua's brightly painted, prudently one-story houses were still punctuated by toppled Colonial churches, which studded the city like Maya ruins. On the main square, the cathedral, once among the grandest in Central America, was more rubble than church, having been only partially rebuilt. But a few grand places of worship survived: On the northern edge of town, graceful, exuberant La Merced still rose like a marzipan wedding cake, with its white tracery of vines, leaves, and flowers set against a soft-yellow background.

There wasn't much happening in Antigua in the 1970s. Siesta was religiously observed, and even when the shops reopened at two o'clock, there was little to buy. Cars were rare, and the few American expats joked that if they needed to locate a friend, they could just walk outside and find the other's vehicle. Like the Johnson sisters in San Miguel, the young Ridingers had trouble adjusting at first. But their father fell in love with Antigua and everything about it—the people, the climate, the lush landscape. To Jay Ridinger, it was a world of Sunday afternoons, with no Monday mornings in sight. In Antigua, he decided, he would realize the long-harbored, romantic vision of life he could never fulfill in Chicago, or anywhere in his native country. He would reinvent himself yet again, on an even grander, more adventurous scale.

He began wearing a loose-fitting safari jacket and a bush hat as his daily uniform. Some said the costume was an effort to make himself memorable. Others considered it a more personal statement, a resolute shedding of the suit and tie he'd worn all those years in Chicago. And still others thought it had a practical purpose, to free him from deciding what to wear each morning. Whatever the motive, the outfit became his trademark, along with the monocle he adopted after corrective laser surgery was successful in only one eye.

Ridinger rented a house on the north edge of town, near the old Convento de Santo Domingo. Built in the seventeenth century, the monastery was once the largest and most opulent in Central America, until an earthquake left it in ruins. Retired American archaeologist Edwin Shook and his wife, Ginny, had bought the property and restored it as their home, encircled by old walls and lovely gardens.

The Shooks invited their new neighbor for cocktails. Jay Ridinger had never developed a taste for alcohol, so he sipped Coca-Cola as he told his hosts about his life in Chicago. But Ginny Shook grew suddenly cold, letting him know that his type—real estate developers—weren't welcome in Antigua. As Ridinger would discover, the couple of hundred foreigners, mostly retirees from the U.S. State Department or the U.S. Agency for International Development (USAID), had a conservative bent in those days. With the near-perfect climate leaving little weather to talk about, dinner-party discussions were dominated by the price of real estate, the trouble finding good help, and the internecine intrigues at the American embassy in Guatemala City. Ridinger began to call his fellow expats "the pachyderms," for their Republican leanings as well as their stodginess.

Personal connections were crucial in Guatemala, in the foreign community as well as among the locals, and there was suspicion of outsiders and a reluctance to go beyond one's circle. In time, Ridinger and the Shooks became close friends, but the rest of the establishment wasn't sure what to make of the flamboyant newcomer. There was no denying his charm or intelligence. But he had a habit of giving advice whether it was solicited or not, and he had an odd way of aggrandizing people when he introduced them, so that army sergeants found themselves promoted to colonels and teachers to superintendents. "If you lift people up, sometimes they'll stay there," he'd explain. Ridinger also had the drive and competitiveness of a natural entrepreneur, and some of his new neighbors suspected him of being a sharp operator.

He began to wonder whether he'd made a terrible mistake, whether he could ever find a place for himself in Antigua. So one evening, he called his new friend Betty Kempe, who by then had installed a telephone in the Villa Santa Monica in San Miguel. Find a housekeeper, Betty told him. Put the girls in school. Study Spanish. Calmed, Ridinger realized he needed something

Jay Ridinger in his trademark bush hat and safari suit.
COURTESY OF MARY LOU RIDINGER

to occupy himself—and he had to find a niche, something that would justify his presence in Antigua to his fellow expatriates. He also began playing in the expat poker game, not only a major social event but also a crucial source of gossip.

There were two antiques stores in the city, and Ridinger stopped in regularly. He bought old furniture to complement the decorative pieces he'd brought from Chicago, his china, crystal, ivory, and miniature wooden boxes. Also in the shops were pre-Columbian jades that had been looted from archaeological sites. In fact, illicit antiquities were so common in Antigua that one American sold them out of his trench coat on the street, like a Times Square pornography peddler. Ridinger especially admired the jades, for their age and artistry, their physical and cultural heft, their sense of mystery.

Like so many before him, he began to wonder where the raw jade for all these carvings had come from. He had never heard of William Foshag or Robert Leslie, didn't know of their discovery nearly two decades earlier. He also hadn't heard that, even as he was preparing to go to Guatemala, a team led by British archaeologist Norman Hammond was finding two more outcrops of jade in the Motagua Valley, at the towns of Usumatlán and El Jute. He just knew that his neighbor Ed Shook had spent years searching for the pre-Columbian jade mines but, to Shook's immense frustration, had found only the occasional rock in a river or field.

Jay Ridinger also met American archaeologist David Sedat. Born in Guatemala of missionary parents, Sedat had teamed up with his former mentor, Robert Sharer, to investigate Preclassic settlements in the nearby Salamá Valley, looking for evidence of early trade in goods such as jade and obsidian. His team had discovered significant greenstone artifacts and a greenstone workshop at El Portón, and they had scouted for jade in the Motagua Valley, close to Foshag and Leslie's outcrop at Manzanal. (Greenstone is a general term for rock that resembles jade but is actually something else;

archaeologists sometimes call it "social jade" or "cultural jade.") At Sedat's invitation, Jay and the girls drove up in the Dodge Travco to San Jerónimo in Baja Verapaz, northeast of Guatemala City, to tour some of the area's archaeological sites.

Sedat was won over by Ridinger's charm and openness to ideas, and impressed by his flair for business. When Jay confided that he was searching for a different direction in life, Sedat thought that his new friend might have the assets—personal, professional, financial—to take up the search for Guatemalan jade. He took Ridinger to an unreported jade workshop in the Motagua, and he showed him a geological map of the country depicting rock formations likely to contain the stone. Though the Guatemalan government had made such information virtually a state secret, Sedat gave Ridinger the name of a man who brokered the maps.

And so the old daydreams came flooding back: Jay in his safari shirt and bush hat, cutting a swath through intractable jungle. Jay the Eagle Scout, sleeping rough, cooking his meals over an open fire. Jay the amateur archaeologist, on the trail of vanished civilizations. Jay the entrepreneur, claiming a treasure that had been lost for centuries. Now he knew what niche he would carve for himself in Guatemala: He would discover the lost jade mines of the Maya.

❈

It was November 1973, and Washington, D.C., was cold, damp, gray. Hugging his overcoat, a tall figure trotted past the statue of Neptune and up the great Renaissance staircase, through a massive bronze door, and into the Great Hall of the Library of Congress. Conceived as a shrine to learning, the library was among the most ornate public buildings in America when it opened in 1897, and it still was nearly a century later—the work of dozens of sculptors and painters and countless craftsmen. Barely slowing his pace, the visitor passed under the gold-leaf ceiling, over the inlaid marble floor, past the busts of Washington and Jefferson, the double marble staircase with its bronze statues raising the Torch of Knowledge. Then he entered the heart of the library, the octagonal Reading Room, with more marble columns, arches, and statues; bronze busts; massive stained glass windows; and rising above it all, the great dome with its mural dedicated to Human Understanding.

In the center of the room was a circular wooden desk. Jay Ridinger approached the librarian stationed there. "Excuse me," he said, "I have a question."

Her eyebrows lifted.

"What's your favorite restaurant in Washington?"

Her brows lifted further, then her eyes crinkled and her dimples showed. She told him.

"I'll make you a proposition," Ridinger said. "I need every journal article and book in the Library of Congress having to do with Mesoamerican jade. If you'll make copies for me, I'll buy you lunch there."

That fall in Antigua, Ridinger had been absorbing everything he could find about jade. Yet, he realized he needed to learn a great deal more. After spending Thanksgiving with his family outside Chicago, he'd left the girls with his parents and had boarded a plane to Washington.

The following day, he returned to the Library of Congress to see what his accomplice had turned up. Taking a seat at one of the wooden desks ringing the Reading Room, he began to scan the stack of photocopies. There were nearly fifty, mostly technical reports from geology and archaeology journals, with polysyllabic titles that meant nothing to him. The librarian's search hadn't uncovered Foshag and Leslie's brief letter to *American Antiquity* reporting the jade outcrop at Manzanal. But toward the bottom of the stack, Ridinger came across a stapled sheaf thicker than the rest. The title was also slightly less opaque: *Mineralogical Studies on Guatemalan Jade,* by William F. Foshag.

Ridinger opened the monograph and began to read. It was an education, more information than he'd ever seen in one place regarding New World jade—its chemical formula, the measure of its hardness, locations where ancient jades had been discovered, techniques used to work the stone in early times. But there was more. As to the source of Maya and Olmec jade, Foshag suggested that anyone searching for the stone in Central America should look for deposits of serpentinite. And Mesoamerica's largest outcrops of that mineral were found in the Sierra de las Minas of Guatemala, just a few hours' drive northeast of Antigua. Ridinger flipped back to the title page. The monograph had been published by the Smithsonian Institution. He collected his papers and coat, made a date to take the librarian to lunch, and hurried out the library's huge bronze door.

He rushed past the Supreme Court and the Capitol, then down Constitution Avenue, skirting the museums on the north side of the Mall. At Ninth Street, the Washington Monument looming closer, he turned left and took a quick right onto Madison Drive. Then he jogged up the wide steps and through the sober classical columns of the Smithsonian's Museum of Natural History. Glancing neither right nor left, he went straight to the gift shop on the building's ground floor.

"I'm looking for a monograph titled *Mineralogical Studies on Guatemalan Jade*," he told the young woman behind the counter. "It was published by the Smithsonian in 1957."

"Nineteen fifty-seven?" she asked dubiously. "The Smithsonian publications are over here," she said, leading him to a set of shelves across the store. They both riffled through the publications, but Foshag's wasn't among them.

"Is there anyplace else it might be?" Ridinger asked.

"Just a minute," she said and disappeared behind a door.

Ridinger paced among the souvenirs. Finally, she returned with a thin paperback. "I found it. It was on a shelf in the back room."

"Is that the only copy?"

"No, there are about a dozen."

"I'll take them all."

✢

William Foshag could not have explained why jade was so often found as veins and nodules within the rock serpentinite. He had died in 1956, the year before the Smithsonian issued his *Mineralogical Studies on Guatemalan Jade.* Had he lived just a few years longer, he would have seen a revolution in our understanding of how the earth works.

As early as 1600, after European voyages of discovery had begun to yield more accurate maps, people began to remark how the continents' coastlines seemed to complement each other. Then, three hundred years later, German meteorologist Alfred Wegner made the startling suggestion that the continents were once joined but had drifted apart, and were drifting still. He couldn't explain how the huge landmasses moved or why, and his notion won few supporters. But by the time of Foshag's death, geologists had begun collecting data and proposing mechanisms to support Wegner's idea. Over the next decade, refined and expanded by other researchers, the concept of continental drift had matured into the theory of plate tectonics, offering a compelling new picture of how the surface of the earth is constantly reshaping itself.

We now know that the brittle, sixty-mile-deep surface on which we walk (the lithosphere) floats over a hotter, more ductile layer (the asthenosphere), which is slowly churning due to differences in density and temperature. The lithosphere consists of about a dozen large, independently moving "plates," which fit together like a poorly made jigsaw puzzle. As the asthenosphere beneath them flows, the plates shift. Where they bump into or slide past each other, they give rise to mountains, earthquakes, volcanoes—and jade.

The top layer of ocean plates (those beneath the sea) consists mostly of basalt, a volcanic rock formed when lava seeps up through cracks in a mid-ocean rift, then hardens. Ocean plates are thinner than continental plates (those under landmasses), but denser. So when they meet a continental plate, they generally dive beneath it, a process geologists call subduction. The resulting increase in temperature and pressure forces some of the water out of the subducting plate, working like the rollers on an old-time washing machine. Since the major components of jade—sodium, aluminum, and silicon—are relatively soluble, they dissolve out of the metamorphosing basalt and are carried away and introduced into the overlying plate.

To achieve jadeite's high density, its light elements have to be packed tightly together within their crystal structure, similar to the way graphite must be subjected to tremendous pressure in order to become diamond. In the case of jadeite, this pressure ranges from 6 to 20 kilobars (six to twenty times the pressure of the earth's atmosphere at sea level), which occurs from about ten to forty miles deep within the earth. On the other hand, temperatures must be relatively low during these processes, less than about 1,100 degrees Fahrenheit, or the jadeite may melt in the presence of water, ceasing to be solid mineral. (Nephrite, the other jade, requires a completely different set of circumstances to form, including only about 1 kilobar of pressure, which is found about two miles beneath the earth's surface—explaining why jadeite and nephrite are not found together, and why jadeite is denser.)

Jadeite's companion serpentine is also formed in the presence of watery liquid, by reaction of the rock known as peridotite, which makes up the earth's mantle (the viscous layer between the crust and outer core). The peridotite forms the ceiling of the subduction channel, and as it cracks from tectonic movements, water squeezes in. The peridotite sucks up the water like a sponge and reacts to form serpentinite. The sodium, aluminum, and silicon dissolved in the fluid crystallize to form jadeite rock, the way that material precipitating out of tap water forms incrustations on the insides of household pipes.

The jadeitite moves along faults created by compression where tectonic plates come together. But it's a long and perilous journey, and much of the mineral can be destroyed before it ever reaches the surface. The problem is that jadeite is not stable under moist, low-pressure, low-temperature conditions. If it doesn't rise relatively quickly, it may combine with the water all around it to create minerals such as albite, which forms a rock called albitite that is often found along with jade. But serpentinite also plays a role in jade's rush to the surface. The jade is embedded in the serpentinite like raisins in a pudding, and though jade is dense, the serpentinite is relatively lightweight; as the lighter rock is buoyed upward, the jade rides along with it.

Geologist George Harlow, curator of minerals and gems at the American Museum of Natural History, calls jadeite "nasty," meaning that its chemistry can make it complicated to track a piece of jade back to its source. Whereas obsidian forms from a more-or-less homogeneous flow of lava, giving it a uniform composition, the chemicals that give rise to jadeite can vary from vein to vein and even within a single vein over time. With jadeite, lots of other elements that were present in the water solutions in very small amounts, called trace elements, can substitute for the sodium, aluminum, and silicon. As a result, each piece of jade carries these trace elements as a kind of birthmark, making it slightly different from every other piece of jade in characteristics such as color, luster, and texture.

It's been said, "As with baked Alaska, the surprising thing is that jadeite exists at all." And the conditions that produce it are rare on earth, accounting for the mineral's scarcity. These prerequisites occur only where an ocean plate slides beneath a continental plate—but most subduction zones don't include jade, which means that other factors must also come into play, although they aren't well understood. It may be, for instance, that not only does the ocean plate have to dive under the continental plate, but that both need to slide horizontally past each other at the same time. One place where these conditions are met is Burma, where the India and Asia plates come together; another is in the Western Hemisphere, where the North American and Caribbean plates are in contact—central Guatemala.

�֍

Back in Antigua after his trip to Washington, Jay Ridinger wrote to Mary Lou Johnson at the Villa Santa Monica in San Miguel.

But she was in Mississippi, where the family owned an old plantation outside Natchez. Called Sligo, after the county in Ireland, the property had been purchased by Mary Lou's great-grandfather, George W. Armstrong, in 1917. Armstrong had been born in 1866 in Texas and had made a fortune there, in oil, banking, steel, and cattle. When he'd gone to Natchez to deliver some mules to the Army, he'd been enthralled with the place and had bought Sligo; later, he added more than thirty other plantations nearby, bringing his holdings to forty thousand acres. Sligo's antebellum house had burned in 1925, and Armstrong had died in 1954; parcels had been sold off, and by the 1970s the property was reduced to three thousand acres. But there were still a caretaker's cottage, a log cabin, and a hunting lodge. This last was a low, rustic building with a huge stone fireplace, where the family gathered for vacations and holidays. A reunion was planned for Thanksgiving, and Mary Lou Johnson had already left.

When Betty Kempe arrived at Sligo, she carried Jay Ridinger's letter. He'd amassed a library of books and articles, he wrote Mary Lou, and was learning all he could about Mesoamerican jade. He related his visit to the Library of Congress and told her that, with the Foshag monograph as his guide, he was going to find jade in

Guatemala. Then the extraordinary proposition: Would she come and be his partner?

Johnson was stunned. As Ridinger knew, she'd wanted to live in Antigua from the moment she'd seen it. And of course she would relish the chance to resolve an archaeological mystery that had stood for centuries. As she thought back over the good times she'd had with Jay and Marilyn and the girls in Mexico, she had to admit that she'd been attracted by Ridinger's distinguished voice and his romantic, child-like enthusiasm. He'd written earlier to tell her about Marilyn's death and the move to Guatemala, and not least, she admired his fearlessness and his ability to reinvent himself time and again; now he'd left everything familiar and, with three young daughters, was starting fresh in a country where he'd never been and knew no one, didn't even speak the language.

But she respected Jay Ridinger too much to see him make a fool of himself. So she wrote back, repeating what her archaeology professors had taught her at La Universidad de las Américas: He was wasting his time; there were no jade deposits in Guatemala.

Jay Ridinger wrote again. Not only was there jade there, but he'd met a Belgian expat named Jean Deveaux, who'd already discovered a supply of the stone—in the Motagua Valley, just where Foshag said it would be. Instead of being disappointed that someone had beaten him to the bonanza, Ridinger was gripped by entrepreneurial fervor. Deveaux had the jade and an idea, but not the money or management expertise to exploit them. So he and Ridinger had agreed to a partnership: The Belgian would provide the raw material, Jay would buy the carving equipment and cut it into manageable pieces, and they would sell the jade on the international market.

Now Johnson was alarmed. Anyone who said there was jade in Guatemala was trying to cheat him, she wrote Ridinger. She'd seen the same thing in Mexico, where naïve gringos would buy what they thought were the lost silver mines of the conquistadors. Don't do it, she warned.

Ridinger wrote back with a proposal of his own: If she would come to Guatemala, she could examine the Belgian's samples and read everything Jay had collected on Mesoamerican jade. If, after that, she still believed he were wasting his time, not only would he stop soliciting her help, he'd give up the project himself.

Mary Lou told her mother about this latest offer. Betty Kempe was still as taken with Jay Ridinger as she'd been that first day in the Villa Santa Monica, when he'd called her "pretty lady."

"He's so handsome and charming," Betty told her. "What do you have to lose?"

Mary Lou knew what her mother really meant: *Careful, or some other woman will snap him up.*

"If you like him so much," Mary Lou told Betty, "why don't you go to Guatemala?"

FIVE

Aventurine

From the air, Guatemala was a brooding landscape of gently pointed hills jutting from an ash-colored mist. Closer to the capital, the peaks grew sharper and greener, before ceding to hives of flat-roofed houses. When the plane tipped its wings over the city, great ravines came into view, with more ramshackle houses clinging doggedly.

At the western end of the capital lay the ancient Maya metropolis of Kaminaljuyu. The place had already been abandoned by the time the Spanish arrived, and in the centuries to come most of the site had been sacrificed to the expansion of Guatemala City. Now only a few grass-strewn mounds remained. But the ancient city (investigated by, among others, Jay Ridinger's neighbor Ed Shook) had once claimed more than two square miles. Straddling a major north-south trade route, it had been inhabited for nearly three thousand years, and beginning about 600 B.C., had dominated the southern highlands for almost a millennium. As one measure of their wealth and power, the kings of Kaminaljuyu had gone to their graves surrounded by carved jade jewelry, masks, and headdresses.

It was February 13, 1974. Mary Lou Johnson had chosen the date because it was her parents' wedding anniversary. She knew there were no jade mines in Guatemala, but still she'd come. And as the plane touched down, she was thinking how happy she was to be there.

At the immigration kiosk, she handed her documents to the uniformed official, then glanced up at the second-floor gallery. Standing behind the glass was Jay Ridinger. He waved, then said something to the man beside him.

When she exited the tiny airport, Ridinger was waiting. He gave her a hug and introduced her to his friend Tommy. Tommy was a pilot, he said; Ridinger knew Mary Lou loved flying, had taken lessons but had never gotten her license. Jay lifted her suitcase into the Dodge Travco, then climbed into the driver's side. Mary Lou took the swivel seat next to him.

They got on the highway to Antigua. Concrete quickly gave way to pine forest, and as Ridinger guided the motor home over the rising, twisting road, Johnson couldn't decide which he resembled more, a tour guide or a deputy from the chamber of commerce. Guatemala was wonderful, he told her. Antigua couldn't be more beautiful. The people were lovely, the culture amazing. He was making friends. The girls were making friends. Everything was perfect. He was so happy she'd told him to come.

He needn't have worked so hard. Mary Lou Johnson had been looking for an excuse to come back to Antigua ever since she'd seen the city two years before. And as she watched Ridinger's confident grip on the steering wheel and listened to his resonant tones, she had to admit another reason for her enthusiasm.

Outside Antigua, the highway crested a hill and became a tortuous, nerve-testing plunge; then, just as abruptly, it deposited the Travco on a dead-flat city street. Jay Ridinger was still renting the Colonial house on the north side of town. His parents were visiting from Indiana, he told Mary Lou, but he'd kept a room free for her. Or if she'd prefer, another friend of his, Bill, would be happy to put her up in his larger house just two doors away. No, she said, she'd rather stay at Jay's.

Ridinger introduced her to his parents. His father, the retired Inland Steel executive, was tall like Jay, with a quiet manner. His mother, once brilliant and opinionated, was drifting into Alzheimer's disease. The next day was St. Valentine's, and when they gathered for dinner that night, Jay had the same gift waiting for all three daughters, his mother, and Mary Lou—a little gold treasure chest filled with raw emeralds.

Over the next few days, Johnson pored through the dozens of books and articles Ridinger had collected. Some, on the Maya and the Olmecs, she'd already known from her archaeology studies. Others, about oriental jade, were handsome but beside the point. And some of the journal articles, on geology and petrology, didn't mean much more to her than they had to him. She was especially intrigued by Foshag's *Mineralogical Studies on Guatemalan Jade*, which linked serpentinite and jade and painted a fat treasure-map *x* over the Sierra de las Minas. At the end, she had to allow that her professors at La Universidad de las Américas may have been wrong; there might be deposits of jade in Guatemala after all. As she worked through the stack of publications, Mary Lou Johnson weighed her choices: She could go back to her mother's house in San Miguel, or despite her misgivings, she could remain in Antigua, "the most beautiful city in the most beautiful country in the world," with Jay Ridinger. She told him she'd stay.

In April, a friend of Ridinger named Jerry Leech came to Guatemala for a visit. With an M.B.A. from the University of Chicago, Leech had been finance director at Hull House and had served on the boards of some not-for-profit housing companies in which Ridinger was involved. The two men had also been next-door neighbors in Chicago. Their wives had been best friends, and Angela Ridinger had babysat for Jerry Jr. While the Ridingers toured in their Dodge Travco before Marilyn died, Leech had taken care of their business in Chicago, paying bills, collecting rents, forwarding mail. In Antigua, Ridinger introduced him to Jean Deveaux and invited his friend to become general manager of their new jade venture. For Leech, the offer came at a good time. He'd just been through a divorce, and like Ridinger, he welcomed the challenge of a new country, a new language, and a whole new industry on which to test his business skills. He went back to Chicago to settle his affairs.

When his friend Bill decided to leave Guatemala, Ridinger rented the larger house, a one-story building with a big patio in the center and another out back, to accommodate the business. Machinery to cut, grind, drill, and polish jade arrived from the States, and Ridinger set it up in the garage, the equipment's metal edges gleaming against the whitewashed walls. On a lot next door, he began constructing his factory, laying a tile floor and raising a translucent plastic roof. In June, Jerry Leech came to Antigua to stay. Jean Deveaux delivered his first load of stone, which they piled in the back patio.

Mary Lou Johnson still distrusted Ridinger's partner. Slender, with a shock of white hair, an aquiline nose, and pointed chin, Jean Deveaux appeared modest of ambition, grandfatherly of mien. Arriving in Guatemala after the Second World War, he'd been dabbling in jade for years, but to Johnson the elderly Belgian seemed an unlikely discoverer of the lost jade mines of the Maya. And though he exuded European culture and charm, she suspected his business dealings had a sharpness to equal his facial features. When Ridinger showed her a sample of Deveaux's green stone, she turned it over in her hand and saw how its crystals glinted in the light. "So this is jade," she said.

At a poker game, Jay Ridinger met another American expat, Bob Terzuola. Dark, heavily built with prominent brown eyes, Terzuola was running an agricultural program for USAID. But like many people in Guatemala, he'd become enamored of jade and he had taught himself to carve small pieces by hand. He'd also discovered a pre-Columbian worksite near the Motagua, just a couple of miles from Robert Leslie's tomato field.

Actually, the site had been discovered by Terzuola's now ex-wife, Gail. The couple had been driving up the Atlantic Highway, which runs from Guatemala City to Puerto Barrios on the eastern coast, when she asked him to stop so she could relieve herself. Around the ninety-three-kilometer marker, he pulled over beside a field of rolling hills. When she came back to the car, she showed him some rock fragments and said, "Bob, this looks like jade." And so it was—a call of nature had led them to a major workshop more than a thousand years old, now known as the Terzuola Site, where tools; fragments of obsidian, jade, and other types of stone; and sherds of pottery have been recovered.

Ridinger brought Terzuola by the workshop and showed him the pile of the Belgian's stone. Terzuola picked up a piece.

"What makes you think this is jade?" he asked.

✢

Mary Lou Johnson was sitting at a long wooden table, a pile of stone chips to one side. In front of her was a flask of a yellowish, sweet-smelling liquid called bromoform. This particular bromoform was nearly three times heavier than water, heavier even than most minerals, and jade's great weight made it one of the few rocks that would sink in it.

Johnson took a chip from the heap on her worktable and dropped it into the bromoform. It floated. Retrieving the stone with a pair of tweezers, she set it to the side. Then she dropped another chip into the flask. It floated too. She fished it out and put it with the first.

From its weight and appearance, Bob Terzuola had suspected that most of Deveaux's stone wasn't jade, but a type of quartz called aventurine. So he'd introduced Ridinger and Johnson to his good friend Josh Rosenfeld, a freelance geologist working for International Nickel and other companies. In his late thirties,

115

Rosenfeld was lanky, with dark hair and beard, glasses, and an accent worthy of his Bronx upbringing. He'd explained to Ridinger and Johnson how to use the bromoform. You had to be careful not to inhale it or to get it on your skin, he'd warned, because despite the syrupy aroma, it was a poison and a carcinogen.

Picking another piece from the pile, Johnson dropped it into the bromoform. This one sank. She eyed the chip, as though waiting for it to spring back to the surface. Well, that didn't prove it was jade, she reminded herself. Even if a stone sank in the heavy liquid, Rosenfeld had said, more tests would be necessary to confirm its makeup.

In the end, fewer than half the chips had sunk in the bromoform. By then, Johnson had tested so many pieces that she felt she could predict whether one would float even before releasing it, which was supposed to be impossible. She began to wonder if she had a special affinity for jade, like the Chinese women who were said to wade through a river and identify jade pebbles with their feet.

Rosenfeld cut some thin slices of the rocks and studied them under a petrographic microscope, exposing them to polarized light to reveal their crystalline structure. Afterward, he told the Ridingers that only about 10 percent of Deveaux's stone might be jade; the rest was a mix of aventurine, serpentinite, and other rocks. The next step would be to ship the promising specimens to a laboratory in the States for an x-ray diffraction study. At the lab, the sample would be bombarded with powerful short-wave x-rays; then instruments would record the pattern the waves made as they ricocheted off. Each mineral produces a distinctive diffraction pattern, depending on its crystal structure, chemical composition, and other properties. So by comparing the pattern made by an unknown sample to a library of patterns made by known minerals, technicians could determine whether the rocks were jade or a worthless imposter.

The Ridingers mailed samples to three different labs and waited for a nervous few weeks. Then the assays came back: Though much of his stone was aventurine quartz, the grandfatherly Belgian had also managed to find jade. Mary Lou Johnson was dumbfounded by the news. Jay Ridinger was ecstatic that his investment seemed about to pay a dividend.

Then, with Deveaux and Terzuola advising, Johnson and Ridinger began to experiment with the carving equipment. Their first task was simple, to slice the jade and polish it into samples they could show to foreign buyers. There was certain to be a vast worldwide demand for Guatemalan jade, Ridinger explained to Mary Lou, and tons could be shipped to places such as New York and London. But the partners would begin in jade's ancient homeland, China, where they would drive Burmese jade from the market and establish (in reverse) the Asian-American trade route that had been postulated for so long.

On October 12, Columbus Day, Johnson and Ridinger left for Hong Kong with their assays and their samples, blocks of polished jade the size of a pack of cigarettes. Neither had ever been to the great commercial center, which the British had seized more than a century earlier to force their goods (especially opium) into the Chinese market. Hoping their own, more modest trade initiative would meet with a warmer response, Johnson and Ridinger began their round of appointments. The first was in a nondescript office in Kowloon, the peninsula extending into the harbor north of Hong Kong Island. The young, abrupt Chinese man mentioned that he'd received their sample in the mail. When they told him they hadn't sent any samples, he took a letter off his desk, signed by Jean Deveaux. He was pleased to enclose genuine jade from Guatemala, the Belgian had written, in anticipation of his partner's visit. But when the Chinese had tested the specimen, it had assayed as aventurine quartz.

There had been a mistake, Ridinger assured him. They'd had some aventurine mixed in with their samples, but they had jade, as well. He took the assay certificates from his briefcase, but the buyer refused to look at them. In any event, he was interested only in imperial green jade, he said.

The meetings had gone no better at the next half dozen manufacturers. Finally, one company agreed to purchase some white jade, but at a price so low that it would barely cover Ridinger and Johnson's travel expenses, never mind the cost of acquiring the stone, cutting it into blocks, and shipping it to China.

On the flight back to the States, Ridinger stared out the window at the empty Pacific. He felt ridiculous, he told Johnson. Now he could see that the Chinese didn't understand New World jade, that they preferred to deal with their longtime partners in Burma. Even the lone trader who had agreed to take their stone was undoubtedly going to pass it off as Burmese. And if the partners couldn't sell their jade in China, with its deep affinity for jade and its long history of importing it, he despaired of any other country buying it. Their venture was over before it had fairly begun.

Back in Antigua, the partners consulted. If there were no international market for Guatemalan jade, they decided, they would have to create a market. And not in Hong Kong or New York or London, but in Guatemala. They already had the equipment; they could carve jade into reproductions of masks and other artifacts and sell them to tourists who wanted to take home an object that was not only handsome but culturally significant. Johnson reminded Ridinger of what their friend David Sedat had once told them, "The story sells the stone." It was jade's association with ancient civilizations like the Olmecs and the Maya that would make it marketable. And Johnson's credentials as an archaeologist made her the ideal saleswoman-in-chief.

They would need to learn how to work jade, but Bob Terzuola and Jean Deveaux would help them. Then, at the earliest opportunity, Mary Lou urged Ridinger, they had to disassociate themselves from the meddling Belgian. But first, they'd have to find their own source of jade.

✦

It was December in the Sierra de las Minas. The rains had ended and with them the cool season known in Guatemala as *el invierno*, "winter." The heat had resurged, with punishing sunshine and temperatures close to a hundred degrees. Shaded only by their broad-brimmed hats, three figures were walking single-file along a narrow hillside trail, through spindly cacti and thorny acacia trees. Every so often, they would stop, incline their ear to a stone, and take a sharp swing with a hammer. Then they would straighten up and trudge on. Jay Ridinger had gotten his wish: He was finally prospecting for jade.

With Jerry Leech focused on the venture's business affairs, the brunt of the search fell to Ridinger and Johnson. Unlike gold, their friend the geologist Josh Rosenfeld had explained, jade wasn't generally located by panning or digging. It would most likely be found in long, roundish pieces called "pods," sitting in riverbeds or on the ground, or jutting from outcrops. But this didn't mean it was in plain sight. When jade is exposed to the elements for long periods, its surface weathers to form a generic brownish crust, or "rind," which gives no hint of the stone's true color—one of the reasons jade was so devilishly difficult to locate. So, the first clues that they had found jade wouldn't be visual, but aural and tactile: Struck by a hammer, it wouldn't produce a flat *thud* as lighter rocks did, but an almost metallic *ping*, and the hammerhead would recoil with a snap they could feel in their wrist. If a stone seemed promising, the next step was to break off a chip with a glancing hammer blow, which required some practice to master. Finally, they would drop the piece into a vial of bromoform for the density test.

They'd driven east from Antigua, through Guatemala City and up the Atlantic Highway. Not far outside the capital, they'd gotten a glimpse of the Motagua. Rising in Guatemala's western highlands, near the ancient market town of Chichicastenango, the Motagua sweeps eastward for almost three hundred miles to the Gulf of Honduras. En route, it incorporates nearly forty tributaries and drains some five thousand square miles, more than any other waterway in the country. To Ridinger and Johnson, the river appeared as a broad ribbon at the bottom of a broad valley. Or at least its course was wide, scoured by the inundations of the rainy season. Now, in the dry time, the Motagua was a meager thread twisting through sandy flats. But over millennia, its floods had deposited millions of tons of rich soil along its banks, and on either side were stands of melons, beans, and corn—and the tomato field where Robert Leslie had run a cultivator over his jade boulder. To the south could be seen a line of violet peaks some 6,000 feet high; to the north was the even more foreboding Sierra de las Minas, jutting nearly 10,000 feet above sea level.

To Johnson, it was a landscape seething with history. Downriver, near the coast, were the remains of the Maya city of Quirigua. And about thirty miles south of that, just across the border in Honduras, the ruins of Copan, where the first royal Maya tomb had been reported opened, by Juan Galindo, in 1834. Now known for its great stelae carved with elaborate portraits of its rulers, Copan had founded Quirigua in A.D. 426 and had held it as a vassal for three centuries. Then in 738, tiny Quirigua, possibly with the help of Copan's longtime rival Calakmul, had managed to slay the great city's king and shatter its control of the region.

Even as Johnson's thoughts drifted back to the past, Ridinger dreamed his mercantile dreams. He'd already been to see Deveaux's lawyer about dissolving their partnership.

"On what basis?" the attorney wanted to know.

Deveaux did deliver some jade, allowed Johnson, who was acting as interpreter. But most of his stone was worthless aventurine quartz.

The lawyer's face drained of color. "You mean," he sputtered, "all those rocks piled in my garage, which this gentleman has paid me for my services, aren't jade?"

After that, the attorney was more obliging, and even represented Ridinger in a few matters. (Ridinger liked to say that you needed three lawyers in Guatemala: One with the clout to negotiate with government officials, one to handle routine matters such as contracts and bribes, and one whom you could call at three o'clock in the morning to get you out of jail; Deveaux's lawyer was of the second variety.)

Ridinger and Johnson also drove into the *campo* and managed to find the Belgian's jade prospector, or "picker." Isaac was painfully thin in his blue jeans and straw cowboy hat, grizzled, with chiseled European features that made him look like the last of the conquistadors. It was clear he didn't know one green stone from another, but thanks to Deveaux, Mary Lou Johnson had had an education on that very subject. More important, Isaac was energetic and eager, and he knew the country and the people. And the Belgian hadn't paid him as promised. So Isaac was happy to show them possible sources of jade and to soothe landowners who might not appreciate strange gringos wandering their property. When jade was discovered, Ridinger and Johnson would negotiate with the proprietors, but until then there wasn't much to discuss.

The first few outcrops that Isaac showed them weren't jade but more aventurine. So the three started combing the wide, sandy banks of the Motagua. When this produced nothing, they cruised the Atlantic Highway, pulling over to examine the deep cuts made when the road was built. After this yielded no jade, they turned to the hot, dry terrain along the Motagua's many tributaries.

Jade prospecting was turning out different from Jay Ridinger's fantasies. For one thing, there was no jungle in sight, only these scrubby hills. The northern, windward side of the Sierra de las Minas was covered in lush cloud forest, where rain fell in an incessant drizzle known as *chipi-chipi*. But here to the south, in the mountains' lee, lay the only arid part of Guatemala and one of the driest areas in Central America, collecting only twenty inches of rain a year.

Searching for jade along the Motagua didn't entail sleeping bags or campfires, either. Ridinger and Johnson stayed at a serviceable motel called the Longarone, complete with an Italian restaurant and swimming pool, and passed their evenings playing gin rummy. But for Jay Ridinger their daily forays were serious affairs. Having resolved to find jade in Guatemala, he focused on the search with the same intensity he focused on everything, from playing poker to speculating in real estate. It was Ridinger who checked the maps, planned the routes, organized the supplies, tried to keep to a schedule.

The area south of the Sierra de las Minas, the only arid region of Guatemala.
PHOTOGRAPH BY THE AUTHOR

Mary Lou Johnson was more relaxed. Not that she was uninterested, but as she wandered the scorching trails, stopping to tap the occasional rock, she found herself daydreaming not about jade's commercial value but its historical significance, about the ancient peoples who had wandered these same paths over centuries, about what they had seen and what the jade had meant to them. She recalled how the Indians said that jade gave off a delicate vapor, like breath, in the early morning sunlight and considered whether there was any scientific basis to the legend. She wondered, could it be because the stone's density made it absorb heat faster than the surrounding rocks?

Johnson was also more fatalistic: If they were meant to find jade, she figured, they would find it. For her, the outings weren't just a means to an end but an adventure to be savored. And she was, in her words, "a diffuse thinker," always "eight-tracking," taking in the big picture, whereas Jay was more fixated on the immediate task. While he would charge ahead, wielding his geologist's hammer, Mary Lou would hang back, stopping to admire the foliage along the river and to chat with curious *campesinos*. She was, she says, "floating along on a little pink cloud."

Mary Lou Johnson was in love, and not just with Antigua or jade prospecting. There were so many things to admire about Jay Ridinger—his virile radio voice; his bearded good looks; his intelligence; his courage; his determination; his panache. And Jay was clearly attracted to her; why else would he have invited her in the first place? Besides her blonde features and open smile, there was her warmth and generosity, her intellect, her deep feeling for ancient cultures; but sometimes she wondered whether her greatest allure for the young widower was that she was, as she says, "healthy as a horse."

Mary Lou had quickly grown fond of Jay's daughters, too. In the beginning, she hadn't been sure what to expect from the girls—seventeen-year-old Renée, fourteen-year-old Robin, eleven-

While prospecting, Mary Lou Johnson would daydream about jade's historical meaning.
COURTESY OF MARY LOU RIDINGER

year-old Angela—but all three had been sweet and welcoming. On Mary Lou's third morning in Antigua, little Angela had served her and Jay breakfast in their double bed. And when Mary Lou had had to return briefly to Mexico, Renée had taken her aside and pleaded, "Please come back; we really need you."

Drifting along on her little pink cloud, Mary Lou Johnson was largely unconscious of the obstacles and perils of prospecting. There was the treacherous heat, which could strip your body of fluids and leave you lightheaded before you realized what was happening; if left untreated, the heatstroke could result in coma and death. The sere hillsides were also home to ticks, scorpions, and snakes. And then there was the civil war, which had been devastating Guatemala for more than a decade.

❖

Since the time of the conquistadors, Guatemala has seen many strong governments but very few good ones. In 1524, the country was effectively conquered by Hernán Cortés's lieutenant Pedro de Alvarado, who may also have given the place its name, possibly from the Nahuatl word for "among the trees." The Spanish put the Indians to work first in the mines, then, when Guatemala's mineral wealth didn't rival that of Mexico or Peru, on plantations of cacao, indigo, and sugar. Though conquered and divided, the country wasn't pacified, and, as in the Yucatan, the Maya would rebel for centuries to come.

The conquerors were also at odds with themselves. On top of the social heap were the *peninsulares,* the Spanish-born bureaucrats charged with administering the colony. At the bottom, just above the unassimilated Indians, were the ladinos, people of mixed Spanish and indigenous blood, who provided the colony's nonslave labor. And in the middle were the creoles, purebred Spaniards born in Guatemala, who controlled the haciendas. Wealthy, landed, but thwarted in their ambition for ultimate power, the creoles resorted to smuggling and corruption to advance their political and economic interests. And as the seventeenth century wore on and Madrid's demands for taxes escalated, the creoles turned increasingly toward extralegal means of redressing their grievances.

In 1700, the Spanish throne passed to the Bourbons, who introduced a variety of commercial and administrative reforms to bolster their authority and increase revenues. Pressed by the demands of the mother country, jealous of the rising fortunes of the ladinos, who were entering trade and the professions, and worried by the influx of even more of the wealthy *peninsulares*, the creoles grew more conservative and obstructionist. By the end of the century, these descendants of the conquistadors were bemoaning the state of the colony and longing for the palmy days of their forebears. Increasingly, they were also considering how to rid themselves of the interloping Bourbons.

Then in 1821, Mexico, their neighbor to the north, achieved independence. Two years later, all of greater Guatemala except for Chiapas formed the United Provinces of Central America. The new nation won its autonomy simply by declaring it, but peace and unity wouldn't be so easily maintained. The impulse to independence had had more to do with self-interest than with patriotic feeling or the desire to extend the fruits of liberty down the social scale, and the new federation quickly became entangled in civil war between the Liberals, who pushed for trade and development (which, not coincidentally, would also benefit their own interests) and the Conservatives, who were dominated by the land-owning creoles. The federation couldn't survive the chaos, and by 1841, five of the constituents—Guatemala, Costa Rica, El Salvador, Honduras, and Nicaragua—had formed sovereign countries. (Chiapas became part of Mexico.)

The new, reduced Guatemala was hobbled throughout the nineteenth century by corruption, legal preference of the moneyed few over the impoverished many, military strongmen, coups d'état, and armed revolts by the Maya, whose enduring rural misery had seen no relief from the change in regimes. In the late 1800s and into the new century, the country's infrastructure and economy improved, thanks to the Liberals' lavish concessions to foreign corporations such as the United Fruit Company, a huge American landowner and grower that also controlled the railways and steamships. But living conditions in the countryside and the urban slums continued to deteriorate.

In the 1920s, prodded by the universities and the labor unions, the country shifted to the left. The trend accelerated in 1944 after the election of Juan José Arévalo Bermejo, who introduced a constitution with new protections for workers, an extension of the vote, more authority for local governments, and expanded education and health services. Predictably, the reforms didn't sit well with foreign investors, wealthy planters, and most crucially, the military, which had been the ultimate arbiter of political fortunes for more than a century, ever since caudillo José Rafael Carrera Turcios had styled himself "the Napoleon of Central America."

Despite more than twenty coup attempts, Arévalo managed to serve out his five-year term. His successor, Jacobo Arbenz Guzmán (elected in a landslide after his opponent was shot to death), accelerated the move to the left and strengthened ties to the Soviet Union, at the same time arresting or assassinating the opposition. Faced with a Communist-leaning state in his own hemisphere, President Dwight Eisenhower later recalled, "Our proper course of action—indeed, my duty—was clear to me." In 1953, he authorized the covert CIA operation "El Diablo," which marked fifty-eight Guatemalans for assassination and provided arms to right-wing exiles in Honduras and Nicaragua. When the rightists invaded the following June, the army refused to come to Arbenz's aid, and the junta named as president Colonel Carlos Castillo Armas—who canceled Arévalo's reforms, outlawed all political parties, purged labor unions, reestablished the secret police, and instituted death squads to eliminate his opponents. "By the middle of 1954," Eisenhower reported with satisfaction, "Central America was free, for the time being at least, of any fixed outposts of Communism."

After Castillo was assassinated by one of his own guards in 1957, General Miguel Ydígoras Fuentes was nominated by the army and duly elected president. Though autocratic, Ydígoras ruled with a lighter touch than his predecessor. But in 1960, a group of junior military officers staged a leftist revolt in Guatemala City. The rebellion was put down, but the leaders escaped to the countryside, where they formed the nucleus of a revolutionary movement that would wage guerilla warfare in Guatemala for the next thirty-six years. In 1963, a coup replaced Ydígoras with military dictator Enrique Peralta Azurdia, who, with American support, continued the reign of terror against even moderate leftists. Three years later, when a rural counteroffensive crushed the revolt in the countryside, the rebels began to launch unnerving attacks on Guatemala City.

On August 28, 1968, American ambassador John Gordon Mein was returning to the embassy after a luncheon for a visiting State Department official, when two cars forced his Cadillac to the curb on the main thoroughfare Avenida de la Reforma. Two men in green fatigues ordered the ambassador from the limousine. When he tried to flee, he was shot in the back with a submachine gun. Mein was the first U.S. ambassador ever assassinated anywhere in the world, but he wasn't the first American to die in the Guatemalan civil war: The previous January two U.S. military advisors had also been killed in the capital.

While Mein's death "naturally shocked Washington," reported *Time* magazine, "Guatemalans were not so startled. Since civilian rule supplanted a rigid military regime in 1966, Communist and right-wing terrorists have killed some 2,000 people in their running crossfire." The attack provided the pretext for more repression, and President Julio César Méndez Montenegro "not only ordered flags to half-staff in mourning, but also temporarily reimposed emergency government powers, including the right to make arrests without a warrant. Outgoing foreign-press dispatches were delayed and censored."

✧

Mary Lou Johnson and Jay Ridinger were beginning their search six years after Mein's assassination. The *campo*, though less violent than the capital, was still tense. So, when it came to the hazards of prospecting, Jay Ridinger was as vigilant as Mary Lou Johnson was carefree. It was Ridinger who insisted that they never do anything to attract the attention of rebels or government troops, bandits or machete-wielding *campesinos*. Not that it was easy to keep a low profile, with the pale foreigners towering over the locals and with Ridinger sporting his trademark safari suit and bush hat.

Though gringos, the prospectors were protected by the fact that they were civilians, with no vested interest in the war. They were also shielded by their patent insanity. With the exception of the loyal Isaac, everyone they came across, from farmers and ranchers to villagers and storekeepers, told them the same thing. They were wasting their time looking for jade. "*No hay,*" they heard dozens of times, "There isn't any." And when the couple refused to listen, the *campesinos* realized the truth—the strangers were *idiotas,* outlandish but harmless. Many of Ridinger and Johnson's expat friends had already come to the same conclusion.

SIX

Jadeite

Jay Ridinger and Mary Lou Johnson had been prospecting around the Motagua for slightly more than a week. Today, December 31, 1974, they were working a parched hillside near a tributary about a two-hour walk north of the river. As always, they filed along in the heat, tapping their geologist's hammers on stones beside the trail. They weren't sure what the *ping* of a jade outcrop would sound or feel like, but whenever a rock seemed to ring a little differently from the others, they'd stop, chip off a piece, and drop it in their vial of bromoform. All the chips had floated today, like the dozens of others they had tested. They decided they would stay in the field one more day, working through New Year's, then head back to Antigua and the girls.

Walking in the lead for once, Mary Lou Johnson brought her hammer down on a partially exposed stone. The steel head recoiled with particular force, she thought, and the ring seemed a bit higher in pitch than the others. As she tried to remove a chip, the rock seemed more tenacious than most. When she finally freed a piece, she fished her vial of bromoform out of the leather saddlebag they used to carry their equipment. She dropped the chip into the container. It sank.

She called to Jay. The fact that the stone was heavier than the test liquid didn't guarantee it was jade, but she had a sense

131

that something was different about this rock, perhaps from her experience testing all those chips from Jean Deveaux. This one was a freestanding boulder weighing about twenty pounds, and they decided to lug it back to the workshop for closer inspection. They dispatched Isaac to find the landowner, a farmer who knew nothing of jade or the sweet-smelling liquid in their vials. No, he told them, he didn't mind if they took the rock.

In Antigua, they sawed into the boulder. Beneath the dull exterior, the stone was a mottled gray-green, similar to what Foshag and Leslie had discovered in nearby Manzanal. They shipped specimens to three different labs in the States. Finally, the typed reports came back: After only one week of prospecting, they had found jade.

True, it wasn't the first jade deposit discovered in Guatemala; Foshag and Leslie, British archaeologist Norman Hammond, even Jean Deveaux had beaten them to that distinction. It wasn't the most desirable shade of the stone, either. But Ridinger and Johnson were ecstatic. They'd done what they'd said they would do, what Jay Ridinger had devoted himself to achieving more than a year ago. Though they found no other jade nearby, they figured that where there was one pod there must be others, so Ridinger and Johnson bought a hundred acres surrounding their find. They also taught the *campesino* to work with a geologist's hammer and the bromoform and hired him to prospect on the rest of his land.

Ridinger and Johnson continued prospecting in the coming weeks and months, sometimes staying at the Longarone, sometimes sleeping in the Travco. They would generally limit their forays to three or four days, so as not to leave Jay's daughters too long in the care of the housekeeper. On school vacations, the girls would come with them, splashing in the motel pool. And so they came to associate jade prospecting not with deprivation, but with amenities they didn't have at home.

On a ridge about a hundred yards from their strike, on the other side of the tributary, Ridinger and Johnson came across a pre-Hispanic worksite. The ground was littered with jagged bits of jade and even a few ancient stone hammers. Ridinger was excited, thinking there might be more jade deposits nearby. But as Johnson closed her fist around the fragments of stone, she was more stirred by the tug of history stretching back a millennium or more, by the thought that she and Jay were just two more in a long line of seekers striding onto this same scene, all searching for jade.

Several weeks later, Isaac led them to a place about half an hour's walk south of the Motagua and showed them what he'd discovered. It was a partially buried pod of jade twice the size of a living room sofa and set in white, crusty albitite. The stone was an eye-catching mélange of dark and light green that Ridinger christened "Maya Foliage Jade." Nearby was more, in an extraordinary spectrum of colors—black, white, gray-green, blue-green, even a little bright green. Ridinger and Johnson bought this land, too, and their workers broke the stone with gasoline-powered drills and hauled it out of the mountains on donkeys.

Throughout the spring, Ridinger and Johnson returned to the Motagua and purchased more parcels of land from the cash-strapped *campesinos*. In the end, they had bought 180 acres and rented another four hundred. But even after taking possession, they asked the previous owners to remain on the land, planting it and prospecting for more jade. Partly, the Americans didn't want to disrupt the *campesinos'* lives or livelihood, and partly, they hoped to discourage outsiders from poaching any jade that might be found. Ridinger recalled how easy it had been to hire the invaluable Isaac away from Deveaux. Despite Mary Lou's urging, Jay still hadn't severed his relationship with the Belgian. But now that they had their own jade to safeguard, he resolved never to allow anyone, no matter how well trusted, to visit their source or to meet their pickers.

Of course, Deveaux and Leech also had to agree never to divulge the whereabouts of their find. But while commerce dictated secrecy, science demanded transparency. Mary Lou

Johnson knew that no academic journal would accept an article about a pre-Columbian jade mine or workshop without a location stipulated—how else could the report be verified or expanded? If she couldn't publish her findings, it would mean the end of her career as an archaeologist. She hesitated, but Jay was adamant. Finally, she consented.

And so, for the first time, the search for the sources of pre-Hispanic jade became the sphere of capitalists rather than enthusiasts and scholars. Most archaeologists and geologists never knew of Ridinger and Johnson's discovery, and those who did generally discredited it—because it hadn't been reported in the scholarly literature. If academics did mention the couple's find, it was usually passed off as unsubstantiated hearsay and the pair described as "entrepreneurs," the term delivered with disdain. When an international archaeology meeting was held in Antigua, Mary Lou Johnson was pointedly excluded. If she happened to run into academics when they came to Guatemala, they greeted her coolly. Some scholars speculated that the couple were dealing in looted antiquities; others accused them of carving their jade into pre-Columbian forgeries.

To a degree, the entrepreneurs were victims of guilt by association. In those days, the forging of artifacts was rife in Guatemala, and some people even suspected Jean Deveaux of such activities. When the motive was lucre rather than learning, the scholars seemed to regard the unethical or illegal as only one slippery step from the merely marketable or profitable. And mixed with that distrust was a generous helping of resentment that the entrepreneurs' secrecy was frustrating the academics' research. As Michael Coe told me, in defense of Edward H. Thompson, the great sin was not to publish. But that was precisely the offense that Mary Lou Johnson was committing, one her former colleagues couldn't forgive. Even David Sedat found himself falling under the suspicion of his peers because of his friendship with Johnson and Ridinger.

And so, Mary Lou Johnson turned away from archaeology and archaeologists and dedicated herself to the new enterprise. Now that she and Jay Ridinger finally had a supply of jade worth carving, their next task was to learn to do just that.

※

In his *Mineralogical Studies on Guatemalan Jade*, William Foshag had described the ancient methods of working the stone. Though some of these techniques had been reported by the conquistadors, most were inferred from studying old jades and the detritus found in pre-Hispanic workshops.

The all-consuming challenge that jade presented to the early stoneworkers stemmed from one of its most desirable characteristics: its extraordinary hardness. As master jade carver Bob Terzuola explains to me, softer stone such as marble can be chiseled into shape, but a hard stone such as jade (or any gemstone) will shatter under such treatment. In fact, carving jade isn't a matter of chipping the stone but of scratching it. This scratching goes by different names—sawing, drilling, grinding, polishing— but for each stage of the process, the artisan needs a substance at least as hard as the jade itself. For the ancient carvers, that material could have been more jade—or garnets, which were collected from the Motagua and its tributaries as pebbles. The pebbles were then ground into an abrasive grit, which was relatively easy because their very hardness made them prone to shattering. (Garnets are still commonly used as an abrasive on sandpaper, and 3M operated a garnet plant in the Motagua Valley for many years.)

The first step in producing plaques, beads, celts, ear ornaments, and most other items was generally sawing. A narrow blade was fashioned of a hard wood such as lignum vitae, so dense that it sinks in water. The blade was dipped in rendered animal fat and coated with abrasive. Then the implement was worked back and forth, scratching the stone again and again until the saw eventually penetrated. It might seem that even an exceptionally dense wood would quickly wear away under this labor, but particles of abrasive lodged in the saw's edge, shielding it from direct contact with the jade and extending its life. Progress was glacial, though: Bob Terzuola had experimented with wooden saws, finding that, using animal fat and abrasive, he could cut through two millimeters (about 8/100 of an inch) an hour; with just water and abrasive, the headway was only half that rate. After sawing, the plaque had a whitish cast, evidence of the violence inflicted on its crystals.

When the ancient carver's blade was halfway through the stone, after perhaps days of effort, he would turn the rock over and begin sawing from the other side. Then, when only a thin bridge remained between the two cuts, he would snap off the plaque, leaving a telltale edge. The two-hundred-pound jade boulder from Kaminaljuyu and smaller pieces from the Terzuola Site had been sawed in just this way. Sawing was also accomplished with string, animal fat, and abrasive; owing to their greater maneuverability, string saws were ideal for intricate work, such as in the exquisite pre-Hispanic plaques of birds, jaguars, and other creatures found in Costa Rica.

The ancient artisans could have engraved jade with a pointed piece of that stone or some other very hard rock, gradually scratching their design into the surface. Or they may have used a sharp piece of wood covered with animal fat and an abrasive powder. To create the holes for stringing beads, they fitted a stone tip to a wooden shaft or used a wooden bit and abrasive. In either case, the shaft was spun by hand or bow. Small beads might be drilled from one side only, but thicker ones were penetrated first from one direction then the other, the way saw cuts were made. Wider openings, such as those for rings, were made with a blunt tip and abrasive. Hollow drills of bamboo, reeds, or bird's bones, again used with an abrasive grit, were an efficient way of making holes. Such drills were apparently also employed to cut circular designs and to fashion the round stems for ear ornaments.

Once a piece was cut to shape, it would have to be ground, that is, rubbed with stone or stone powder until the coarse scratches left after carving were replaced by finer scratches, giving a smoother edge and surface. Finally, the artisan would polish his creation, perhaps the most demanding part of the entire process. The polishing may have begun by rubbing a hard stone, such as a jade celt, over the piece. But, judging from the high polish found on some artifacts, the ancient stone workers also used a stone dust as fine as talcum powder, which couldn't have appeared in nature but must have been manufactured especially for this purpose.

The modern-day carvers had electric saws, drills, and grinders to work their jade. Yet, despite all their technology, the process still consisted of making incremental scratches in the stone, just much more quickly than could be done by hand. Whereas the ancients had used loose abrasive, the modern equipment was fitted with blades, tips, and belts to which abrasive was already bonded. In the beginning, the Ridingers' carvers used silicate carbide, which was relatively inexpensive; but before long, they switched to harder (but much more costly) diamond as their abrasive of choice.

Despite coaching from Bob Terzuola, it took months for the carvers to learn how to work the stone. As in ancient times, the first step was generally to saw a flat plaque from a rock, like a piece of bread sliced from a loaf. For this, they used a circular saw mounted in a metal box. Beneath the abrasive-coated blade was a pan filled with lubricant; as the blade spun, it would pick up the liquid, which eased the saw's passage against the stone. Whereas it could take pre-Hispanic workers days to cut through a good-sized rock, the modern equipment performed the same feat in a couple of hours—although, even with the lubricant, the saw sometimes had to be shut down for thirty minutes or so to keep the blade from overheating. A diamond blade could cut for only about 250 hours before needing to be replaced.

The next step was to trace onto the plaque the object to be carved—say, a simple round pendant. Eventually, they discovered that a thin bronze rod was ideal for this, because its yellowish line stood out against the stone; although the jade remained unscathed, the softer bronze wore down like the tip of a pencil. The drawn outline was sprayed with lacquer so it wouldn't rub off before the cuts were made; then the plaque was placed on a diamond-tipped table saw with a reciprocating blade. Beneath the cutting platform was a tank of water, which the blade would dip into on its down stroke. The water acted as a lubricant, but it splattered everywhere, requiring the operators to wear goggles and rubber aprons.

As the workers followed the outline with the saw, at times their fingers would come within millimeters of the oscillating blade, and it seemed that a slip would result in a severed finger. But this was an illusion: The edge of the saw was coated with diamond dust, but the blade was perfectly smooth, since teeth wouldn't have survived more than a couple of seconds against the stone. So even modern sawing was a process of incremental scratches. And paradoxically, though the blade could penetrate one of the hardest stones known, since it had no teeth, casual contact presented no danger to delicate human flesh. More prolonged contact would produce not a cut, but a burn.

After the piece was cut out, it was pressed against a metal wheel coated with diamond dust to grind down its edges. Then came the final step, polishing, which, as in ancient times, proved one of the most tedious and challenging, mastered only after long experimentation and the use of machines fitted to Bob Terzuola's specifications.

The process of polishing takes the scratches that have been made in the course of carving and grinding and gradually replaces them with finer and finer scratches until they're no longer visible to the human eye. The key word is gradually. Whereas softer stones such as marble take a polish relatively quickly, jade, thanks to its great density, must be coaxed to a luster. At the beginning, the carvers used abrasive powder and some polishing bits that Terzuola fashioned from lignum vitae, whose resin produced a honey-like aroma as the wood warmed to its task. Later, they substituted metal bits electroplated with abrasive. And for the final polish, they used a series of five consecutively finer leather wheels smeared with an abrasive paste of chrome oxide or aluminum oxide. Terzuola instructed the workers not to quit polishing until they could hold a lightbulb to the piece and read the wattage reflected in its surface; only then would the jade shine like the gemstone it was. There's nothing more "heartbreakingly beautiful," Terzuola tells me, than the polish on a piece of jade, and its ability to take such a sheen is one of the reasons that the stone is "the king of gems." And diamonds? As far as he's concerned, the best use for them is to carve jade.

If a hole were needed in an item, such as a bead, it was drilled with a diamond-tipped bit about the size of a sewing needle. This proved a surprisingly expensive part of the process, because the delicate bits needed to be replaced after only an hour or two of use. As Terzuola pointed out to the partners, in a sense they weren't in the jade business but the business of drilling holes. The holes went by different names, according to whether they were round (circles), or curved (crescents), or tube-shaped (grooves), but they were all created by removing material. There was an old adage among Chinese jade carvers: "Our job is to subtract; we cannot add." And now the entrepreneurs discovered for themselves how arduous this subtraction could be, burning expensive blades and bits.

The more material to be removed, the more costly the item to produce. Even making a plain round bead was deceptively demanding, consisting of sawing a cube from a plaque, then rounding its eight corners on the grinding wheel, drilling a hole in the center, and finally polishing it. But the most expensive items to produce were hollow, such as bowls, with a tremendous volume of material to be extracted and only a thin shell of jade remaining. (Perhaps this was one reason why the ancient Maya generally produced life-size masks not from a single piece of stone but from a mosaic of thin plaques affixed to a wooden or plaster base.) One of the first items Ridinger and Johnson made was a set of poker chips, as a gift for Jay's uncle. All those round edges ate up lots of diamond, and in the end they figured their expenses in the thousands of dollars, not even counting the value of the stone.

❖

The more practice they had in working jade, the more respect the modern carvers felt for the ancient craftsmen. They discovered that the stone wasn't apt for exceptionally detailed carving, owing to its large crystals. But they also found that it was a joy to work, with a substantial, sensual feel in the hand. True, its exceptional density made it demanding—not so much in the carving, thanks to their diamond-tipped instruments—but later, in the care required to polish it. As Bob Terzuola says, "When you finish a jade carving, you know you've accomplished something." But jade's hardness also makes it forgiving of mistakes. Whereas a slip of the chisel can ruin a marble statue-in-progress, the gradual scratching necessary to carve jade makes it difficult to commit a serious error, as each movement is too incremental to do much damage.

Even while their carvers were still mastering their technique, the entrepreneurs were eager to start selling some pieces—and to mark the return of the jade industry to Guatemala for the first time in five centuries. They painted the exterior of their factory/showroom jade green and installed some elegant wooden displays in a front room. But in the beginning, there wasn't much merchandise to fill them. For their premier products, they chose the simplest and most economical to produce—jade blocks in a variety of sizes. In July

1975, there was a gala grand opening of their enterprise, which they named the Jade Factory. Friends came and admired the merchandise, but the blocks made for pricey bookends or doorstops. Had they ever thought of carving something else from jade, the friends asked delicately—say, jewelry?

So they ordered a supply of wire, gold beads, and freshwater pearls from a company in the States, and jewelry making became a family pursuit. Ridinger's youngest daughter, Angela, recalls walking home from school on those quiet, car-less streets of Antigua, doing her homework, then sitting at the kitchen table and assembling necklaces and bracelets. Her girlish designs tended to be delicate, combining diminutive jade beads and pearls, while Johnson's tended to use larger, more rustic beads closer to the ones strung by the ancient Maya.

Jay Ridinger was among the first foreigners invited to join the Antigua Rotary Club, and one day he had them in to tour the jade factory. His Spanish was still rough, but Johnson happened to overhear a conversation between two Guatemalan businessmen standing behind her. It takes an American to invest in something like this, commented the first man. Yes, said the second, you'd never find a Guatemalan starting a jade business. Johnson realized it was true. Guatemalans with money to invest tended to put it in coffee fincas or textile factories or other traditional ventures rather than in something new and unproven. There had been admiration in the exchange, she realized, but also a tinge of resentment that left her with an uncomfortable feeling.

And so Jay Ridinger discovered that, like prospecting for jade, owning a jade mine was not what he had imagined. For one thing, it wasn't a mine or quarry in the usual sense, since the stone wasn't dug out of a great hole in the earth but was collected from boulders or small outcrops at ground level. And people were still skeptical that what he and Johnson had found was jade at all. Even those who should have known better were among the most vocal doubters. One of their first sales was a simple beaded necklace, purchased by a tourist from Washington, D.C. Returning home, the client happened to be seated at a formal dinner next to the wife of the Guatemalan ambassador. When the woman showed off her necklace, the *señora* contemptuously informed her that she'd been cheated: Everybody knew there was no jade in Guatemala.

But the natural market for their stone, Johnson believed more firmly than ever, was not in Washington or Houston or Chicago but in Guatemala—and not among skeptical Guatemalans, like the ambassador's wife, but among foreign tourists, who would be more susceptible to jade's charms while vacationing in the land of its origin. They weren't really selling jade, she realized, but like the purveyors of any luxury good, were trading on an image. Yes, diamonds were beautiful, but what induced young men to spend thousands of dollars on them? Not the stones' sparkle, but the conviction that diamonds were "forever," reinforced over generations of clever marketing. And so, she resolved to play to jade's strength, the same qualities that Johnson herself had found so affecting—its deep history and its ties to the great civilizations of the past. David Sedat's slogan, "The story sells the stone," became her mantra.

Since tourists didn't come to Guatemala with these associations preformed, the entrepreneurs would have to create the image they desired. When their workers became more skilled at carving and they expanded their merchandise beyond simple blocks and beads, they eschewed the elephants, Buddhas, and hearts that were mainstays of Chinese jade vendors and resolved to carve only reproductions of Mesoamerican figurines and masks (which made some archaeologists even more suspicious).

For this kind of work, Bob Terzuola outfitted their workshop with flexible-shaft drills. These consisted of a motor, about the size and shape of a large coffee mug, which was hung from the ceiling above the worktable. Attached to the motor was a flexible shaft about two and a half feet long, like the kind that dentists used before they switched to compressed air to power their implements. The motor was regulated with a foot pedal, and at the end of the shaft was fitted a carving tool whose shape varied according to its purpose. Dentist's drill bits often proved ideal.

In the showroom, rather than locking their merchandise behind glass, Ridinger and Johnson displayed everything on open counters and shelves, so browsers could experience for themselves jade's cool, heavy feel in the hand. And, drawing on her archaeology credentials, Johnson began an educational barrage, lecturing about Mesoamerican jade to anyone willing to invite her, and some not so willing—the Chamber of Commerce, the Rotary Club, the American diplomatic corps, the postal workers' union, the fifth-graders in the local schools, and cruise ship passengers. They would later build a small museum in the back of the store, exhibiting their reproductions along with the ancient tools and stone fragments they'd found.

As they honed their marketing strategy, sales improved, and the partners gradually added employees—a truck driver, more carvers, salespeople. They also yielded to the market and began to carve elephants, Buddhas, and hearts.

In January 1976, they appeared to get the break they'd been waiting for. Ridinger and Johnson were in the shop when an American tourist burst in wanting to know, "Is this the place?"

"The place for what?" Johnson asked.

The man took a newspaper clipping from his pocket. "Is this the jade factory that was in the *New York Times*?"

Ridinger and Johnson stared at the headline: "Brilliant Traces of Maya Civilization Are Newly Etched in Guatemalan Jade." Beside it was a photo of Jean Deveaux, bent over his grinding wheel. Apparently, a *Times* reporter had happened into the store when the others were out. Despite Johnson's urging, Ridinger hadn't severed his partnership with the Belgian, whose pieces were sold in the shop, but by then relations were so strained between the associates that Deveaux had never even told them of the visit.

Deveaux was the hero of the story ("a Belgian stone-carver has rediscovered an ancient Maya jade quarry in the jungles of Central America"), and Ridinger and Johnson weren't even mentioned by name. But otherwise the piece hit every note they could have wished: jade's significance to vanished civilizations, the long mystery of its sources and their recent rediscovery, the return of the jade industry to its homeland. "It is all a delight to the eye," the article went on. "But what is most striking is what looks like traditional Maya jewelry set out on soft felt counters and tagged for sale, instead of in a museum or the back room of an antiques shop. The jewelry not only looks like something a Maya priest might have worn, but it comes from the very soil he once walked." Who wouldn't want to bring home a piece of that? If the eager American were any indicator, more tourists would be finding their way to the partners' shop.

Then, just a few days later, at 3:01 a.m. on February 4, 1976, Guatemala was struck by one of the worst earthquakes in its history. Centered about a hundred miles northeast of Guatemala City, the 7.5-magnitude quake shook the country for thirty-nine seconds, followed by hundreds of aftershocks. When it was over, nearly twenty-five thousand people were dead, more than seventy-five thousand were injured, more than three hundred towns were leveled, and more than a million people were homeless. Casualties were reported in seventeen of the country's twenty-two administrative departments, with most suffered in the countryside, when thick roof beams and heavy tiles collapsed on *campesinos* sleeping in mud-brick houses. Said one farmer to *Time* magazine, "We cannot build of adobe again. It is of earth and it is our coffin."

In the hardest-hit department of Chimaltenango, not far from Antigua, a quarter of the population was killed or injured and 97 percent were homeless. Throughout the country, roads were closed by landslides, making access to the affected areas nearly impossible. Electricity and drinking water were cut off for days. Food soon became scarce, and there were reports of people eating rats. Nearly half of Guatemala's hospitals were destroyed, and emergency morgues were set up in soccer fields and alongside roads, with bodies wrapped in bed sheets or scraps of plastic. Many victims were buried, unidentified, in hasty graves, where some were exhumed by packs of hungry dogs.

In Antigua, which had been abandoned in the eighteenth century after repeated earthquakes, houses were destroyed and public buildings were toppled. At the Jade Factory, the front walls collapsed, exposing the store to the street; inside, the display cases tumbled forward, spewing their contents on the floor. Around the corner, the kitchen wall of the Ridingers' rented house fell in and the tile roof slid into the garden. Jay and Mary Lou started sleeping in the Travco until they could find another house to rent, while Angela slept outdoors in the patio of the factory/showroom. Many people with the means simply left. Those who remained responded with paranoia, generosity, or greed, depending on their character. Jay Ridinger found a farmer with a supply of carrots for sale and started a soup kitchen; Mary Lou Johnson set up an earthquake information center, displaying maps of fault lines and summarizing the latest seismological research.

Originating in the Motagua Valley, where the Caribbean and Central American tectonic plates grind together, the earthquake was provoked by the same forces that had created the country's spectacular volcanoes—and its jade. But no one was thinking of luxuries like jade any more. Although President Kjell Eugenio Laugerud García assured his people, "Guatemala is wounded but not to death," it would be years before the country recovered.

It would also be a long time before tourists returned to Antigua. With a slow market for their jade in Guatemala, Ridinger and Johnson carted some of their jewelry to Texas and the Midwest and held trunk shows at the homes of friends and relatives. But they found there was little demand for Guatemalan jade in their native country, either. Americans, like Europeans, had no cultural affinity for the stone, and the few collectors concentrated on oriental jade. The irony was not lost on Mary Lou Johnson: Ridinger had been attracted to jade not only by the challenge of rediscovering the lost sources, but by the promise of building a lucrative business. They had managed to find jade, fill a workshop with equipment, and learn to carve the stone, only to discover that it was nearly unsalable—first in Hong Kong, then in Antigua, and now in the United States. Guatemalan jade may have been the most precious substance on earth to the Maya, but a millennium later, no one seemed to want it.

With the investment in land and equipment and the overhead of the store and factory, the business had exhausted Jay Ridinger's savings as well as an infusion of cash that Jerry Leech had raised from investors in Chicago. The partners cut staff to a minimum, and Ridinger finally extricated himself from his agreement with Jean Deveaux. But the business wasn't generating enough revenue to maintain itself. Leech and Ridinger had a falling out, and Leech returned to the States. Then, in December 1977, Ridinger began a new joint venture: After nearly four years of living and working together, he and Mary Lou Johnson were married in an outdoor, Renaissance-dress ceremony at Betty Kempe's Villa Santa Monica in San Miguel de Allende.

⁘

The area around the Motagua Fault was the one place in Latin America where deposits of jade had been discovered. But the question remained, since the days of William Foshag: Was the Motagua the only source of that stone for the ancient Mesoamericans? Mexico and Costa Rica were both rich with carved pre-Columbian jades, and espousing the so-called criterion of abundance, many experts believed there must be deposits of jade in those countries as well. The way to resolve the issue was to analyze geological specimens from the Motagua and carved jades from museums, and compare the two groups. If all the museum jades matched stone from the Motagua, that would suggest that the Maya and others had mined only that area; if not, it would imply that there were other pre-Columbian sources still waiting to be discovered.

Counting Foshag and Leslie's jade from Manzanal, Norman Hammond's from Usumatlán and El Jute, and the Ridingers' stone, geological samples from five different locales were available for study. Hammond and his colleagues subjected the specimens to electron microprobe and neutron activation analysis. In the first test, the rock is bombarded with electrons, causing it to emit x-rays; since each element produces a distinctive x-ray pattern, researchers can determine which elements are present in the stone and in what proportion. In neutron activation analysis, a sample is exposed to a source of neutrons, causing some of the atoms' nuclei to become radioactive; the radiation released similarly indicates the chemical composition.

Most of the elements would be the same across all samples—the silicon, oxygen, aluminum, and sodium that are jadeite's main constituents. But minute traces of other elements should also be found, holdovers from the stone's formation, and these, the researchers hoped, would give each specimen a unique chemical "fingerprint." In the end, though, the trace elements fell into no clear pattern, and the samples proved largely indistinguishable, forcing Hammond and his colleagues to "a somewhat indeterminate conclusion." They held out the hope that one day investigators would be able "to characterize at least some jade sources firmly," but first, a wider selection of jade deposits would have to be found for testing.

In 1976, the Boston Museum of Fine Arts and the Peabody Museum at Harvard took up the challenge, launching an ambitious study known as the Mesoamerican Jade Project. This time, the plan was to analyze a wider selection of geological samples as well as some museum jades; when the compositions of the raw jade and those of the artifacts were compared, it was hoped that some would match, showing that the jade in a certain carving had come from a specific location. The museum jades would be tested with neutron activation analysis, since that technique didn't damage the samples. But even so, the curators would have to wait six months to get their items back, once the induced radioactivity had dissipated.

The first field director of the Mesoamerican Jade Project, charged with traveling Guatemala and collecting the geological samples, was a man named Russell Seitz. Then Seitz was succeeded by Ron Bishop, an archaeologist also trained in chemistry, who was working at Brookhaven National Laboratory, on Long Island. But for both men, the results were disappointing. "After five years of work," Bishop found, he "had more questions than answers."

For one thing, their search hadn't turned up any significant new deposits of jadeite. This meant there were still only a few geological specimens available for testing, most provided by the Ridingers, along with Foshag and Leslie's samples, some borrowed from museums' gem collections, and a few discovered by Bishop. And, like Hammond, et al., Bishop found jade an inapt candidate for such a study, since two specimens taken just feet apart could present different chemical profiles.

Bishop did discover, though, that the differences in jade taken from distinct sources was greater than the differences among samples taken from the same source. So, even though there was no trace-element "fingerprint," no foolproof way to track an individual artifact to a specific location, certain similarities did emerge—just as members of the same family, though they have different fingerprints, may share an inherited resemblance. And based on this looser criterion, only about a third of the museum jades—excavated as far north as Chichen Itza and as far south as Copan, Honduras—were similar to the stone currently being taken from the Motagua. The artifacts fell into six clusters, suggesting that their jade may have originated in half a dozen distinct locations.

The Ridingers' jade was in the same group as about 10 percent of the jades that Edward Thompson had raised from the Sacred Cenote at Chichen Itza. Mary Lou Ridinger was amazed to think that some of their stone may have been carried all the way to the Yucatan, some four hundred miles distant, perhaps a thousand years before. But just as startling was the study's other implication: If the raw material for the antique jades had come from six different places, and the Ridingers' mine accounted for only one, then five more pre-Hispanic sources were still unaccounted for.

In 1977, after the start of the Mesoamerican Jade Project, tourists had begun to trickle back to Antigua. By the following year, the Ridingers believed they had survived the worst of their financial crisis, and, despite natural disaster and civil war, they continued their search for new deposits of jade.

Around this time, Mary Lou Ridinger was prospecting in the eastern Motagua Valley with her friend Charlotte Thomson, one of the instigators of the Mesoamerican Jade Project. Driving rough dirt roads, they were scouting tributaries south of the river and using geological maps to trace serpentinite outcrops and tectonic boundaries. But with daylight fading and gasoline running low, they headed back to the Longarone Motel for the night.

On the television in their room, they heard a news flash about the chronic border dispute with British Honduras, as Belize was then known. For centuries, Britain and Spain had quarreled over this scrap of land straddling Mexico and Guatemala on the Caribbean coast. In 1862, it had become a Crown Colony of Great Britain, and when British Honduras was granted self-government in 1964 (full independence would come in 1981),

Guatemala was still claiming the territory for itself. Now the feud had reached yet another crisis, and the Guatemalan government was declaring a state of siege and threatening to confiscate any private vehicles found near the border. So the next morning, the prospectors bowed to diplomacy and skulked back to Antigua. Other matters intervened, and Mary Lou Ridinger didn't return to the promising site they had seen the day before.

Then all prospecting was put on hold when the civil war, now in its third decade, took a new, even deadlier turn.

⁘

At 9:30 on the morning of January 31, 1980, thirty-four indigenous farmers protesting the kidnapping and murder of peasants in the department of Quiché occupied the Spanish embassy in Guatemala City. Spain was singled out not because it was involved in the atrocities, just the opposite—it was considered sympathetic to the rebels because Spanish missionaries had been among those killed by federal forces.

The protestors occupied the embassy peacefully and announced a press conference for noon. But before the meeting could be held, police stormed the building, over the objections of the Spanish ambassador. The dissidents, along with Spanish embassy workers and some Guatemalan officials, fled to an inner office. Accounts of what happened next are conflicting, but fire broke out inside the occupied office, either when one of the protestors' Molotov cocktails exploded or when the army launched the incendiary agent white phosphorous.

However the fire started, the police blocked the protestors' escape, and thirty-six persons were burned alive, including two embassy employees and two Guatemalan diplomats. Afterward, the Spanish ambassador excoriated the government for "extraordinary brutality," and Madrid accused it of violating "the most elementary norms of international law," the inviolability of a country's embassy. Spain broke off diplomatic relations, and hundreds of thousands of Guatemalans turned out for the victims' funeral.

Later, President Fernando Romeo Lucas García ordered a brutal crackdown in the *campo*, ushering in the most violent phase of the war and prompting some forty-five thousand Guatemalans to flee to refugee camps over the Mexican border in Chiapas. On March 7, the army's chosen candidate, former defense minister and brigadier general Ángel Aníbal Guevara, was elected president in patently fraudulent balloting.

On the 23rd of that month, junior army officers led a coup to prevent the new president from taking office and instead installed General José Efraín Ríos Montt, an evangelical Christian, who proclaimed, "Thank you, my God. You have put me here." The new president proceeded to dissolve Congress, abrogate the constitution, outlaw political parties, and suspend further elections. He also continued his predecessor's brutal policy in the countryside, including drafting *campesinos* into pro-government civil defense forces on pain of death; rebels responded by killing the draftees along with their families. In July, Ríos Montt told an indigenous audience, "If you are with us, we'll feed you; if not, we'll kill you." The strategy was known as *Frijoles y Fusiles*, "Beans and Rifles," and the born-again president was as good as his word: Among the atrocities committed by his troops, three of the most notorious were at the villages of Dos Erres in the Petén, where more than two hundred people were murdered; Plan de Sánchez, in Baja Verapaz, where more than two hundred fifty were killed; and Río Negro, also in Baja Verapaz, where more than four hundred were slaughtered. All told, during Ríos's tenure hundreds of indigenous villages and tens of thousands of *campesinos* were annihilated.

Shortly after the new president took office, American ambassador Frederic Chapin had commented, "We consider President Ríos Montt a significant improvement over the previous president, and we hope to be able to work constructively with him." Increasingly alienated by its ally's abysmal human rights record, the Carter administration had cut military support and reduced economic aid to a trickle. Then, taking office in 1981, Ronald Reagan increased assistance, including military aid. Even so, the Guatemalan economy continued to stagger under violence and recession; foreign investment and lending dried up, exports dwindled, and tourism was virtually nil.

In Antigua, it would be a long time before government atrocities in the *campo* became general knowledge. But the intensified campaign brought the war home as never before. An army tank appeared in the *plaza principal* for the first time, silhouetted against the quaint Colonial buildings. And anyone who dared to venture out of town might hear the *pop-pop* of gunshots along the road, as federal troops and rebels battled in the woods.

Despite the escalation, Mary Lou Ridinger still felt oddly detached from the civil war, was still riding her "little pink cloud." But there was no denying the effects that first the earthquake and now the worsening violence were having on the jade business. About this time, she recalled, "It all came crashing down." The tiny team was working fourteen hours a day, seven days a week— marketing, designing, attending to legal matters, struggling to keep the enterprise solvent. In the eight months they had trudged through the arid hillsides prospecting for jade, Mary Lou had never lost faith, had always felt she was living a life of "high adventure." But these days, she was fearful of what the future might bring. Unable to market the jade they had, they gave no thought to prospecting for new sources.

The rising violence did touch Antigua eventually, not with gun battles in the streets but in more insidious ways. Occasionally, a resident who had done something to offend one side or the other would find a corpse on his doorstep, a hint that he should leave town for a while. A gang threatened death to more than a hundred local business owners, including the Ridingers, if they didn't leave ten thousand U.S. dollars in cash at a specified location. The notes were addressed to "Whom It May Concern," and after consulting with their neighbors, most recipients ignored them. But one merchant, the Chinese owner of a dry-goods business, fled the country. Then, a couple of weeks later, the bodies of eight of the gang members were discovered on the edge of town, apparently victims of an intramural dispute.

Another incident, personal and painful, touched the Ridingers deeply: Their driver was kidnapped. Taking the company truck to Guatemala City to pick up Mary Lou at the airport, he was intercepted by armed bandits, who blindfolded him, drove him to a hiding place, and pressed him to reveal the whereabouts of his bosses' mine. Thanks to the Ridingers' secrecy, the driver didn't know the location, and less than a day later, he was released uninjured. But he returned with a message specifically for Mary Lou Ridinger: *We will get you,* the thugs warned, *and you won't be able to hide even in San Miguel de Allende.*

Apparently, the kidnappers were trying to terrorize the Ridingers into leaving the country and ceding control of their mine. The attack seemed strangely timed, considering that first the earthquake and then the escalating civil war had made their jade virtually unmarketable. But in Guatemala, even more than in other places, perception was more persuasive than reality, and clearly anyone with a jade mine must be a latter-day King Solomon. And to appear wealthy in Guatemala was, Mary Lou Ridinger says, "to paint a target on the side of your car or the front of your house." Whereas in the States, the well-to-do might buy a Mercedes to flaunt their success, in Guatemala they would drive a battered pickup so as not to attract *envidia,* "envy"—including that of government officials. Ever since they had discovered jade, Jay Ridinger had been dreading that a man in an army uniform would wrap an arm around his shoulder and tell him, "I'm

Colonel So-and-So, and I'm your new business partner." But it hadn't happened, presumably because they were fish too small to tempt the seriously corrupt.

The day after the kidnapping, the Ridingers hired a security consultant, who advised them to vary their routine—drive different cars; leave the house at different hours; keep their plans to themselves, even in small matters such as whether they would attend a friend's party. For their own safety, they began spending more time outside the country, in Natchez and San Miguel de Allende. On these trips, the Ridingers would take merchandise, holding more trunk shows, educating people about Guatemalan jade, and hoping to send enough money back to Antigua to meet their payroll.

Even as the Ridingers were coming under siege, Guatemala was finally inching toward peace. In August 1983, Ríos Montt was deposed by his minister of defense, Óscar Humberto Mejía Victores. (The first sign that yet another takeover had begun was that radio stations would start broadcasting nothing but patriotic tunes. Expatriates in Antigua had a name for the programming, "coup music," and they took it as their signal to stock up on groceries and stay indoors.) In 1984, elections were held for an assembly to draft a new, more liberal constitution, which took effect in May of the following year. Two years later, Marco Vinicio Cerezo Arévalo would be elected president—the first civilian to hold that post in sixteen years—and would put forth reforms including the introduction of habeas corpus and the establishment of a human rights commission. Though the war hadn't ended, political and economic progress was being made, and violence was on the wane.

Tourists still hadn't returned to Guatemala, and financially, 1984 was the Ridingers' worst year yet. But even through these dark times, they resumed the hunt for new sources of jade. They hired a young cousin, Andy Duncan, a graduate student in geology, to prospect during school vacations. For two summers, Duncan pored over Foshag's publications, Ed Shook's notebooks, and the Ridingers' own field notes. Though he conducted a grid-like search over the Motagua Valley, he found no new deposits of jade.

By Duncan's third summer, 1987, his search had led him westward, about thirty miles outside Guatemala City. And there, thirteen years after the Ridingers' initial discovery, about forty feet from the Motagua, on the flat alluvial plain running along the river, he came upon a second source—a ton of jade boulders in a handsome blue-gray shade similar to that favored by the ancient Olmecs. The Ridingers announced the find in the English-language Guatemala City publication *This Week*, but in keeping with their protocol, didn't reveal the location.

Along with the blue jade, Duncan found a striking black stone flecked with gold-colored metal, different from anything the Ridingers had ever seen and different from anything they had ever heard reported in Asia, the Americas, or Europe. When they mentioned the stone to their daughter Angela, she recalled that in his account of his travels to the Orient, Marco Polo mentioned seeing jade with flecks of gold. Their factory foreman, who handled more stone than anyone else in the company, insisted the rock was jade. The carvers had experimented with the piece, he said, and it worked like jade, with the same toughness and density. And so the Ridingers shipped a sample to the Gemological Institute of America for an x-ray diffraction study, which confirmed that the stone was jade. The metal flecks were three-quarters pyrite, or "fool's gold"; the rest consisted of half a dozen other minerals, including gold, silver, and platinum. The Ridingers christened the discovery "Galactic Gold Jade" and began to carve some into jewelry. But they wondered, why had none of this conspicuous jade ever been discovered in an ancient Maya city?

Not long after, Jay Ridinger received a phone call from the United States. "I've heard of you," the man said, "and I have some secrets of jade I'd like to share." He would divulge nothing more over the telephone, and since he was too old to travel, he invited Ridinger to come to his house in suburban Maryland. Ridinger's curiosity was sufficiently piqued that he flew to Washington.

The man had traveled to Guatemala many times, he explained, and in his basement he had dozens of ancient black jade celts he'd collected. He also had a rock saw, and when he showed Ridinger a cross-section he'd made of one of the celts, gold flecks were plainly visible. Apparently the stones' outer surfaces had also been flecked, but over centuries the softer metal had oxidized and abraded, leaving only the more durable jade. Of course, no museum would sacrifice its artifacts to such an experiment, but the Ridingers were certain that some of the black celts on display in Guatemala City and elsewhere were also carved from Galactic Gold. Again, Mary Lou Ridinger submitted no article to an academic journal reporting the find.

A couple of months later, *National Geographic* published a cover story on jade. Though the lion's share was devoted to Asian stone, New World jade was included, along with Mary Lou Ridinger ("an archaeologist who mines Guatemalan jade") and Ron Bishop, by now a curator at the Smithsonian, who was testing Mesoamerican museum pieces to see which were jade and which were greenstone. After the article, Mary Lou noticed a shift in attitude, even on the part of academics. The warming had actually begun after she'd furnished geological samples to the Mesoamerican Jade Project in the 1970s. But now that their business had been brushed with the imprimatur of *National Geographic*—who'd acknowledged Mary Lou as an archaeologist, no less—even skeptics had to concede that the Ridingers were selling bona fide jade and that the stone was a legitimate part of Guatemala's heritage.

In late August 1987, Mary Lou Ridinger attended a week-long international conference in Denver, where some thirty geologists and archaeologists met to share the most recent findings about Mesoamerican jade and to consider avenues for further research.

She brought along a dozen samples of their newly discovered blue-gray jade, which the Ridingers were calling "Olmec Blue," and passed them out to some of the attendees.

One of the crucial questions for the conference went back to Ron Bishop's work for the Mesoamerican Jade Project, several years before. He'd suggested that the museum artifacts and geological samples formed six distinct clusters based on the trace elements they contained, although it wasn't certain how many geological sources they represented. Since then, he and his colleagues Edward V. Sayre and Joan Mishara had analyzed more than a hundred artifacts from Costa Rican museums. Only half a dozen were found to resemble geological samples from the Motagua, reinforcing their conclusion that other, undiscovered jade sources must exist.

Many experts had long suspected that jade deposits would be found in Mexico and Costa Rica, since both areas were rich in jade artifacts and had known deposits of serpentinite. But William Foshag had searched the Mexican state of Puebla without success, and in subsequent years, no jade had been documented either in that country or in Costa Rica. Now another conference attendee, geologist George Harlow, from the American Museum of Natural History in New York, declared those efforts futile: "Based on geologic interpretation," he stated, "the prospect of Mexican and Costa Rican sources is extremely poor," since there were none of the tectonic plate boundaries required for the stone's creation. In fact, he concluded that the region around Guatemala's Motagua Valley was the only place in Mesoamerica meeting the geological prerequisites for the formation of jade.

As for the trace mineral research, which had suggested a variety of sources for the jade, Harlow believed that Bishop's clusters were artificial, the result of studying too few samples and failing to consider the stone's heterogeneous nature. Instead of focusing on trace elements, Harlow did his analysis with a microscope and electron microprobe, concentrating on more general characteristics such as color, texture, and mineral content. And with this forest-instead-of-trees approach, he found that most of the jade artifacts were actually similar to geologic samples taken from the Motagua.

Harlow's analysis was thorough and, to some, persuasive. Attendees from Mexico and Costa Rica were crestfallen to hear the world's leading expert on the geology of jade say that deposits would never be found in their countries. But the Ridingers were excited that undiscovered sources might lay tantalizingly close to the two sites they were already working in the Motagua. With the war winding down and the *campo* becoming safer, and with tourists finally returning to Guatemala, it was time to resume their prospecting.

SEVEN

Jade Guatemalteco

It was a hazy afternoon toward the end of the rainy season. The Bell Jet Ranger helicopter hovered over the scrubby ridge. Sitting in the copilot's seat, Mary Lou Ridinger took her eyes away from the window and peered again at her map. Then she trained her binoculars on a stone outcrop several hundred feet below. Finally, she turned to Jay, sitting in the back seat beside his daughter Robin, and shouted over the *thwack-thwack* of the blades, "That's the place!"

The Ridingers' prospecting was more sophisticated than it used to be. They were now expert with geological maps and could trace the fault lines and serpentinite deposits where jade was liable to lurk. Like the ancient Mesoamericans, they knew that the ground over serpentinite was generally barren, because when the stone broke down it released few nutrients and even some chemicals that were poisonous to plants.

The Ridingers were also more astute at recognizing jade when they found it. Because the stone wraps itself in its nondescript rind when exposed to the elements, appearances counted for little in this type of prospecting. The hunt was necessarily more tactile and aural, more intuitive. Over thousands of hours in the field, the Ridingers had mastered the language of the hammer bounce, had learned to parse its recoil and *ping*.

Mary Lou was the ex-flying student, but it was Jay Ridinger who'd suggested they hire a helicopter, despite the extraordinary expense. On the map, the area they were searching wasn't far from the site of their first jade discovery back in 1974. But it was much higher in the sierra, up a sheer cliff with a waterfall, several days' walk from any road. The Ridingers knew because they had already hiked it. They had found some jade there, including a little of the coveted imperial green, but on foot they'd been able to carry out only a few small samples. So they'd come back today in search of more. This morning they had spent reconnoitering another location, then had flown west to yet another place where they'd heard reports of jade. It was that second area they were flying over now.

The sky was pocked with high thunderheads. As the helicopter skittered under the clouds, the Ridingers traced the corrugated contours on the ground. Mary Lou glanced at her map, then at the earth again. Yes, this was the spot. But if they set down, they would expend the little remaining daylight, and they wouldn't make it to where the imperial green was waiting. And since they weren't sure they could ever afford to hire another helicopter, they might never have the opportunity to return. Still . . . what if there were jade here as well?

They were mulling the dilemma when Robin, now in her twenties, spoke up. Why didn't they drop her off to take a look? They could go on, then come back and pick her up later. Mary Lou and Jay hesitated. Not that they doubted her prospecting abilities—she was accomplished with a geologist's hammer and a vial of bromoform—but they were reluctant to let her down alone in strange territory. Robin pointed out that she often wandered off by herself when they were prospecting on foot—what was the difference? No *campesinos* or combatants came up this high in the sierra. And the helicopter would be back in an hour anyway. What could possibly go wrong? Eventually, she persuaded them. Mary Lou signaled to the pilot, a round, bespectacled man named Ricardo, who brought the craft down on the ridge. Robin hopped out with her equipment bag and scurried from under the blades. As the helicopter took off, her parents could see her waving up at them.

Mary Lou Ridinger held the map out to Ricardo and pointed to their next destination. He nodded, the helicopter turned to the east, and a few minutes later, they were circling the other site. They landed in a clearing and began chipping out some promising samples. But after an hour, they became aware of a dense fog forming around them. They grabbed their gear and jogged back to the helicopter. Ricardo started the rotors before they were even settled in their seats, and in a moment they were racing toward Robin.

In the short time it took to get there, the earth had vanished; not even the flat tops of the mesquites and acacias poked through the mist. It was impossible to get their bearings. And even if they could find the ridge again, landing was out of the question. They circled for a long time, but the weather only worsened. They were getting low on fuel, Ricardo told them. Finally, he said that if they didn't find Robin in ten more minutes, they'd have to leave without her.

Sitting alone in the back seat, Jay felt paralyzed at first. Then he remembered an ancient legend that if two people were wearing jade cut from the same boulder, they could communicate through the stone. Jay, Mary Lou, and Robin all wore plain pendants, about the size of a half dollar, made from a single piece of green jade. Now, clutching his charm, Jay closed his eyes and focused fiercely on his daughter. After a few minutes, he pointed to a spot in the clouds and told Ricardo, "Go down there—she's going to be standing right down there!" The pilot looked at him as if he were mad, but Ridinger insisted.

The helicopter began a wary descent, with Ricardo watching the altimeter. And in that instant, the clouds parted just enough to reveal Robin, who was waving frantically—and standing precisely where Jay had pointed. They set down on top of the ridge, and Robin jumped in. Then, as they rose, they glanced down at the place where they'd landed; it was totally consumed by fog again.

At least, that's how Jay Ridinger described the incident to a reporter for *Lapidary Journal.* By nature, Ridinger had long been a searcher for more than jade. He'd dabbled in yoga, gone to Esalen, taken a course for shamans. Charismatic and intuitive, he was suspected by more than one person of having psychic abilities. And he believed in the mystical power of jade. He told how a Maya shaman had once explained to him that jade had to be "awakened." "Jade is very lazy," the wise man had said, "and being old, sleeps a great deal." To demonstrate how to bestir jade, the shaman had taken two pieces from a pouch and clapped them together. That afternoon in the helicopter, Ridinger hadn't struck his pendant, only clutched it and concentrated in order to rouse whatever power the jade possessed. But he told the reporter, "I am convinced this is a subject that deserves serious research and study."

Supernatural abilities have been ascribed to jade for thousands of years—the power not only to communicate with the spirit world, but to cure disease, revive the dying, even to ensure immortality. Over that long span, dozens of legends have illustrated the stone's supposed faculties. In his classic book *Jade: Stone of Heaven,* Richard Gump, of Gump's department store in San Francisco, recounts two stories from China in which jade serves as the agent of divine will. In the first, from the Han dynasty (about 200 B.C. to A.D. 200), a solid-jade coffin materializes inside the imperial palace. When the casket proves too heavy for even the brawniest of royal retainers to lift, the emperor accepts it as an augury of his death and takes his place inside. As soon as he's situated, the top slams shut, the coffin suddenly is light enough to carry, and the ruler is buried with all the honors attendant to his rank.

Gump's other legend has to do with a carved jade seal that for two thousand years was considered an essential emblem of imperial power. In the 1700s, with the unruly Yangtze River again over its banks, Emperor Qiánlóngdì cast the seal into the current in a desperate attempt to appease the gods—and the floodwaters miraculously ebbed. Then, years later, as the emperor rested beside a jade fountain near Beijing, the gods saw fit to return the offering, and the seal appeared in the burbling waters.

In Mesoamerica, mystical powers were attributed to jade for more than three millennia—and still are. Many of the Ridingers' friends and employees in Antigua have their own tales about so-called jade magic. Gail Terzuola, ex-wife of master carver Bob Terzuola and co-discoverer of the Terzuola archaeological site, tells of a friend who was wearing a jade necklace that Bob had made. When a drunken policeman fired a stray shot, the bullet struck the woman in the neck—but ricocheted harmlessly off the heavy jewelry. Jane Swezey, wife of Bill Swezey, Mary Lou Ridinger's professor from La Universidad de las Américas, tells how Jay Ridinger once insisted that she wear one of his oversized jade necklaces; finding it a bit gaudy, she politely resisted but ultimately ceded to his power of persuasion. And as soon as she slipped the jade over her head, she felt a strange, harmonious feeling that stayed with her the rest of the day, like nothing she'd ever experienced before or since.

The Ridingers' dynamic manager, Raquel Pérez, is also an advocate of jade magic. "Jade is history," she says in her excellent English. "It's part of us, our ancestors." On her desk, she keeps a disk of Galactic Gold jade, which she rubs whenever she mulls an important decision. She believes that jade protects her and her family, and so her seven-year-old son has carried a coin-sized piece of jade in his pocket since the age of three. Raquel and her boyfriend also wear heart-shaped pendants carved from the same piece of jade, which they believe facilitate communication between them.

The scientifically trained Mary Lou Ridinger was skeptical of jade magic at first. When Bill Swezey died, she did give Jane a piece of jade to place in his coffin—that was a tribute to her mentor, though, not an effort to confer immortality. But when she became pregnant and doctors warned her about the possibility of a premature delivery, she began to rub a piece of jade over her womb. Jake was born in May 1984, exactly at term, weighing nine and a half pounds. "Who knows if it was the jade?" Mary Lou laughs. But, she says, "Jade is an obsession. I believe in it. It brings fortune when given away. It's a mystical thing. It's my religion."

Geologist Josh Rosenfeld hasn't lived in Guatemala for thirty-five years, but he still wears a jade ring and a large jade bead around his neck that was carved by his friend Bob Terzuola. Not only is jade beautiful, it makes him feel good. It's a "very spiritual stone, as close to alive as a stone can be." Does that mean he believes that jade has supernatural properties? "No," he demurs, "I'm a scientist."

Bob Terzuola doesn't believe in jade magic, either. To explain the stone's preternatural coolness, he summons the laws of physics—because of its density, the stone takes a long time to warm up and to cool down. But that's not to say he doesn't have a special regard for jade. He's always felt in harmony with it, in a way that he hasn't with any other type of stone he's worked, he tells me, and he's always felt that jade has been generous to him.

A scientist who does believe he was touched by jade magic is Olaf Jaime-Riverón, a Mexican archaeologist completing his dissertation at the University of Kentucky. Several years ago, when he was surveying an Olmec site in the state of Veracruz, Jaime-Riverón was overcome by heatstroke and fell into a coma. By the third week, it seemed he might not regain consciousness. But, he tells me, when one of his professors touched an ancient blue celt to Jaime-Riverón's forehead, he awoke. Ever since, he's been convinced of the medicinal properties of jade—like Chinese sages and Mesoamerican kings before him.

As for the Ridingers, they never did get back to Guatemala City that afternoon after rescuing Robin. Out of fuel, they made an emergency landing in the parking lot of a Pepsi plant in Teculután, just east of Manzanal. Robin reported that her outcrop showed no sign of jade. But her parents had better luck; based on the samples they took that day, they were able to expand their mining license to include that site as well. To extract the stone, they returned with burros, not a helicopter.

※

Despite the sophistication of the Ridingers' prospecting, no additional jade deposits deigned to reveal themselves. So, through the rest of the 1980s and into the 1990s, the Ridingers mined just two license areas—the one that they had found in 1974 and later expanded with their helicopter prospecting and the site with Olmec blue and Galactic Gold that Andy Duncan had discovered in 1987. The Mesoamerican Jade Project had suggested several other possible sources of pre-Hispanic jade in the Motagua, but if they existed, their location remained a mystery.

Meanwhile, the Ridingers' business continued to grow. By the early 1990s, they had opened five stores—three in Antigua, one in Guatemala City, and one in the Petén, near Tikal—and the family had become the largest purveyors of jade in Central America. At the risk of flaunting their prosperity, they had also bought a large, walled Colonial home on the south edge of town, once the center of a coffee finca. In typical Guatemalan fashion, success had bred imitation, and several other jade factories/showrooms had opened in Antigua. Some were operated by former associates of the Ridingers, including Jay's ex-friend Jerry Leech, who had begun mining jade from two quarries of his own.

The growth of the Antigua jade industry would have been impossible without the gradual resolution of Guatemala's civil war.

When reformist Marco Vinicio Cerezo Arévalo had been elected president, his administration had been met with renewed hopes for peace. But by the end of his term, the country was suffering under a stagnant economy and rampant corruption, and labor unionists and *campesinos* were complaining that they had seen no betterment in their lives.

Cerezo's successor, the right-wing evangelist Jorge Antonio Serrano Elías, invigorated the economy and initiated peace talks with the insurgents. Then in 1993, when he grew exasperated with the slow pace of progress, coup music sounded again. Serrano dissolved the government and seized dictatorial control, but this move was met with widespread protests, and he was forced to flee the country. As his interim replacement Congress named Ramiro de León Carpio, a liberal who attacked corruption, introduced constitutional reforms, and continued negotiations with the rebels; over the course of his truncated term, a number of agreements were signed, including those on indigenous rights, resettlement of displaced persons, and agrarian reform. The year 1996 saw the election of Álvaro Enrique Arzú Irigoyen, known for his strong commitment to human rights, and on December 29, accords were signed bringing the civil war to a close. During thirty-six devastating years, two hundred thousand Guatemalans had been killed, the great majority of them rural Maya; another forty thousand people had disappeared, overwhelmingly the victims of government death squads; perhaps a million more were refugees.

Peace wasn't a panacea for all that ailed Guatemalan society. In the ensuing years, the economy continued to improve and the modest middle class grew, but again the benefits didn't trickle down equally to the lowest strata of society. Instead of disbanding, the government's newly unemployed security agents turned to organized crime. Today, corruption, crime, violence, and drug trafficking remain endemic, and Guatemala City finds its way onto some lists of the world's most dangerous metropolises.

Meanwhile, Guatemala still struggles to sort through two generations of civil war. In 2005, the archives of the former national police force were discovered in an abandoned munitions depot in Guatemala City—eighty million pages of documents, including some in cabinets neatly labeled *Asesinos* and *Desaparecidos*, "Assassins" and "Disappeared." Researchers have been organizing the files into a digital database, an enormous project that will take several more years. Even with only a tenth of the documents scanned, the archive has exposed atrocities committed by the national police force, and several arrests have already been made. Not everyone in Guatemala is eager to see the truth emerge. There was an attempt to firebomb the archive, and after the government's human rights ombudsman released a preliminary report on the project, his wife was kidnapped and tortured. But work continues, and it's hoped that the files will finally give victims' families, and the nation, long-awaited closure on this particularly abysmal chapter in Guatemala's tortured history.

✤

In 1998, toward the end of the rainy season, Mary Lou, Jay, and Angela Ridinger, along with fourteen-year-old Jake and one of their local pickers, were searching for jade near the border of Honduras, a region notorious as the drug-trafficking capital of Guatemala. They had come because the prospector claimed to have found some boulders of lavender jade, an idea that Mary Lou met with skepticism.

Jay Ridinger pulled their pickup off the side of the road, and the group began walking up one of the Motagua's many tributaries. Mary Lou Ridinger had a sense of déjà vu. They came to an area just below a road, set on a tight curve with a steep cut on one side. Then she remembered. The road hadn't been paved when she'd last been here, twenty years before almost to the day, and the dirt track had been nearly impassable even in their four-wheel-drive pickup. She told Jay, "This is where Charlotte Thomson and I turned around that time we were prospecting in 1978, and it looked like there was going to be war with Belize." Mary Lou had meant to go back to the place, but something had always seemed to interfere.

Their prospector led them to the boulders, which did have a lavender tint, veined with white.

"That's jade," Jay Ridinger said.

Mary Lou was still doubtful. Lavender jade, which owes its unusual hue to the presence of manganese, had never been reported in Guatemala—or as far as she knew, in any Olmec or Maya site.

Lavender jade was mined in Burma, Jay persisted. Why not here? He said he'd always expected they would find stone of that color in the Motagua.

When the assay came back from the States, they had their verdict: It was jade. In the meantime, Mary Lou had tracked down a single example of carved lavender jade in the archaeological record—a celt discovered on the Mexican island of Cozumel. But however beautiful or distinctive lavender jade might be to us, it doesn't seem to have made much of an impression on the Olmecs or the Maya. Although the color isn't common around the Motagua, the ancients must have stumbled over some of the stone during thousands of years of prospecting. But it appears the Olmecs had an overwhelming preference for blue stone and the Maya for green—the brighter, the better. And if Maya artisans couldn't obtain green jade, rather than resorting to lavender or other colors, they would generally work softer greenstone such as serpentinite.

And so the Ridingers discovered their third jade source. Mary Lou had a large oval ring made from the lavender stone, with a white, x-shaped vein in the center. She calls it her x-marks-the-spot ring, and she wears it every day to remind her of the value of persistence.

Jay and Mary Lou Ridinger pose with pieces of lavender jade; it was the first time the rare stone had been reported in Guatemala. COURTESY OF MARY LOU RIDINGER

It had taken the Ridingers more than two decades to locate their first three sources of jade, but beginning in 2002, they discovered another four in just two years. The new finds ranged over a wide area, from far north of the Motagua to far south, and from high in the mountains to the banks of the river itself. Most of the new jade lay in outcrops, and most was the typical gray-green. But source number five, the one nearest the Motagua, consisted of river boulders in a striking range of colors, including reddish-orange and blue-green; that site also had extensive evidence of ancient celt-making.

The run of new discoveries, coming after such a long hiatus, wasn't the result so much of skill or luck as competitive pressure. Early in 2002, the Ridingers learned that an American company called Ventana Mining was planning to enter the jade business in Guatemala, and the Ridingers decided to stake out as many new sources as possible before the interlopers' arrival. The new venture did find jade and apply for some government licenses, but nearly a decade later, it's still in the process of finalizing permits and securing funding. The company's plans, once it does start operations, are to sell non-gem-quality jade for tile and similar uses, not to make jewelry or reproductions to compete with the Ridingers. Yet, thanks to Ventana's ongoing interest in Guatemalan jade, the Ridingers more than doubled their inventory of sources.

At this point, Mary Lou and Jay Ridinger were doing little prospecting themselves. Though they reviewed geological maps and suggested areas to search, most of the on-the-ground work was done by their staff geologist, Jaime Godoy, along with local pickers and the young Jake Ridinger. The lanky, towheaded Jake had been accompanying his parents on prospecting trips since the age of five, and by the time he was eleven or twelve, he'd been making overnight forays into the mountains with the Ridingers' collectors, in what his mother calls "a jade initiation rite." Eighteen years old and grown to six foot seven, Jake went off to college in the States. But on school vacations, wearing a lucky piece of jade around his neck, he would drive himself up the teeming Atlantic Highway, meet a local guide or prospector, then hike into the searing backcountry. Sometimes, they'd venture thirty or forty miles from the nearest road, spending four or five days, picking wild plants and shooting game to supplement their rations. What drew the young Ridinger to prospecting? Partly it was his love for the outdoors, and partly a desire to contribute to the family business. On one of his excursions, Jake Ridinger came across a boulder with a vein of the rarest jade of all, imperial green. Another time, he found some blue jade on one of the family's license sites, but only scraps—the lion's share had already been broken up and carried off by poachers.

A few hours' hike from the poached blue jade, a farmer led Jake to a previously unreported archaeological site. With a gorgeous hilltop setting, it consisted of a series of mounds whose centers had been dug out by looters. There were also two long, parallel mounds that may have been a ball court, and nearby were caves with ancient inscriptions. Based on that discovery, a friend of the family sponsored Jake for membership in the Explorers Club, the New York organization whose mission is to study "unknown or little known destinations or phenomena in order to gain knowledge for human kind," and whose three-thousand-name membership roll includes Edmund Hillary, Robert Peary, Roald Amundsen, and Neil Armstrong. Ridinger's find was also reported to Guatemala's Instituto Nacional de Antropología e Historia, which added it to its registry of thousands of sites awaiting excavation. The Instituto's listing conferred legal protection, though the place's remoteness makes it impossible to defend against more poaching.

✣

In 1999, the Ridingers received some favorable publicity, when Mary Lou played a prominent role in a Discovery Channel special called *The Mysteries of Jade,* focused on the scourge of looting. In March of that same year, Bill Clinton visited Guatemala and spent a couple of hours at the flagship store in Antigua, chatting with Jay Ridinger and their employees (Mary Lou was out of the country). For Hillary, he bought a green necklace, and for himself a carved frog. For Chelsea, he designed a necklace of lavender jade; perhaps trying to send a message to his White House staff, he bought them bags of strong Guatemalan coffee. The visit came a year after the Monica Lewinsky scandal had broken and just a month after the Senate had voted to acquit Clinton on impeachment charges. Jay Ridinger took the opportunity to present the president with a long, pointed piece of jade—a reproduction of the penis perforators that Olmec and Maya kings had used to sacrifice their blood to the gods. By then, having survived the scandal, Clinton could laugh at the gesture.

But the Ridingers still faced challenges. The greatest remained educating prospective buyers about Guatemalan jade and its three-thousand-year history. Also, being dependent on tourism, their business was periodically buffeted by world events—recessions, terror attacks, hurricanes, anything that kept people at home. Poaching was another perennial problem.

The mining laws had changed since the Ridingers had begun their prospecting. Back then, any minerals found on private land, including jadeite, were the property of the landowner. Now all minerals, even those on private property, belonged to the state. So the Ridingers no longer had to buy or even rent land in order to mine its jade. When they discovered a deposit, they would substantiate the claim by filing assays and sometimes escorting a mining inspector to the site. Then the federal government would issue them an exclusive license to collect jade within a defined area, perhaps several square miles, in exchange for an annual fee and a royalty (based on the type and quantity of stone extracted), which would be shared with the municipality where the mine was located. By law, the landowner received nothing. However, the Ridingers signed contracts with the proprietors, agreeing to compensate them for any jade the *campesinos* collected. Jerry Leech had also secured government licenses for his quarries, but less scrupulous merchants were dispensing with the formalities and acquiring jade on the black market.

Though the Ridingers continued to guard the location of their mines, they resolved never to post armed lookouts to prevent *campesinos* from pilfering their jade. For one thing, the amount of stone lost that way was minimal. For another, the Ridingers knew that the value of jade lay not so much in the raw material as in its working—the sawing and carving and grinding and polishing that turned it from a rock into a thing of beauty.

But large-scale commercial poaching was another matter. Now that lavender and other uncommon colors had been found in the Motagua, Asian dealers took a new interest in Guatemalan jade, with Chinese poachers becoming particularly aggressive. A Chinese group invaded one of the Ridingers' sites with earth movers, dynamite, and guns to intimidate the locals. But the Ridingers appealed to the Department of Mining, which expelled the invaders. So, whereas they had once feared that corrupt officials would impose themselves as silent partners, they now enjoyed the government's protection. At least to a point: Sometimes the foreign poachers simply bribed officials and exported illicit stone by the containerful.

Besides poaching, the Ridingers had to deal with even more brazen forms of theft. In July 1993, there was an armed robbery of their shop in the upscale Hotel Camino Real near Tikal, in the Petén, a part of Guatemala known for drug trafficking and violence and often compared to the American Wild West. It was their second robbery from the store. A year earlier, bandits had crept in at night, grabbed whatever they could carry, and fled. The second time, they also entered in the early morning, but with guns drawn; they fired at hotel security guards, disabled the shop's alarm system, smashed display cases, and stole every piece of jade in the store, some sixty thousand dollars' worth. Then they vanished into the forest. The police made no headway in the case, and when the Ridingers' manager in the Petén, a strapping retired Army first sergeant named John Mann, tried to investigate, it was suggested that he stop asking so many questions if he cared for his own safety.

Two months later, Mary Lou Ridinger happened to be in the Petén at the invitation of two nonprofit groups, Pro Petén and Conservation International. The organizations were sponsoring a project in which carvers from Honduras would teach Guatemalans how to knap arrowheads and carve bone to sell to tourists at nearby Tikal. The nonprofits had courtesy visas to enter Belize for the day to collect flint that the artisans-to-be would use for raw material.

And so Mary Lou Ridinger, two members of Conservation International, and a man named Chico, a talented carver who had worked for the Ridingers for years, left Guatemala in their pickup truck at six o'clock in the morning.

In 1991, Guatemala had finally recognized Belizean independence, though the border between the two countries was still unratified (as it is even today). But Ridinger's group showed their visas and crossed into Belize without problem. They easily located the flint, following a geological map that Mary Lou Ridinger had brought along. By one o'clock, they'd loaded the stone into the pickup and were headed back to Guatemala.

About five miles from the border, they decided to stop for lunch at a roadside restaurant. Sitting at their table and chatting with the owner's wife, they asked about the local craft of slate carving, in which flat slabs were incised with bas-relief figures and landscapes. As a matter of fact, the woman said, she had some slate carvings in the shop next door, and after they ate, she'd be happy to open it for them.

When she entered the store, Mary Lou Ridinger was dumbfounded: Not only were slate carvings on display—but so were the jade masks, plaques, and jewelry that had been stolen from her shop near Tikal. Chico also recognized the merchandise instantly, since he'd carved much of it himself. The only things missing were small items—earrings, pendants, and key chains.

Ridinger confronted the woman, who called in her husband. The robbery was unfortunate, the man said, but that had happened in Guatemala, not Belize, and he and his wife weren't at liberty to say where they'd gotten the pieces. Ridinger offered to pay a reward and to deliver other jades for them to sell. Then, when the couple still protested, she began scooping up the merchandise, talking all the while. "Thank you so much for returning our jade. This is really such a wonderful gesture on your part. I'm going to make sure you receive recognition for what noble people you are."

Meanwhile, under her breath she was saying, "Pack it up, Chico. Get it on the truck." The wife started sobbing. The thieves had left the jade on consignment, she said, and they would kill them when they found it missing. "You can't do this," she pleaded. "Think of our children." But Mary Lou and Chico kept collecting the jade, while the members of Conservation International looked on with mouths agape.

They carted every piece to the pickup, dropped it in the open bed, and jumped into the cab. "Drive!" Mary Lou ordered. They sped toward the frontier, watching their rear view mirrors. But no one followed, and when they reached the border and showed their courtesy visas, the Guatemalan guards didn't so much as glance in the back of the truck.

The next day, John Mann went to the restaurant/gift shop to make good on his boss's promise. Not long after, he heard of two men arrested for car theft in Flores, in the Petén. Rumor was that the car was full of small jades—the key chains, earrings, and other merchandise that Mary Lou Ridinger hadn't recovered. But when Mann went to see the local police chief, he was informed that no jade had been mentioned in the arrest report—most likely, Mann suggested, because the officers had taken the items for themselves. In the end, the Ridingers recovered all of their merchandise except for about two thousand dollars' worth. But they never discovered what punishment, if any, was meted out to the bandits and the corrupt policemen. And they never learned whether the thieves took their revenge on the owners of the roadside gift shop.

❖

Over the years, the Ridingers' relationship with the archaeological community had warmed. Though some academics were still skeptical of them as "entrepreneurs," most were now satisfied that the couple weren't selling forgeries or looted antiquities. The thaw had begun as far back as the Mesoamerican Jade Project, which the Ridingers had provided with many of its geological samples. Around that same time, when the first meeting of Maya epigraphers was held in Guatemala, the Ridingers had invited several of the scholars to tour the jade factory.

Among the group was Linda Schele, the doyenne of Mayan epigraphers, who'd played a crucial role in reconstructing the royal lineage of Palenque, working from the glyphs that Alberto Ruz had discovered on the sarcophagus of Pakal the Great. In the Ridingers' shop, Schele mentioned that she'd always wanted to learn to carve jade. Mary Lou Ridinger had always wanted to learn to read Maya glyphs, and she suggested that they exchange lessons. And so began a warm friendship between the academic and the entrepreneur. When Schele died of pancreatic cancer in 1998, at the age of fifty-five, the Ridingers dedicated a corner of their in-store museum, depicting Maya cosmology, in her honor. Included in the display was one of the last photos ever taken of Schele, in which she's holding one of her pieces of carved jade, her putative passport to immortality.

An event in 2001 further raised the Ridingers' standing among archaeologists. Mary Lou was in the shop in Antigua when a Guatemalan woman came in offering to sell a small, crudely carved greenstone mask. Ridinger was on her way to lunch, but when she glanced at the mask, she thought she recognized it as one that had been stolen from a museum at La Democracia, on Guatemala's Pacific Coast.

She recalled that the mask had been excavated at Monte Alto, a Preclassic site also on the Pacific. In fact, Marian Hatch, the archaeologist who'd found it, lived in Antigua, a couple of blocks away. Ridinger called Hatch to confirm the identification before contacting the police, though even as she dialed, she was certain her friend would be in Guatemala City at La Universidad del

Valle, where she was chair of the archaeology department. But Hatch answered the phone and agreed to come right over.

Ridinger took the mask into the store's office/library, while the woman waited in the patio outside. Marian Hatch arrived and immediately identified it. On Hatch's advice, Ridinger called not the local police but the Instituto de Antropología e Historia, which said it would dispatch some men from the capital, about an hour away. To stall for time, Ridinger began peppering the woman with questions.

"Where do you think the mask is from?"

"The south coast."

"Do you think it's old?"

"Oh yes, it's Preclassic."

"What do you think it's worth?"

"I want thirty-five thousand American dollars for it," the woman said, though Ridinger figured the mask was worth millions.

Time was passing, and the authorities still hadn't arrived. Ridinger and Hatch were wondering how much longer they could stall. Finally, Mary Lou Ridinger confronted the woman. "Look, we know the mask is stolen. The police are on the way. So we'll give you a choice. You can either leave it here and walk out the door, or you can wait for the authorities."

The woman answered that she'd have to consult her husband, who was waiting in a car outside. But as she walked out the front door, the officials finally arrived. The husband sped off, and the woman was arrested. The story made national news, and Mary Lou Ridinger testified at the trial. "What were you thinking?" her friends asked her. "This is Guatemala. There will be reprisals. They could kill you." By this time there were armed guards posted at the store, and for the next week they did report suspicious cars cruising in front. But no one ever tried to exact revenge. As for the mask, it didn't go back to La Democracia but was taken for safekeeping to the Museo Nacional de Arqueología y Etnología in Guatemala City.

❖

The Guatemalan jade business has come a long way since Mary Lou Ridinger's excited arrival in 1974, and it's now possible to buy jade jewelry in dozens of shops throughout the country. The Ridingers are the industry's acknowledged founders, and they, along with associate-turned-competitor Jerry Leech, are the leading purveyors of the stone in Central America. Even so, production is still relatively small, and Mary Lou Ridinger is adamant that it remain "non-invasive and ecologically sustainable."

This is in contrast to what has reportedly happened in Burma (or Myanmar, the name conferred by its military dictators in 1989), where jade is mined on a large commercial scale, in a process that has proven destructive not only of the environment but of human lives. In their powerful book *Stone of Heaven: Unearthing the Secret History of Imperial Green Jade*, Adrian Levy and Cathy Scott-Clark, two British investigative journalists who managed to get access to the Hpakant mines in northern Burma, report how impoverished peasants are recruited with promises of easy money. But at the huge quarries, which are ringed by military checkpoints, they are forced to toil fifteen-hour shifts and to live in overcrowded, filthy conditions. Workers are also systematically cheated of their pay, and when they have lost all hope of reuniting with their families, they are offered, in lieu of wages, a potent form of heroin direct from Burma's Golden Triangle. And after their early death from malnutrition, malaria, overdoses, and AIDS, they are replaced by the next crop of naïve arrivals.

In Guatemala, Mary Lou Ridinger's business benefits from the limited production that she advocates, which discourages new competitors and helps prevent a glut of jade on the market. It's not idealism or self-restraint that keeps the industry small, but the weak worldwide market for the less-salable Guatemalan stone.

So the same fact of entrepreneurial life that has bedeviled the Ridingers for years now also helps them maintain their position as market leader.

As she approaches her fourth decade in Guatemala, Mary Lou Ridinger, the ex-archaeologist, is still very much the "entrepreneur." Does she ever wonder how things might have gone if she'd pursued her original career instead of embracing Jay Ridinger's more commercial vision? "No," she answers immediately, "never." Hers has been "a life of magic," blessed with "the joy of adventure."

Robert Leslie, perhaps more than anyone the modern "discoverer" of jade in Guatemala, left the country more than fifty years ago, but when he returned on vacations, he would often stop by the Ridingers'. On one of these visits, he told Mary Lou that if he were the Christopher Columbus of Guatemalan jade, then she and Jay were the Hernán Cortés. Like Columbus, he said, he'd made his breakthrough, then sailed away, leaving it to the Ridingers to stay on and revive an art that had been forgotten for nearly five centuries.

Mary Lou Ridinger is amused by the comparison to the conqueror of the Aztecs. But she says it's precisely this idea that gives her the greatest satisfaction—not just that she and Jay located more jade sources than anyone else, but that they returned jade carving to its homeland. Part of that satisfaction lies in the employment they've given to hundreds of Guatemalans, from pickers to carvers to salespeople. But even more fulfilling is the impact she believes that jade has had on national pride. Though it was a vital part of Guatemala's history, jade had been lost so thoroughly that people doubted its existence. With its restoration, she believes, "every Guatemalan has something of world-class value that belongs to Guatemala and to their heritage." Apparently President Álvaro Colom concurred: On his inauguration in 2008, he ordered forty reproduction jade masks from the Ridingers to present to visiting heads of state.

Several years ago, Mary Lou Ridinger traveled to San Antonio, Texas, for an exhibition of artifacts from the Maya ruins at Río Azul, located in northern Guatemala, not far from Tikal. It had been proclaimed Guatemala Month in San Antonio, and archaeologists, the editor of *National Geographic*, and other dignitaries had flown in for the opening. Among them were the Guatemalan ambassador and his wife—the same woman who years before had assured one of the Ridingers' first customers that there were no jade deposits in Guatemala. The diplomat and his *señora* were standing in the receiving line, and as Mary Lou made her way toward them, she saw that the woman was bedecked with jewelry purchased from the Ridingers. When Mary Lou reached her, she thanked her for wearing *jade guatemalteco*. To which the ambassador's wife replied, "I wouldn't wear anything else."

⁜

Though the ancient jade fields have given up some of their secrets, they still guard others. One has to do with the bright, wonderfully translucent stone known as imperial green. A freak of geology, created when a tiny bit of chromium is added to the mix, imperial green was the most coveted of all jade in Maya times, preferred for the greatest works of the wealthiest kings. Today, it remains the most-prized gemstone in the world, breathtakingly rare in Burma and rarer still in Guatemala. Over nearly four decades, the Ridingers have handled hundreds of tons of jade, ranging from blue to black to lavender to dozens of shades of green. But during all that time, they have come across just three small cobbles with veins of imperial jade. Their competitors have fared no better. So where did the Maya obtain this most desirable of all hues—and is more waiting, somewhere, to be discovered?

What bright green jade was to the Maya, translucent blue was to the Olmecs. And in a way, Olmec jade is even more beguiling.

Not only was it the choice of that great early civilization of Mesoamerica, but Olmec blue is even more of an enigma—not because it was rarer than imperial green in ancient times, but because it was more common. Hoards of gleaming blue stone artifacts have been uncovered in Mesoamerica, from southern Mexico to Costa Rica, often fashioned into elegant, highly polished celts. But in all their years of prospecting, the Ridingers have discovered only one significant cache of the raw stone—the hundred or so river boulders weighing about a ton. It's this discrepancy, remarked by Alexander von Humboldt, between its ancient abundance and its modern rarity, that makes the stone so tantalizing. Where did the Olmecs find it? Are those sources depleted? Had the Ridingers stumbled over the very last of the Olmec blue?

PART III

THE STORYTELLERS

EIGHT

Los Jaderos

Russell Seitz hadn't been to Guatemala in years. But in early 1999, the one-time field director of the Mesoamerican Jade Project was back in Antigua, on holiday with his fiancée. Making the rounds of the city's jade and jewelry shops, he inquired about the stone the merchants had been getting from their pickers in the *campo*. "Have you seen any funny-looking jade recently?" he'd ask the proprietors. In the heart of the Antigua tourist district, at a shop called *El Reino del Jade,* he was told to take a look on the roof, where the stone was piled while waiting to be carved.

When he began to poke around the heaps of rock, Seitz was astonished: Among the run-of-the-mill shades of grayish green, he spied one about the size of a human hand, blue and translucent, to his eye nothing like the "opaque," "oatmeal-colored," "worthless," and "inexportably bad" jade he generally saw around town. In fact, the stone struck him as the finest jade he'd ever seen in Guatemala. "Lordy," he thought, "this is Olmec type. Where did it come from?"

Seitz pressed the store's manager, Carlos Morales Cornejo, for the source of the jade. Morales didn't know, because it had come in from one of his prospectors and had been dumped with all the rest, but he agreed to try to trace the mystery stone. His vacation over, Seitz returned to Boston.

It was nine months before Morales and his prospector Carlos González tracked down the picker who'd found the blue jade and persuaded him to lead them to the source. Seitz went back to Guatemala, and he and Morales drove out the Atlantic Highway to González's town of Teculután, where the Ridingers had made the emergency landing in their helicopter. Then the party left the road and, guided by González and a man named Cerminio León, continued on foot northwest along the Río Blanco. For two days, they trekked into the desolate Sierra de las Minas, skirting a half-mile-deep canyon and climbing more than five thousand vertical feet, until they reached a grass-covered clearing at a place called El Ciprés.

Seitz was "thunderstruck" by what they saw there: Prospectors had dug a shallow trench fifty yards long by two yards wide, exposing a mass of blue-green jade—"not just a bunch of boulders," Seitz reckoned, but "a competent vein of jadeite." Though it was "not grade A," he judged it "better than what you get in the valley and better than anything that we saw in the 1970s," when he was working for the Mesoamerican Jade Project.

Seitz returned to the States with a hundredweight of the stone packed in his luggage. After Harvard's Hoffman Laboratory for Experimental Geophysics confirmed that the samples were jade, he sent specimens to George Harlow, at the American Museum of Natural History, for corroboration. Then Seitz gathered a team to return to Guatemala. Other commitments kept Harlow from joining on this visit, so Seitz was accompanied by Karl Taube, an archaeologist at the University of California at Riverside, and Virginia Sisson, a geologist from Rice University. Though their motives were academic, not mercenary, the band at first dubbed themselves "the Jade Raiders." Then, eager to avoid any piratical connotation, they adopted the tamer "*Los Jaderos*," "the Jade People."

Arriving in March 2001, *Los Jaderos* followed González to a mass of jade boulders along the Río Hondo. They climbed into the sierra until they reached El Ciprés, where they were excited to find an old stone roadway as well. Then *Los Jaderos* heard rumors of even more jade some thirty miles away, at a place called Quebrada Seca, in the mountains south of the Motagua. But they had run out of time and would have to wait till June to return to Guatemala and verify the reports.

The Quebrada Seca site was especially intriguing, because at one time only the north side of the Motagua Fault was thought to meet the requirements for the formation of jade. For the past several years, there had been hints of jade to the south—pink and lavender near the village of La Ensenada, blue-green in the Río El Tambor and near the towns of Carrizal Grande and San José—but none of this prepared *Los Jaderos* for what they saw at Quebrada Seca in June. It was "the big one," announced George Harlow, who joined the group for this second trip. Nearby, they found other important deposits of jade scattered over many square miles, leading *Los Jaderos* to estimate they had expanded the range of known jade deposits in Guatemala by at least sixfold.

Most of the stone was of indifferent purity with no commercial value—a "dull sea of pastel blue-green and gray," as Russell Seitz described it. George Harlow agreed: "It's stuff that you could slice up and make nice tile out of. But you couldn't make much jewelry." Some of the jade, though, was a spectacular translucent blue. "We had worked for a month in Burma," said Virginia Sisson, "and didn't see anything as good as this." And whereas the Ridingers had found only small cobbles of blue jade, here there were "bus-sized" boulders of it, including one estimated to weigh three hundred tons, among the largest jadeite rocks ever discovered.

Why hadn't the huge source been unearthed before? With geologists telling them that jade would be found only on the north side of the Motagua, prospectors had been concentrating their efforts across the river. And located a two-day, uphill hike from the valley, the new find lay in a remote region not often traveled. But since the end of the civil war in 1996, more people had ventured into the area, to farm and to prospect for jade.

Ultimately, the explanation lay not so much in geology or topography or demographics as in meteorology. In October 1998, Hurricane Mitch had lingered over Central America for five devastating days, loosing more than six feet of rain and spawning floods and avalanches that killed nearly twenty thousand people. In Guatemala, where the Motagua crested a ruinous thirty-one feet above flood stage, almost three hundred people had died and damage had been counted at three quarters of a billion U.S. dollars.

But for jade prospectors, the hurricane was, as Russell Seitz put it, "a perfect storm," sweeping away feet of soil and exposing jade boulders along tributaries both north and south of the Motagua. Locals traced the trail of stones back up the mountains to the outcrops stripped of soil by the hurricane. Then they sold the jade to shops in Antigua, where the vacationing Russell Seitz had happened to see it.

✦

Los Jaderos reported their find in the December 2001 issue of the journal *Antiquity.* "Some of the recently recovered jadeitites," they wrote, "have the combination of composition, minor minerals, and visual characteristics . . . that point to these newly discovered (or rediscovered) deposits as excellent candidates for an 'Olmec-blue' jade source." Behind the scientific detachment, their meaning was clear: They believed they had discovered the lost jade mines of the Olmecs.

The story wasn't picked up by the general press until the following May, when the *New York Times* published a piece under the headline, "In Guatemala, a Rhode Island-Size Jade Load," giving the impression that the jade was scattered over some 1,200 square miles. Within days, *Los Jaderos'* find attracted more attention than the discoveries of all their jade-hunting predecessors combined. "Source of Olmec Treasure Discovered in Guatemala," the Associated Press reported. "Since the 18th century, collectors, geologists and archaeologists have sought the answer to a frustrating mystery: The ancient Olmecs fashioned statues out of striking blue-green jade, but the stone itself was nowhere to be found in the Americas. Now scientists believe they have discovered the source—a mother lode of jade in Guatemala that could tell much about ancient American civilizations and about the formation of the continent where they lived."

Academics not involved in the expedition were also impressed. "It's an early step but a very important one," said Jeremy Sabloff, then of the University of Pennsylvania Museum. "I think it's very exciting and has a huge amount of cultural and historical potential." Archaeologist Héctor Escobedo, then of Guatemala's Universidad del Valle but now minister of culture and sports, called the discovery "one of the most significant" in decades and suggested that it accounted not just for the Olmecs' stone but for "all of the sources for Mesoamerican jades," making it "the new jewel of our cultural heritage."

But the Guatemalan government cast a more critical eye. Guillermo Díaz, director of the Instituto de Arqueología e Historia, complained that *Los Jaderos* hadn't secured a permit for their research and hadn't submitted a report to the authorities, putting them on a par with "vulgar thieves." Philip Juárez-Paz, director of the Department of Mines, grumbled that the first he'd heard of the find was in the pages of the *Times*, more than a year after the fact. He was also miffed that *Los Jaderos* hadn't paid the requisite fee to export jade from the country.

Decades before, academics had condemned the Ridingers for refusing to divulge the whereabouts of their quarries. Now the Guatemalan government was claiming that *Los Jaderos* declined to reveal the exact location of their discoveries, supposedly to discourage additional poaching. (Russell Seitz calls this assertion "utter bilge" and claims that his group showed the locations to a pair of GPS-equipped archaeologists from two different Guatemalan universities.)

The Department of Mines expressed its displeasure at the alleged lack of transparency and claimed that its own prospectors couldn't locate the new sources, leading it to suspect that the jade was spread over an area much smaller than the 1,200 square miles reported. (The figure was apparently an exaggeration by one of *Los Jaderos*; George Harlow estimates the size at closer to 160 square miles.) The department worried that the overstatement would set off a stampede of prospectors into the protected biosphere where the jade was claimed to lie. Explained Juárez-Paz, "We at the Ministry want the mining sector to grow, whether through gold, silver, nickel, jade, whatever. If something like this really exists, it will be wonderful, it will represent economic growth for the local communities. . . . But we believe it's necessary to set the record straight and not exaggerate the news. And if people want to request permission to search an area, let them do so following the steps that the law requires."

George Harlow responded that the Instituto de Arqueología e Historia had told *Los Jaderos* that a permit wasn't required, since they weren't doing a formal excavation. To the Department of Mines, he apologized, explaining he didn't realize permission was needed to export the stone and in fact had never requested a permit to take jade out of the country in the past. For his part, Seitz claimed that the government had known about his prospecting since the 1970s, when he was accompanied into the field by a state geologist, but had never requested him to secure a permit. "Does looking at rocks require a license?" he asked. But, mindful of museum politics and the need for diplomacy, he also e-mailed an apology to Juárez-Paz, who asked *Los Jaderos* to take more care in the future.

In Antigua, the newspaper reports also peeved the Ridingers, who'd considered themselves the discoverers of Olmec blue jade since 1987, when their cousin and employee Andy Duncan had found that ton of bluish boulders along the Motagua River. In August of that year, Mary Lou Ridinger had passed out specimens at the Denver Jade Conference, and after *Los Jaderos'* find was publicized, she told a reporter for the *Miami Herald* that one of her samples had been given to George Harlow. But apparently, the Ridingers' blue stone had slipped his mind by the time of *Los Jaderos'* discovery, some dozen years later. For the Ridingers, the *Times* article constituted "a lightbulb going off"; in fact, it was their competitive regard for Seitz's team, as much as the rumored plans of Ventana Mining, that would prompt their extraordinary burst of prospecting beginning in 2002.

But Russell Seitz wasn't impressed by the Ridingers' claim. Most of the jade they sold was green, black, and other colors, he pointed out, and the little blue they did have, had been collected from river rocks, not from an outcrop. (Whereas prospectors prefer their jade as loose boulders, already free of other rock and often conveniently sized for transport, scientists like to find their jade in the ground, where the stone's surroundings tell a bigger story about the local geology—just as archaeologists want to see an artifact in its "context" to appreciate its significance.) Whoever found the blue jade first, Seitz concluded, "One thing's for sure." The Antigua merchants "haven't been selling good-quality, blue-green jade in any significant quantity."

⁂

For geologists, *Los Jaderos'* find offered a rare window into the collision of tectonic plates, since rocks formed through such processes are generally driven deep underground and not to the surface where they can be studied. "The material exposed [in the mountains around the Motagua Fault] is probably one of the best records on Earth of this kind of event," George Harlow pointed out. Moreover, most such stones didn't have the historical and cultural significance of jade. "It's exciting," Harlow added, "because it's an opportunity to connect the archaeology and the geology together."

From a geological point of view, the most puzzling aspect of *Los Jaderos'* discovery was that the jade on the north side of the Motagua Fault seemed to be only about seventy million years old, while the jade on the south side appeared to date back to about 125 million years ago. Why did the jade seem to form at two different times?

These ages were measured by a technique called argon-argon dating, not of the jade itself but of minerals such as mica and hornblende, which are thought to have formed around the same time as the jade. Because rocks aren't alive, they don't absorb carbon from the environment, the way plants and animals do, and therefore can't be dated through carbon-14 testing (which in any event, isn't accurate for objects older than sixty thousand years). But some minerals do contain other radioactive isotopes that can be measured. One such isotope is potassium-40, which decays very slowly (with a half-life of 1.25 billion years) into argon-40 and calcium-40. Because argon is inert, meaning it doesn't readily combine with other elements, rocks contain no argon at formation; so any argon found within them must result from this decay of potassium. Using a mass spectrometer, researchers can precisely measure the amount of argon in a rock and from that calculate how long ago it was created; the more argon relative to potassium, the older the rock.

The situation became more complicated when Hannes Brueckner, professor at Queens College and research adjunct at both the Lamont-Doherty Earth Observatory of Columbia University and the American Museum of Natural History, retested the Motagua rocks using a different method that relies on the decay of another radioisotope, 147-samarium, into the element neodymium. According to Brueckner's measurements, the rocks on both sides of the fault formed around the same time after all—about 120 million to 140 million years ago. How to account for the different results? Although the argon-argon method is very precise, its "clock" resets to zero when rocks are heated to high temperatures, which causes all the argon to escape; samarium-neodymium decay, on the other hand, isn't affected by such changes. So it appears that the jade on adjacent sides of the fault formed at the same time, but that something happened about seventy million years ago to reset the age of the stone to the north. It could have surfaced later than the southern stone, for instance, in a kind of reshuffling of the geologic cards, or it could have been reheated by some event that didn't affect the rocks to the south.

But this explanation raised another question. Jade isn't normally found directly across both sides of a fault like the Motagua (known as a strike-slip fault, meaning that virtually all motion, in the present and the recent past, is horizontal rather than vertical). The jade may be produced on both sides, but because the segments are continually sliding past each other, over time the movement of the fault should separate the deposits by hundreds of miles. That was why, after jade was discovered on the north side of the Motagua, geologists had discouraged prospectors from searching directly to the south.

In the case of the Motagua Fault, the north side is sliding westward, while the south creeps eastward. So why, after millions of years of such slippage, were the jade deposits found adjacent to each other? It seems that they were actually created far apart, on an unusually long section of the Motagua Fault, when it was a subduction zone rather than the strike-slip fault it is today. So, while the northern jade was forming near the Caribbean, the southern jade was forming closer to the Pacific (for convenience,

I'm using present-day references here, although the geography was very different 140 million years ago, when the Caribbean plate was just beginning to form). Then, over many millions of years, the motion of the fault, instead of separating the two deposits, brought them together in a kind of meeting of the mines. So as a result of *Los Jaderos'* discovery, the geology of the Motagua has been rewritten, showing it to be more distinctive and more complex than had been thought and providing geologists with years of additional research to better their understanding not just of that region but of tectonic action around the world.

Los Jaderos' discovery also bolstered George Harlow's suggestion that all the Mesoamerican jade had come from the area around the Motagua. One argument against that idea had been that some of the museum jades didn't match the stone currently mined in that part of Guatemala, implying that the raw material for those pieces had originated elsewhere. George Harlow's counterargument had been that it was just a matter of looking more diligently—that as more geological sources were discovered, jade would be found that was similar to the problematic artifacts. One kind of archaeological jade with very little corresponding stone from the Motagua had been Olmec blue. But now that *Los Jaderos* had uncovered a huge deposit of that type, it seemed to support Harlow's claim that the resources of the Motagua were large and varied enough to eventually account for all the jades in museum collections.

If *Los Jaderos'* sources had been mined in Olmec times, why had the sites been abandoned with untold tons of the precious stone unexploited? Did the quarries fall into disuse when Olmec civilization passed its crest, to be surpassed by the Maya, with their predilection for green jade? Or had the mines been buried by some violent upheaval until Hurricane Mitch exposed them again? Landslides are common in the area, for example. Or maybe the sources were covered in ash from the region's many volcanoes. Russell Seitz leans toward the latter explanation, telling *Archaeology* magazine, "The [jade] deposits have been Pompeiied several times." Even after Hurricane Mitch, deep layers of ash still cover the south side of the fault. It would be a simple matter to date the ash to see whether it fell during the Olmec era, but such a project might be hard to fund, suggests *Jadera* Virginia Sisson, since it could be considered a novelty area out of the academic mainstream.

However the deposits came to be hidden, Seitz believes that if the late-arriving Maya had known about the treasure of blue jade buried in the sierra, they would have exploited it. In fact, he makes the radical suggestion that the Maya carved mostly green jade not for cultural reasons, as is generally supposed, but because the Olmecs had already collected the blue jade from streams and accessible veins, the way "the Forty-niners scarfed up all the conspicuous gold nuggets in California's riverbeds, leaving it to latecomers to go after the slimmer pickings in them there hills." He believes that, eschewing the undistinguished gray-green stone left in the "many ugly outcrops" around the Motagua, the Maya suffered a shortage of gem-quality jade. "Jade mining dwindled under the Maya," he claims. "By Aztec times, some mines were already lost."

Some scholars find the idea of a Maya jade shortage credible. For example, a lack of raw material could explain why the Maya's carvings are generally smaller than the Olmecs' and why the Maya often fashioned their masks as thin mosaics rather than from solid stone—not just to save labor but to conserve a scarce resource. And a shortage of jade could explain why some Maya artifacts were worked in less valuable greenstone.

Other scholars demur. Huge waste deposits in the Early Classic city of Tikal and the Late Classic city of Cancuen suggest that, at least at some places and some periods during their long history, the Maya had raw jade in abundance. And the Maya may have made mosaic masks not due to a shortage of jade, but because that technique helped artisans in the lowland cities, where the jade-working tradition was less developed, to achieve a greater likeness of their subject. The Olmecs' larger carvings, similarly, may have resulted not because the Olmecs had more jade than the Maya, but because they wanted to show their stone's striking transparency to full advantage.

As for the Maya's use of less desirable greenstone, it does appear that the pre-Hispanic artisans could tell the difference between jade and similar rocks. Bob Terzuola claims he can generally identify jade on sight, and he can always tell whether a stone is jade once he starts working it. Jade is so distinctive in its appearance, density, and texture that it's inconceivable to him that the ancient carvers (if perhaps not their patrons) couldn't also recognize it. And the fact that the Maya's greatest works were generally reserved for jade show that they could discriminate between that and lesser stone.

So it may have been that for the Maya, color trumped every other quality. They apparently preferred to carve jade, but when it was unavailable, any green stone was better than blue, no matter how dense and lustrous the latter might be. But if the Maya knowingly carved non-jade greenstone, doesn't that imply a shortage of the genuine article? Not necessarily. It could just be that certain individuals who wanted jade didn't have the resources, financial or otherwise, to get it. Of course, this is always the case with high-status goods—if they were too readily available, they'd lose their cachet. Just because today some people buy cubic zirconia doesn't mean that there's a worldwide shortage of diamonds, only that for some people, the real thing is out of reach.

Then, too, if the Maya did suffer a lack of jade, it could have been caused not by a falloff in supply but by an increase in demand, as every Maya king and noble insisted on having his own cache of the ultimate status symbol. Or producers or traders could have withheld stone to create an artificial shortage and manipulate the market. Or warfare or some other disruption in trade routes could have been to blame. None of this necessarily implies a dearth of jade at the source.

As for Olmec blue, Virginia Sisson doesn't believe that there was ever a shortage of that type of jade in ancient times, either. Despite the possibility of volcanic eruptions and landslides, the sheer quantity of stone that she and the other *Jaderos* discovered makes her doubt that the enormous jade field was ever totally buried. So if the Maya had wanted blue jade, she suspects they could have found it. And indeed, as twentieth-century prospectors have demonstrated, there are still millions of tons of jade of all colors in the Motagua that the Maya never availed themselves of. Is it plausible that all these deposits escaped the notice of the ancient prospectors? Or if the Maya knew the jade was there, is it likely they would have thought it "too ugly" to bother with?

Another argument for a jade shortage is that, even when the Maya did carve genuine jade, the quality of their stone was generally inferior to the Olmecs', as though the Maya had to content themselves with the dregs that their predecessors had passed over. I often heard people who work with jade arrange the various types into a kind of lapidary pecking order, so that among ancient jades, Olmec was said to be better than Maya, which was supposedly better than modern jade from Guatemala; among modern jades, Burmese was also judged of higher quality than Guatemalan; and among Guatemalan stone, *Los Jaderos'* blue jade was judged better than the green stone generally offered for sale in Antigua. So I started to wonder, what does *quality* mean in a piece of jade, anyway?

As I began to canvass archaeologists and geologists, I found that many have trouble pinning down the concept. It's a cultural term with no objective meaning, they say, an aesthetic decision, a value judgment we make, an overlaying of our cultural preferences on the past. Ron Bishop of the Smithsonian, who has done more scientific analysis of jade than perhaps anyone, tells me he doesn't know what the word *quality* refers to—hardness, luster? To him, it's a term more for gemologists and art historians than for archaeologists.

George Harlow finds that so-called differences in quality are really matters of individual preference, an aesthetic appraisal about a stone's color and transparency. That's not to say that judgment doesn't have a mineralogical basis. For instance, visible cracks diminish the perceived quality of a piece of jade, as do inclusions (foreign bodies of other minerals). And translucency depends partly on the size of the crystals—the smaller they are, the more translucent the stone appears to the human eye. Purity can also enhance perceived quality, because the more different minerals found in the stone, the more light is diffracted, further reducing translucency. But the crucial word in all of this is *perceived*: Although it's a fact that a particular stone has a purity of such-and-such percent or crystals of such-and-such size, it's the opinion of the beholder that translates that perception into *quality*.

In terms of pleasing color and transparency, Harlow admits that Olmec jade could be argued to be of higher quality than most Maya stone. But that doesn't mean that Olmec stone was universally better. In fact, the Maya had more emerald green jade, he points out, which is generally considered the most desirable type of all. Score a quality point for them. But if you look closely at carved Maya plaques, you can see that they often have an irregular surface, because they've been cannily carved to expose a thin vein of bright green set in a less desirable color. So even some of the most spectacular Maya artifacts are less uniform in terms of "quality" than they might appear.

Olmec pieces are often said to show a higher level of craftsmanship than Maya carvings. Some people find the Olmec workmanship more consistent, and many confess a preference for Olmec jades, which though older, seem more "modern" for their simplicity of form. But on the other hand, Maya figures are carved with more detail and movement. In terms of polish and finish, Bob Terzuola finds that both Olmec and Maya carvings generally range from good to very good. It's hard for him to decide, as a craftsman, who were the more skilled carvers. The Maya definitely invested more time, creating more, and more complex, objects. But above any differences between the two bodies of work, what impresses Terzuola is their underlying similarity: Both the Maya and the Olmecs could have picked other beautiful stones that would have been infinitely easier to carve, but they chose the most difficult material possible as the medium for their highest art.

What about the variation in the so-called quality of jade being sold today? Though Burmese jade is often said to be of higher quality than Guatemalan jade (partly because Burma has more emerald green), there is no objective yardstick, George Harlow points out. Though some experts consider that a stone should be at least 90 percent jadeite to be sold as jade, there is no industry standard, and to be considered of gem quality, jade only has to have an appealing color, some transparency, and the strength to withstand carving. And so some unscrupulous merchants, in Guatemala and elsewhere, take advantage of people's ignorance and pass off what Virginia Sisson calls "junk" to unsuspecting tourists. In other words, some of the jade being sold in Antigua now is good, some not so good.

Was Maya jade really of higher quality than what is being offered now? It's true that the Maya had more emerald green than today's merchants, but as William Foshag reported more than fifty years ago, most of the ancient Maya jade was not emerald green and is comparable to what is being mined in Guatemala presently. And Bob Terzuola reminds us that today's artisans have an exceptional type of black jade that Terzuola judges as fine a jade as you'll see anywhere in the world, based on its lack of inclusions; great purity; dense, tight crystals; evenness of color; and its ability to hold "a polish that will take your breath away." (The term is a misnomer, by the way: Black jade appears to be that shade because of its great depth of color, but if you cut a thin plaque and examine it under a lamp, you'll see that it's really very dark green.) And the lion's share of this fine black jade comes, not from Burma, but from Guatemala.

In the end, I realize, it's no simple matter to tease out the meaning of *quality* in jade, and declaring one piece as "better" than another involves a host of judgments and assumptions. Which makes it hard to argue that the Maya of twelve hundred years ago would have preferred to carve blue jade because of its superior "quality." So the consensus is still that the Maya had a genuine preference, religious and cultural, for jade that was green—the color of water, of breath, of life itself. And it's very difficult to conclude that Olmec jade is better than Maya jade, that Maya jade is better than modern jade, or that *Los Jaderos'* Olmec blue is better than the green jade being sold in Antigua today. Ultimately, as George Harlow says, such judgments come down to differences in "taste and commerce."

❖

Meanwhile, in the years since *Los Jaderos'* discovery, research has continued in Guatemala. In February 2004, Karl Taube returned to the Motagua with a team of archaeologists to inaugurate El Proyecto Arqueológico del Jade, an ambitious effort to "document archaeological sites and jadeite sources in the upper Río El Tambor drainage area," which includes the territory around *Los Jaderos'* discovery. In its first season, Taube's group found seven more sites with the remains of stone buildings and jade workshops. The workshops didn't surprise them, because jade is so heavy that it was generally reduced to smaller pieces very close to where it was mined. From the shape of the fragments, it appeared that, as at similar sites throughout the Motagua, the stone had been formed into celts, presumably for shipment to cities where it would be rendered into finished items under the direction of Maya nobles.

Why take the trouble to carve celts instead of just knocking the stone into rough but portable chunks? Taube, who's written extensively on Olmec and Maya symbols, believes the shape may have been dictated by a combination of practicality and ideology. For one thing, celts served as a more-or-less uniform measure for jade, the way bullion does for gold today. The celts also made it easier to judge the jade, since flaws are more apparent in the smaller, more translucent celts than in an uncut block. And finally, the celts had a ritual significance, especially for the Olmecs, because their shape called to mind the husks of the sacred corn plant, the crop that had made Mesoamerican civilization possible and whose *masa,* or dough, had even served as the raw material for the mythical creation of mankind.

Other research is being conducted by the Cancuen Archaeological Project, led by Arthur Demarest of Vanderbilt University. Built at the point in northern Guatemala where the Río La Pasión becomes navigable, the Maya city of Cancuen ("Place of the Serpents") was a major trading center where goods such as jade, pyrite, and obsidian were gathered from the highlands and transferred to canoes for shipment to the northern lowlands. The city grew wealthy, building a port on the river, an expansive market, and one of the grandest palaces in Mesoamerica. Cancuen reached its zenith in the seventh century A.D., until its nobles were massacred and the city sacked about the year 800, a victim of the violence and unrest around the time of the Maya collapse.

The ruins at Cancuen were littered with jade fragments, including a thirty-five-pound boulder in the process of being sawed into plaques. But archaeologists discovered that the city's jade didn't resemble stone from the Motagua as much as it did carved artifacts found in the Salamá Valley, northeast of Guatemala City. So they began to wonder whether there might be unreported jade sources in the Salamá. The Ridingers confirmed that they were mining jade in the area, and they furnished samples for testing. Preliminary findings showed that the Salamá stone did resemble the fragments from Cancuen, and now the archaeologists are searching for evidence of trade routes that might have been used to move the jade.

Meanwhile, fundamental questions remain. The Ridingers believe they have found the lost jade mines of the Maya, just as *Los Jaderos* think they have discovered the jade mines of the Olmecs. There's no question that both teams have found jade. But have they found "mines," and are those sources really Maya or Olmec?

NINE

"The Most Mysterious Stone of the World"

In Antigua, Guatemala, 4:00 a.m. seems even earlier than it does
in most places. On this particular morning, the sky is the color
of obsidian, and the air is frigid owing to the altitude. During the
day, the narrow streets are hemmed by parked cars, but at this
hour, the vehicles are all hidden away for safekeeping.

At 4:20, Mary Lou Ridinger pulls in front of my hotel in her
white Ford F-150 pickup, or *picop,* as they're known here. We've
arranged to meet at this hour hoping to slip through the capital before
the horrendous morning rush begins. On the outskirts of Antigua, we
stop to pick up Raquel Pérez and Vinicio Jérez, the Ridingers' general
manager and production manager. Wearing baseball caps and jackets,
they climb into the back seat. We're headed to the *campo* to inspect
some jade. Though Mary Lou still doesn't grant anyone access to her
mines, she's agreed to make an exception and let me come along on
this trip to meet some of her pickers.

At first, the road is unlit and deserted, but in time, the pine
trees give way to an untidy concrete sprawl. We've left too late. As
we approach Guate, as Guatemala City is familiarly known, there's
a blue smudge on the horizon, and traffic is already creeping. In the
old city center, goats are still herded through the streets dispensing
milk, and indigenous *campesinos* still gather in the *plaza principal,*
selling brightly colored textiles. Here on the outskirts, we pass the

less picturesque offerings of a developing economy—luxury hotels; junkyards; convenience stores; flat-tire fixers and car-rim emporia; American big-box stores and fast-food franchises; vendors laden with newspapers, peanuts, fresh fruit, toys, air fresheners. Finally, we turn onto the four-lane Atlantic Highway, surrounded by tractor-trailers, military trucks, and wildly painted "chicken buses," all emitting the blackest exhaust I've ever seen. Just east of the capital, we come to the first roadblock, but the police wave us through.

The highway is all curves and hills, and as the tractor-trailers compete to pass on the upgrades, they hold back everyone else. For two hours, we crawl past truck stops and repair shops. Then the road forks and some traffic exits left, toward the coffee and cardamom fields of Las Verapaces. The Atlantic Highway levels out along the Motagua's slender floodplain, but the sierra looms on either side, the peaks as jagged as a saw blade. Sixty miles from the capital, we come to the eponymous workshop that the Terzuolas discovered back in the 1970s. We pull onto a grassy track, slip the rope off a chicken-wire gate, and drive in. For the next hour, we comb the rolling hills along the river, inspecting fragments of jade knocked loose by workers more than a millennium ago.

A few miles farther on, we pass the one-time tomato field where Robert Leslie uncovered his jadeite boulder. The earth is barren now, and in his soft, serious voice, Vinicio explains that, like much of the land in the area, it belongs to a *narcotraficante*. But the man has been arrested, and so the field remains unplanted, the *campesinos* out of work. Next, we come to the tiny town of Manzanal, where Leslie discovered the jade outcrop that he and William Foshag published in *American Antiquity*. We see the towering modern sign for the Longarone Hotel, where the Ridingers used to stay while prospecting, and the Pepsi plant where they made the emergency landing in their helicopter.

Just beyond, we come to another roadblock. This time, the policeman signals for us to stop, but deep into an explanation of how serpentinite suppresses plant growth, Mary Lou doesn't catch his signal. As we speed by, I see the surprised look on the official's face. I tell Mary Lou what's happened, and a couple of hundred yards farther along she finds a parking lot to turn into. A police *picop* pulls alongside, and officers with automatic rifles order us out while they search the truck. Meanwhile, a heavy-set, middle-aged man with gold braid on his hat brim approaches each of us in turn, taking down our identities and nationalities. I'm the last, and when I pronounce my exotic name, he looks up from his clipboard with a bewildered expression. I tell him, "*Se escribe G—*" "It's written *G—*" but before I can get any further, he sets down his ballpoint and tells me, "*No importa.*" "It doesn't matter."

We turn off the highway onto a winding secondary road, mostly blacktopped but in places just strewn with gravel. Off to one side, there's a deep, guardrail-less ravine, and sometimes Mary Lou has to navigate around a landslide blocking one lane. She tells me that when she first started coming here, some thirty years ago, there were no bridges, and she would ford the streams in her truck; in the rainy season, the all-dirt roads were all but impassible. She points to a hillside planted with corn. Deforestation is the inevitable consequence of blacktop, she explains, because it encourages farmers to expand their acreage and ship their produce to market in the city.

We drive through modest but well-kept villages, including Hulté, the butt of jokes in Guatemala for the supposed idiocy of its residents; they say it has something to do with uranium in the water. In front of one house is a heap of bluish rocks, but Mary Lou assures me they're not jade. A little farther on, we pass the outcrop where she and Charlotte Thomson turned their truck around before rushing back to Antigua when war threatened with Belize. That's the same area where the Ridingers later found their lavender jade and where Asian poachers arrived with guns and dynamite, until the government ran them off.

Not long after, we park above a high cliff and begin walking up a steep dirt lane. The temperature is ninety degrees, and though the way is shaded by trees, we start to break a sweat. We pass modest stands of corn and beans, all tilled by hand, because the terrain is too hilly to plow with tractors; most is too rugged even to work with a horse or mule. It's been two years since Mary Lou has been here, and she notices the new concrete houses with cars parked in front: The *campesinos* are doing well in this corner of Guatemala.

Toward the crest of the hill, we come to an older house with a wide front porch and a roof of *lámina,* corrugated sheet metal. The three pickers are waiting. All are thin, and all are dressed in T-shirts, jeans, and white straw cowboy hats—the two brothers and a son who work this land. One of their wives is called out to greet us, and we shake hands and fill a few minutes with small talk. Inside, two young boys are watching soccer on their new cable TV. Their sixteen-year-old sister, congenitally lame, attends school in Antigua, her tuition paid by a scholarship and her books, uniforms, and incidentals supplied by the Ridingers.

Our hosts lead us down off the porch. In front of the house, next to the smoldering fire where trash is burned, are two modest piles of stone. The larger one, two feet square and just as tall, is made up of green rocks; the other, about half that size, has stones of bluish green and lavender. Vinicio squats to take a look. Usually he makes these trips alone, sometimes with Raquel. But it's been six months since anyone from the company has been here. Under the pickers' contract, someone is supposed to come every two to three months to inspect the stone that's been collected. But the recession and plunge in tourism have cut into sales, and the Ridingers aren't looking to expand their inventory of jade. They're under no obligation to take the stone, but they know the collectors rely on the extra income.

The older brother acts as spokesman. Moving to the larger pile, he takes a white enamel basin and splashes some water onto the green stone to bring out its color. Vinicio picks up several pieces and turns them to catch the light. Then he points to the network of fine cracks running through them. In a soft voice, he tells the prospectors that the stone is too fractured to use. The damage isn't from their pneumatic drill, he explains; the defect was there long before.

Turning his attention to the other pile, he holds up a piece of blue jade to gauge its translucence. The stone is about the size and shape of a raw tuna steak, and it has the same tight grain and uniformity of color. Conferring in murmurs, Vinicio and Raquel pick out some stones. In the end, they choose about a quarter of the smaller pile, clearly less than the prospectors hoped. The son fetches a woven plastic sack that once held corn seed, and the rocks are dropped inside. Straddling the bag, the older brother hefts it. Sixty kilos, he pronounces, 132 pounds. Vinicio accepts the measurement, but they have yet to settle on a price. Under Guatemalan law, the stone doesn't belong to the farmers but to the government, and the Ridingers have the exclusive license to take jade from this area. So the question doesn't hinge on the value of the jade but on the fee for finding it, digging it out of the ground, and carting it here. If the Ridingers don't want the stone, or if they can't agree on a price, the collectors can't offer it to anyone else, at least not legally. The *campesino* goes into his pitch, lauding the quality, color, and rarity. Vinicio responds in a hushed tone. Then he and Raquel confer, the brims of their baseball caps nearly touching, and she takes out of her wallet 1,300 quetzales, about 160 U.S. dollars.

Raquel walks down to fetch the pickup. While we're waiting, a neighbor, wizened and nearly toothless, stops by on his horse. He's heard of our visit, and he's brought a piece of blue stone that he's dug from his property. There's more, he says; are they interested? Vinicio takes the rock and examines it with polite interest. Possibly, he answers, but first they have to assay it to confirm that it's jade. Is it all right if they borrow it for testing? "*Claro,*" the old *campesino* tells them. "Of course."

Raquel backs the truck up the narrow road. The sack of jade is dumped in the bed, and we start toward Antigua, hoping to make it through Guate before the evening rush.

�֍

On the drive to Antigua, I wonder whether our meeting with the jade collectors replayed a transaction enacted over thousands of years in Guatemala, maybe on that same hillside. It's easy to imagine such a scene, with hopeful sellers laying out their stone for inspection, touting its virtues, haggling over its value. Yet, like so much that's written about jade, my imagined marketplace is just conjecture. Was the stone sold on the open market back then, or was it mined under royal control? What would the buyers have traded for it? How did it get from quarry to workshop, from workshop to palace? I consider what has, and hasn't, been learned about Olmec and Maya jade since the day that Robert Leslie discovered his outcrop near the town of Manzanal.

For one thing, it's finally been proved that Mesoamerican jade was mined in Guatemala, not in China or Atlantis. And it's clear that most came from around the Motagua River, with its extensive sources and its worksites where the jade was fashioned into celts and other artifacts. Another crucial issue—fifty years after Leslie's discovery—is whether the Motagua was the only pre-Columbian source of jade, or whether it was also collected in places such as Mexico, Costa Rica, and the Caribbean. Despite George Harlow's argument that the geology isn't right in Mexico or Costa Rica, some of his colleagues, such as Ron Bishop, were never convinced. Archaeologists Michael Coe and Clemency Coggins believe that the state of Guerrero, in southwestern Mexico, can't be written off. There's evidence that the Olmecs were there, Coe points out, because Olmec-style paintings have been discovered in caves in the area. And so much carved jade has been found nearby that he doesn't believe the local people would have had the resources to acquire it all through trading (the "criterion of abundance" again).

Coe knows an entrepreneur in the Mexican state of Chiapas who carves and sells what he claims is jade and who once showed Coe a map depicting four Aztec forts forming a protective square around the stone's supposed source, a location whose Nahuatl name translates as "Place of Jade." Mexican archaeologist Olaf Jaime-Riverón tells me that small amounts of stone from Chiapas, as well as from Guerrero and the state of Puebla, have preliminarily assayed as jade. He also says that the sites have yielded pottery sherds dating to Late Classic and Postclassic times, from about A.D. 800 to 1500, and he believes that new evidence may push the timeline even earlier. But these findings haven't been published in an academic journal, and to date no jade deposits have been documented anywhere in Mexico.

In the Caribbean, ancient jade carvings have been discovered in the Bahamas and on Cuba, Puerto Rico, and Antigua (not to be confused with Antigua, Guatemala). But was this stone mined locally, or was it imported from the mainland? Two decades ago, George Harlow allowed that jade might turn up in the Caribbean, along the eastern edge of the same fault that also runs through Guatemala. And in 2008, jade deposits were discovered in Cuba and the Dominican Republic and duly reported in academic journals.

But opinion differs on whether the geological jade from the Caribbean matches the archaeological artifacts discovered there. Harlow argues that the carved stone resembles that from the Motagua because both contain quartz, a relatively rare component of jade. But quartz has also been found in the jade deposits on Cuba and the Dominican Republic, leading other scholars to argue that the carved stone originated on those islands. And the sources on Cuba are reported to show evidence of having been dug in pre-Hispanic times.

So, for the moment, the best we can say is that, while small deposits of jade have been documented in the Caribbean, Guatemala seems to have been at least the principal source for ancient Mesoamericans. Still, what exactly have the Ridingers and *Los Jaderos* discovered there? Have they really found the jade mines of the Maya and the Olmecs? What does *mine* mean in this context, anyway?

When we think of a mine, we usually conjure up the image of a tunnel or a pit in the ground. But the pre-Columbian prospectors didn't obtain their jade that way, any more than the Ridingers and their competitors do now. Instead, the ancients would have collected loose boulders or, at most, dug jade from outcrops or veins near the surface. If they removed a pod of jade from an outcrop of, say, albitite or serpentinite, as modern miners often do, they may have left no more indication of their work, a thousand years further on, than if they had picked the stone out of a riverbed. And if they pried jade out of a vein, centuries of weathering can make it impossible to distinguish manmade fissures from natural ones.

For Olmec or Maya miners, veins of jade would have been even more problematic than for present-day prospectors. With earth or other rock often covering the veins, how would the ancients have known that the deposits were even there? If they did come across an exposed vein, perhaps after a storm had carried away the topsoil, how would they have mined it with stone tools? (Even metal tools wouldn't have helped much, since jade is harder than steel.) The miners might have taken advantage of natural fissures to pry out pieces, but jade is resistant to such coercion; when it fractures, it makes a noise like a gunshot. They may have used a technique known as spalling, heating the stone until the difference in external and internal temperatures caused it to crack.

But that would have damaged the stone closest to the fire, which then would have had to be chipped off with a heavy hammer. So at best, spalling would have been a laborious, inefficient way to mine for jade.

It seems likely, then, that the ancient miners—prospectors, after all, not scientists—got most of their jade the way modern pickers do, not by arduous excavation but by collecting loose stones (or "float") that had washed down from the surrounding mountains. Not only were such boulders easier to find, extract, and transport, but they offered another advantage. Jade pried from outcrops may be marred by tiny cracks, like the green stone that Vinicio rejected from his collectors. And if these defects were hidden in the center of the stone, they might have been discovered only much later, after a great deal of effort had already been expended on a carving in progress. On the other hand, river stones are relatively free of such flaws, since any weak bits tend to be sheared off in the tumble down the mountainside.

Whether they were digging jade from outcrops or just picking up river boulders, the best evidence that ancient miners give of their activity is generally the stone fragments, tools, and potsherds (and occasionally buildings and roads) that they left behind. Based on such clues, the Ridingers believe that four of their jade sources were worked in ancient times. But the evidence is indirect, and Ron Bishop of the Smithsonian says that such leavings would have to be found awfully close to a jade source to persuade him that they and the mining were from the same era. Conversely, the absence of such clues doesn't mean that a site wasn't exploited in prehistory, since it may be that no such evidence was left behind; or if it were, it could have been buried or swept away in the centuries since.

And whether those ancient workers were Olmec, Maya, or later arrivals can also be hard to establish, since that assessment usually hinges on clues such as the radiocarbon dates of plant matter or the style of ceramic objects. It's difficult to say when a quarry was worked, since each new digging destroys evidence of previous activity. Some present-day researchers discovered what they thought were signs of Maya mining, only to realize that they had stumbled across one of the Ridingers' sources.

So are the Ridingers and other jade merchants in Antigua taking their stone from the same sources once exploited by the ancient Maya? Archaeologist David Sedat tells me it would be "conceited" of us to make that assertion. Instead, it seems that the ancients, like today's prospectors, happily took their jade wherever they found it over a wide area (now recognized to be even wider, thanks to *Los Jaderos'* discovery).

What about *Los Jaderos'* sites? Is there evidence that they were worked by the Olmecs? Russell Seitz would be "astonished" if Olmec evidence weren't discovered there, and scholars such as Olaf Jaime-Riverón, Michael Coe, and Clemency Coggins also suspect that *Los Jaderos* have found at least one of the sources of the blue jade carved by the Olmecs.

One problem with this theory is that there's no sign of workshops in the area where the jade would have been reduced to transportable size. Of course, any evidence could have been washed away by the same floodwaters that exposed the veins and boulders of jade. And by the time *Los Jaderos* arrived, more than two years after Hurricane Mitch, the site was already being worked by locals, which likely would have destroyed any lingering evidence of pre-Columbian digging. Or there may be no Olmec artifacts because the Olmecs themselves never ventured into the mountains; the jade could have been mined instead by local people who exchanged it through a trade network extending to the Olmec cities hundreds of miles away.

But the stone roadway at El Ciprés proved impossible to date, and Taube now believes it might be from as late as the nineteenth century. He and his colleagues have found only one pottery sherd that could possibly date to Olmec times, and the great majority appear to be from the Late Classic period, more than a thousand years after Olmec civilization had collapsed. It's true that the rugged terrain may be concealing Olmec sites and that Olmec evidence could still be buried at El Ciprés. But the mountain soil is thin and therefore unlikely to hide undiscovered artifacts. So there's no conclusive archaeological evidence that *Los Jaderos'* sites were mined in ancient times. As Karl Taube says, "There is no smoking axe." He believes that, even if the outcrops above the Motagua were the ultimate source of Olmec jade, the ancient prospectors may have gathered it only after the boulders had come to rest in the valley below.

Who would have collected the stone? Michael Coe suggests that the Olmecs may have mounted armed expeditions to seize their jade, because he can't believe their rulers would have left the extraction, transportation, and carving of such a valuable commodity to others, any more than a government today would allow counterfeiting of its currency. But Taube points out that no fortresses or administrative centers have been discovered in the region, from which central control over mining would have been coordinated. He thinks it unlikely that the Olmecs and Maya would have traveled to an inhospitable backwater such as the Motagua in search of jade. Instead, he suggests they would have been content to leave the hard, heavy work of collection to locals, stepping in themselves to direct the more lucrative trading and carving of the stone (much as the Antigua jade merchants do now).

Taube also believes that raw jade was relatively plentiful and hence not terribly costly at the source, that the real value was added only in the skilled labor of transforming it from raw stone into items of ritual meaning and beauty. This is also what happens in Guatemala's jade industry today. As I saw in my visit to the *campo*, raw jade commands little in comparison to the prices charged for jade jewelry and carvings. It's partly this discrepancy between what is paid collectors and what is charged tourists that has led some to disparage the Antigua merchants (though this criticism doesn't take into account the dealers' considerable overhead—license fees, salaries, and all those diamond saw blades and drill bits).

If the archaeological evidence doesn't prove that *Los Jaderos'* or the Ridingers' sites were worked by the Olmecs or the Maya, how can the issue be resolved? In search of an answer, some researchers have turned to the laboratory and to analytic techniques borrowed from chemistry.

✣

In the national anthropological museum in Mexico City, there's a gorgeous spearpoint of glossy black obsidian, nearly a foot long, with edges sharp as glass. And obsidian is glass, formed when a particular type of lava flows from a volcano then cools too quickly to form crystals. This gives obsidian an exceedingly fine texture that allows it to hold an edge sharper than any razor; even today, scalpels made from obsidian are sometimes used for delicate eye surgery. In pre-Columbian times, obsidian tools and weapons were highly sought-after and eagerly exchanged. Hoping to learn about the movements of ancient people, their social organization, and the economic relationships among them, archaeologists were keen to retrace the obsidian trade route. The questions were the same as for jade: Who mined it? Whose hands did it pass through? What was it exchanged for? Where was it worked, and by whom?

Fortunately for the scientists, every volcanic eruption, even from the same mountain, releases a unique cocktail of chemical elements. And because obsidian is thoroughly mixed in an underground reservoir before being ejected to the surface, it's remarkably uniform in its constituents. Thanks to both these factors, scientists were able to trace any given piece of obsidian back to the deposit where it originated.

It was a similar scenario with the clay used to make pottery: The exact mix of chemicals is also unique to a specific location, a fact that archaeologists have exploited to study important issues. Opinion was divided, for example, on the influence that the Olmecs exerted over their neighbors. Did Olmec culture develop first, then spread throughout the region, or were the Olmecs simply one of many cultures developing simultaneously in Mesoamerica?

Pottery with Olmec-style decoration has been found in a wide swath of Mexico. But was it all made by the Olmecs and traded across vast distances, or did different groups produce their own ceramics, perhaps borrowing Olmec designs? Archaeologists, including Hector Neff from California State University at Long Beach, analyzed the pottery clay using neutron activation analysis, which bombards a specimen with neutrons, then measures the radioactivity emitted to determine its chemical composition. Neff and the others discovered that most of the clay had been dug near the first Olmec capital of San Lorenzo, leading them to infer that the pottery had been made there, then exported to other, presumably less developed cities. Though not all experts are in agreement with this conclusion, the research does show how this powerful technology might be used to shed light on important archaeological questions.

Could the same impressive results be obtained with jade? In the 1970s, scientists such as Ron Bishop had begun addressing the problem. In the intervening decades, researchers have assembled an imposing armamentarium of techniques, some of which, like neutron activation analysis, can penetrate a piece of jade down to the atom's nucleus. Whatever technology is used, the fundamental question is: Do pieces of jade fall into a clear geographical pattern (the way obsidian and pottery clay do)? Based on its chemical composition, can we say that it came from here (whether "here" is as wide as the Motagua Valley or as narrow as a specific boulder)? The answer hinges on two factors: First, the composition of jade must vary from place to place. And second, that geographic variation has to be strong enough to stand out above the "noise" of non-geographic differences. Obsidian and clay meet both of these criteria because each deposit is unique, showing strong geographic variation, and each deposit is homogeneous, minimizing the background noise.

But the geological forces that form jade are more localized and variable, and its deposits are more dispersed and harder to find. So with jade, it's extremely difficult to assemble a reasonable library of sources. No matter how many samples are collected for analysis, there will always be some that remain undiscovered. This means that when an artifact is tested, its composition often isn't a close match to any known geological sample. Conversely, if an artifact does resemble a particular source, there's no proof that it wouldn't match some other, unknown deposit just as well. And the problem is compounded by a bias in the geological samples that have been tested so far—most have been provided by the Ridingers, whose sources are hardly distributed scientifically throughout the region. No wonder that many archaeologists and geologists who work with jade consider the lack of geological specimens the single greatest obstacle to their research. To Hector Neff, sampling is still so spotty that he isn't even confident there is any geographical pattern in the chemical composition of jade.

Then there's the problem of jade's heterogeneity, caused when it incorporates trace elements at the time of its creation, resulting in a "nasty" rock that forever bears the accident of its birth. The variable nature of jade's formation is a boon to the gemologist, because it means that the stone is found in many different colors. But for the scientist, it's a nightmare, because it means that two pieces can vary significantly in their chemical composition—even if they come from the same outcrop. Faced with this deafening "noise" in their data, it's impossible for researchers to conclude with certainty where a piece of jade originated.

To get around the problem, some scientists use statistics to establish the likelihood that two jade samples came from the same place. When you do this, you want to see your data clumped into nice clear groups—and this is exactly what happens with obsidian and pottery clay. But Hector Neff confesses that when he examines plots of jade samples, he has to study them at length before he can organize the data into even tentative clusters. For this reason, he finds it more satisfying to work with other materials that are inherently less messy. Ron Bishop is more blunt. He calls the technique "pseudoprobability analysis" and pronounces the state of the art "God awful." It's "horrendously difficult," he tells me, to pin a specific artifact to a given location within the Motagua.

Just as it can be hard to find a good selection of geological samples of jade, it can be difficult to get testable jade artifacts. Museum curators are protective of their wares, reluctant to take pieces off display and to let researchers subject them to analysis even with nondestructive techniques. If the method removes even minute quantities of material from the artifact, the museum may well withhold permission, even when the piece is already broken or of only limited archaeological interest.

Sometimes researchers get lucky, though. When curators at the anthropology museum in Mexico City were restoring Pakal's mask, which Alberto Ruz had uncovered at Palenque, they found themselves with a few tiny pieces of broken jade left over. They sent them to Hector Neff at Cal State, who subjected them to a method with the inelegant name of laser ablation inductively coupled plasma mass spectrometry, also known as laser ablation ICP-MS, or for our purposes, laser ablation. In this technique, the laser vaporizes a small specimen of the sample, which is then introduced into a hot ionized gas called a plasma, where the extreme conditions strip electrons and create positively charged ions, allowing researchers to make a near-complete inventory of the elements and their proportions in the vaporized sample. In the case of Pakal's mask, the test showed that its stone was similar to fragments from the Maya workshop at Cancuen. And when Neff was asked to test a carved jade discovered at the Pyramid of the Moon at the great city of Teotihuacan in central Mexico, he was able to determine that it resembled jade from the Motagua Valley. Note that in both cases, though, the jade was judged to be similar, not identical.

Are there any technological advances in the offing that might allow scientists to match geological samples with archaeological carvings once and for all? Hector Neff points to isotope testing as one method that may hold promise. Whereas techniques such as neutron activation analysis and laser ablation measure trace elements present in tiny quantities in the stone, isotope testing exploits the fact that some elements, such as oxygen and hydrogen, come in different "flavors," with a variable number of neutrons in their nucleus. These are called stable isotopes, meaning they're not radioactive and don't decay or transform into other elements. During chemical reactions and physical changes, the lighter and heavier isotopes separate, leaving a characteristic proportion of each, which can be measured using a mass spectrometer. In the case of minerals, the host environments in which they formed, and even slight changes in environmental conditions such as temperature, leave a permanent, measurable record in the proportion of stable isotopes.

Do stable isotopes constitute the long-sought "fingerprint" that will positively link pre-Columbian jade artifacts to their geological sources? Researchers have already had success with isotope testing of turquoise and marble. In the case of turquoise, geologist Mostafa Fayek and archaeologist Sharon Hull of the University of Manitoba were able to differentiate thirty-five out of thirty-eight geological samples (and the other three they were able to distinguish with trace element analysis). With marble, other investigators were able to trace the stone in ancient Greek and Roman statues back to the exact quarry where it originated.

But jade isn't marble or turquoise. Because jade is harder, it's more difficult to prepare a sample for testing and more difficult to remove tiny amounts from an artifact without noticeable damage. Before even requesting permission to touch any museum pieces, Fayek and Hull would test their methodology on geological samples, as they did with turquoise, to see whether any meaningful geographical pattern emerged. If they did discern a geographical pattern, they would need to build as comprehensive a catalog of geological samples as possible—a crucial step that has stymied other investigators. Finally, they would need to persuade curators to let them test their artifacts, since a sample ranging from one to five milligrams needs to be removed from the specimen. But before any of this work could even begin, they would need to secure funding. In other words, any isotope testing of jade is still years in the future.

In the meantime, present techniques remain more helpful in ruling out matches between jade samples than in definitively ruling them in. That's because, even with current tools, some pieces of jade have such radically different constituents that the specimens seem unlikely to have originated in the same place. The jury is still out on how useful elemental analysis of jade will prove, and in the end the stone may turn out to have no discernible pattern to its geographic distribution. As Hector Neff says, "Sometimes the world just isn't cut up in the way you hope it is."

As for *Los Jaderos'* jade, George Harlow confesses to being disappointed with the chemical match between Olmec artifacts in museums and the geological samples brought back from Guatemala. He doesn't believe that the jade in the carvings came from the site they discovered, and he suspects that either the Olmec mines have not been found, or they were depleted in ancient times and therefore will never be found. In fact, Harlow doubts that Olmec jade will ever be traced to only one location, since like the Maya, the Olmecs most likely gathered their jade from a variety of sources, both north and south of the Motagua. And this idea certainly coincides with the opportunistic ways of prospectors: If jade is to be found in hundreds of places, why collect it in only one?

Immediately after *Los Jaderos'* discovery, Ron Bishop commented, "There is no demonstrated evidence that we have found the source for the Olmec blue jade. I look forward to seeing some scientific data come out, but until then the mystery continues." A decade later, he hasn't changed his opinion. "There is no evidence," he tells me. "It's still an open question."

So have the jade mines of the Olmecs and the Maya been rediscovered, or not? On one hand, it appears that there were no jade mines near the Motagua, in the sense of a few discrete, central sources. But on the other hand, the entire valley and the sierra above it can be seen as one great jade mine, providing the ancients with many different types and colors of the stone, which they extracted from many different places. Knowing the specific outcrop or boulder where a piece of jade originated would doubtless fill in many gaps in our understanding of the pre-Hispanic peoples (as would being able to confirm that a particular piece of carved jade came from a non-Motagua source such as the Caribbean), but at this point, that kind of fine discrimination simply isn't within the reach of even the most sophisticated scientific analysis. For now, the proposition that the Olmecs once mined the sites discovered by *Los Jaderos* and the Maya once mined the sites quarried by the Ridingers lies more in the realm of faith than science.

�֍

In piecing together this account, I've come to realize that archaeologists, like writers, are in the business of taking the facts as they understand them and trying to weave a convincing storyline. As Hector Neff tells me, "Archaeology is one of the historical sciences, along with geology and evolutionary biology. All have an element of narrative." Says Karl Taube, "There's lots of narrative in archaeology, which is one of the exciting things about it; you're trying to reconstruct the past."

It used to be, in the days of, say, Edward H. Thompson and J. Eric Thompson, that archaeologists enjoyed wide artistic license in drafting their stories. And so Edward Thompson could decide that Chichen Itza's High Priest's Temple was "not merely the tomb of a great priest, but the tomb of *the* great priest, the tomb of the great leader, the tomb of the hero god, Kukul Can, he whose symbol was the feathered serpent," and J. Eric Thompson could insist that the Maya were a peaceful, docile people, a more primitive, uncorrupted version of ourselves.

But today, archaeology considers itself a science, bound by the methods of scientific inquiry. Instead of the sit-down-and-let-me-tell-you-a-story approach, explains Jeremy Sabloff, now of the Santa Fe Institute, "Archaeology is a hypothesis-driven, dynamic process. It's true that evidence is open to interpretation, but the question is, can you refine questions and devise research to test hypotheses?" To be scientifically meaningful, archaeologists' hypotheses about the human past, like geologists' about the formation of the earth or biologists' about the evolution of life, need to be what philosophers of science call falsifiable: In order to be provable, they need to be capable of being disproved. With an experimental science such as chemistry, researchers can devise tests to determine whether the real world supports or contradicts their theories. But in the case of a historically oriented science like archaeology, falsifiability can be harder to come by. As David Sedat says, "You can take a very complex set of materials that have been found [such as Olmec-style potsherds] and you can weave three or four different stories about that data, and some of those scenarios will be quite different from others." The Olmec pottery research is a good example of falsifiability in action: If the clay is from an Olmec city, the hypothesis went, the pottery is Olmec and testifies to a certain influence that the Olmecs exerted over their neighbors; if the clay is from non-Olmec cities, the pottery is not Olmec and doesn't demonstrate such an influence. Other investigators may disagree with the methods or conclusions, but at least the research is designed to be either supported or contradicted by the data. (In fact, further analysis suggests that the Olmecs may also have imported pottery from their neighbors.) The pottery study is also a good example of how traditional fieldwork, such as excavating potsherds, and newer laboratory techniques, such as neutron activation analysis, can work in tandem. In the words of Ron Bishop, a pioneer in this high-tech/low-tech partnership, "You make up the best possible story you can with the data you have. You want the best fit of all possible kinds of information." David Sedat is more pointed: "You can make up stories, but you want them grounded in evidence."

And yet quantifiable evidence isn't always forthcoming. Sometimes, "the world isn't cut up the way you'd like." And so, being a "nasty" stone, jade yields only so far to chemical analysis, and the data points just don't fall into neat clusters. We now know that the Maya and Olmecs got most if not all of their jade from the area around the Motagua. But as such large questions are resolved, they splinter into a host of finer, more pointed ones: Did the jade come only from the Motagua? What parts of the Motagua? From both boulders and outcrops? How was it collected? By whom? What was it traded for? How did it find its way into cities? Where was it carved?

And so the questions multiply. For instance, what role did jade play in the shifting alliances among the Maya city-states? In A.D. 738, Quirigua successfully revolted against larger Copan; could the rebellion have been inspired, at least in part, by a desire to control the Motagua jade route? Did superpower Calakmul back the revolt to weaken its archrival and Copan's ally Tikal, just as in later centuries the United States and the Soviet Union would enlist battling factions in Central America in their own game of realpolitik? The consensus remains that the decline of Maya civilization was caused by a variety of factors, especially climate-related environmental disaster. But did jade hasten that decline, for example by fomenting conflict among the city-states? Michael Coe points out that trade disruption played a crucial role in the Maya collapse and that such a disturbance would most likely have included the jade route. Though it may not have been a prime mover, David Sedat believes that "there would certainly have been competition for jade and prestige for those who could command it, especially the highest-status emerald green jade. Jade is one of the commodities that would have been in play; it would certainly have been a strategic good," since it was recognized as "a storehouse of spiritual energy."

If we could trace Maya jade back to its geological sources, we might go a long way toward resolving such questions. If all the jade was mined around the Motagua, that would suggest a certain model of how the stone was acquired and moved to its destination. If the jade came from a broader area, encompassing Mexico or the Caribbean, the story might be more complex, involving longer trade routes and more buyers and sellers along the way. Similarly, being able to trace the journey of a single piece of jade from quarry to royal tomb could provide enormous information about the movements of goods and peoples, greatly expanding our knowledge of the pre-Hispanic world and perhaps reshaping our understanding of its cultures. How can we know whether Quirigua and Copan were founded to guard the jade route if we don't even know where the jade was coming from?

These questions aren't a matter of simple academic curiosity, because through broadening our understanding of ancient cultures, we come to a greater appreciation of our own. Archaeology seeks to explain the where, when, why, and how—not of abstract beings but of our ancestors. In rooting out the story of the Olmecs and the Maya and all the other people who have come before us, we are discovering our own story, piecing together how we got to be the way we are. Just as with jade, the answer depends on tracing the narrative back to its source. As Ron Bishop says, in the pursuit of archaeology "we're dealing with a huge mystery. It defines what happened in the past and who we are." Yet, until we have the technology to cut through jade's heterogeneity and trace it to its geological origin, the stone will robe itself in what David Sedat calls its "magical mystery."

The image of the Humboldt Celt that I keep on my computer desktop is a persistent reminder of its undeciphered message and unexplained disappearance. Two centuries after Alexander von Humboldt carried it back from the New World, the celt still seems an apt metaphor for the enigma of Mesoamerican jade. Despite all that we've learned over the past fifty years, jade still guards its secrets, perhaps forever. Edward H. Thompson recognized it over a century ago, and it's as true now as the day he wrote it: Jade is still "the most mysterious stone of the world."

EPILOGUE

Another spring evening in Antigua, Guatemala. Again the sun slips behind the volcanoes, and again my wife, Teresa, and I find ourselves in the Ridingers' Colonial house there. This time, instead of sitting under the colonnade, we've arranged ourselves in the spacious garden, in lounge chairs positioned at each end of a long wooden table. The table is built in the shape of an *x,* its four arms oriented toward the north, south, east, and west, in a nod to the Maya's reverence for the cardinal compass points. As I call my questions down the table to Mary Lou Ridinger, the shadows swallow the jumble of tropical plants, the fireflies begin their dance, and I have to strain to hear her answers over the exuberance of the crickets.

When it grows too dim to write, I set down my notebook. There's to be a birthday party later, for the Ridingers' granddaughter Andrea, who's turning twenty-five. Three generations will gather on the house's wide colonnade for *chilaquiles* and chocolate cake. But Jay Ridinger won't be among them. Almost a year before, just two weeks after Teresa's and my first visit, he lost his long battle with multiple myeloma, a rare cancer of the blood. The causes aren't well understood, but the family wonders whether it could have something to do with decades of handling those poisonous liquids to test for jade.

Jay's loss is felt keenly, both in the business and in the family. Among the most affected are grandchildren Andrea and Christian and general manager Raquel Pérez, who calls him her "*faro de luz,*" her guiding light. In Mary Lou Ridinger, the company still has a strong hand on the tiller, but she, too, has lost her *faro de luz.*

We make our way to the colonnade. In one corner hangs a faded poster in a simple metal frame. It's a photo of two golden retrievers sitting side by side on a beach, shot from behind so the dogs appear to be contemplating the ocean. Printed over the picture is a quotation from Antoine de Saint-Exupéry's *Little Prince*: "Love does not consist in gazing at each other, but in looking outward together in the same direction."

"That's you and Jay," I once said to Mary Lou.

"Yes," she answered.

Did Jay Ridinger fulfill his mission to discover "the lost jade mines of the Maya"? That depends on your definitions—and in any case, he was more concerned with managing his business than with debating technicalities. But tonight, standing in this old house filled with collections and mementos, and soon to be filled with his children and grandchildren, I'm confident that, whatever the archaeologists and geologists might have to say, Jay Ridinger found what he was seeking.

It's dark now. Toward the far end of the colonnade, yellow rays spill out a doorway and across the tiled floor. Walking ahead of us, Mary Lou Ridinger strides through the gloom, following the light toward her big whitewashed kitchen, to prepare the family celebration.

AUTHOR'S NOTE

All the events recounted in this book actually happened. As detailed in the Notes, I've changed the chronological order of some incidents and have invented minor details in a few scenes. All persons and places portrayed are real, and no names have been changed. All thoughts or emotions ascribed to characters are as reported in interviews or their own writings, or as reported by persons close to the principals; none have been invented by the author.

Concerning Spanish-language place names, I've dropped the accents where commonly accepted English spellings exist—Mexico, for example, not México; the Yucatan, not Yucatán. Where there is no generally accepted English form—El Ciprés—I've used the Spanish spelling, accents and all. Similarly, I've dropped the accents in the names of ancient cities and archaeological sites—Chichen Itza, not Chichén Itzá, as it is written in Spanish. On this last point, I've followed the sixth edition of the classic work *The Ancient Maya* by Robert J. Sharer with Loa P. Traxler. And I've adopted Sharer and Traxler's transliterations from Mayan to English—*haah, k'in, Pakal,* and so on. For Spanish personal names, I've retained the original spelling—Hernán Cortés. (Note that none of this applies to direct quotations, where I've followed the spellings in the original text.)

ACKNOWLEDGMENTS

This book would not have been possible without the help of the following persons, who graciously shared their time and expertise, by consenting to interviews, by writing e-mails, and/or by reviewing all or part of the manuscript: Chloé Andrieu, Centre National de la Recherche Scientifique, France; George J. Bey III, Millsaps College; Ronald L. Bishop, Smithsonian Institution; Hannes K. Brueckner, Queens College of CUNY and the Lamont-Doherty Earth Observatory at Columbia University; John Cleary, Ventana Mining Company; Michael D. Coe, Yale University; Clemency Coggins, Boston University; Andrew Duncan; Byron Estrada Straube, Casa del Jade; Mostafa Fayek, University of Manitoba; William F. Foshag III; George Harlow, American Museum of Natural History; Susan Haskell, Peabody Museum of Archaeology and Ethnology at Harvard University; Olaf Jaime-Riverón, University of Kentucky; Vinicio Jérez; Betty Kempe; Gerald Leech, Casa del Jade; John Mann; Hector Neff, California State University at Long Beach; Thomas and Alma Olson; Raquel Pérez; Angela Ridinger; Jake Ridinger; Josh Rosenfeld; Jeremy Sabloff, Santa Fe Institute; David Sedat, the University of Pennsylvania Museum and the Copan 2012 Botanical Research Station; Russell Seitz; Robert J. Sharer, the University of Pennsylvania Museum; Virginia Sisson, University of Houston; Maria Elena Streicher; Jane Swezey; Karl Taube, University of California at Riverside; Renée Ridinger Taylor; Bob Terzuola; Gail Terzuola; and Ralph Lee Woodward Jr., Tulane University. If, despite this generous assistance, any errors remain in the text, the responsibility is wholly mine.

Thanks to the dedicated staff of the following institutions: Biblioteca Pública, San Miguel de Allende, Mexico; Wilson Library of Millsaps College, Jackson, Mississippi; National Geographic Society Image Collection Office; New York Public Library; Ricks Memorial Library, Yazoo City, Mississippi; and the Smithsonian Institution Archives.

To Deirdre Mullane of Mullane Literary Associates, thank you once again for your intelligence, judgment, determination, generosity, friendship—for everything I could expect from an agent and for some things I have no right to expect.

At Lyons Press/Globe Pequot, many thanks to my editor, Keith Wallman, for your enthusiasm at the inception of this project and for your thoughtfulness and professionalism in bringing it to fruition. Thank you also to production editor Ellen Urban, for making that part of the process a pleasure.

To my friend Tom Bosworth, thank you for introducing me to Georgeann Johnson and Betty Kempe. And to Georgeann, thank you for your impeccable taste in giving *Humboldt's Cosmos* as a Christmas gift to your brother-in-law Jay Ridinger, without which I would never have made my way to his house in Antigua and would never have heard the story of jade that launched me on this project.

To Mary Lou Ridinger go my special thanks for the inspiration to begin this book, as well as the knowledge, generosity, and patience you showed over the course of its writing.

As always, my deepest thanks and greatest love go to my wife, the writer Teresa Nicholas, my partner in all things.

NOTES

With these notes I acknowledge my debts to those who have gone before and point the way to those who wish to follow. For most published sources, only the authors' names and page numbers are listed below; see the Bibliography for complete information. Within each citation, I've tried to list the sources from most germane to least. In general, I haven't included notes for information that is noncontroversial and readily available from a variety of sources.

PROLOGUE:

xiii. Background on the Humboldt Celt: Aguilar.

xiii–xiv. Interpretation of the Humboldt Celt: Valentini.

xiv. Humboldt quotation: Humboldt, pp. 38–39.

CHAPTER ONE:
"THE MOST ROMANTIC OF ALL GEMS"

3. Thompson's dive into cenote: Thompson, 1932, pp. 280–85. This introductory section, as well as the passages below on Thompson's first entry into Chichen Itza, his excavation of the High Priest's Tomb, his investigations into Chichen Itza's other mysteries, and his dredging, include close paraphrases of his account and even several brief expressions that I have cited without quotation marks, so as not to hinder the readability of

the text. All thoughts attributed to Thompson throughout the chapter are as he reported them (or in a few cases was said to have reported them to his biographer, T. A. Willard) and are not the result of my own speculation. Some events in this chapter have also been presented out of chronological order.

3. "Still as an obsidian mirror": Thompson 1932, p. 271.

5. "There is where the palace of the rain god lies": Thompson 1932, p. 284.

5. Landa quotation on Sacred Well: Landa, p. 194. The translation is mine.

6. Landa quotation on superstition and lies of the devil: Sharer, p. 126.

6–7. Sarmiento quotation: As cited in Thompson 1932, pp. 275–76; for original Spanish text, see La Real Academia de Historia, p. 20.

7–8. Quotation from "Atlantis Not a Myth": Thompson 1879.

8. Thompson's chagrin at his audacity: Thompson 1929, p. 4.

8. Thompson theory only one in a rash of similar ones: Sharer, p. 6.

8–9. Thompson quotation about daughters of whaling captains: Thompson 1932, p. 15.

9. Description of Mérida on Thompson's arrival: Thompson 1932, pp. 36–37.

9. Thompson's house-building; "white heat" quotation: Thompson 1932, pp. 38–39.

9. Thompson's entry into Chichen Itza: Thompson 1932, p. 193. See first note in this chapter.

10–11. History of Chichen Itza: Schele and Freidel, p. 349ff; Sharer, p. 558ff; Ringle, Negrón, and Bey.

11. Montejo anointed the pyramid his "castle": Thompson 1932, p. 216.

12. Putnam quotation: "1893 World's Columbian Exhibition Collection," website of the Field Museum (http://fieldmuseum .org).

12. Quotation on the near ruin of Thompson's health: Thompson 1929, p. 7.

13. Quotation from the Massachusetts Board of Managers: Cited in Thompson 1932, p. 149.

14. Henrietta gave birth to seven more children: Reports of the number of Thompson children are conflicting, but this is according to "Ancestors of Ernest Hamblin Thompson" at www.ancestry.com.

14–16. Excavation of High Priest's Temple: Thompson 1938. See first note in this chapter. Thompson identified the white vase as alabaster, but subsequent tests have shown it to be marble.

15. "Sprawled out like a lizard": Thompson 1938.

15. Dialogue concerning the mouth of hell: Thompson 1932, p. 262.

16. Thompson quotation concerning the "tomb of the great priest": Thompson 1932.

17. Thompson quotation regarding Yankee riggers: Willard, p. 104.

17. Thompson quotations regarding "average native" and "fertile zone": Thompson 1932, p. 270.

19. Thompson quotation regarding "muck and rocks": Thompson 1932, p. 271.

19–20. Description of dredging and quotations regarding the "weirdest part of the weird undertaking" and "many deeps and hollows": Thompson 1932, p. 271ff. See first note in this chapter.

20. Wise man's quotation regarding *pom* and Thompson's quotation that he "slept soundly and long": Thompson 1932, p. 274.

20–21. Thompson's bailing out of fishermen and report on *chicle*: *New York Times* 1901 and 1906.

21. Thompson limited himself to two hours' diving per day: Willard, p. 128.

21. The greatest treasure ever recovered in the Americas: Orrin C. Shane III, curator of archaeology, Science Museum of Minnesota, quoted in Blake.

21. Inventory of items removed from Sacred Well: Coggins and Shane; Willard, p. 284.

22. No other collection of jades covers such a wide period of time or such a variety of styles: Proskouriakoff, p. ix.

22–23. Announcement of Thompson's find, and Merriam and Saville's assessment: *New York Times* 1923.

23. Anecdote of broken statue: Thompson 1932, p. 178.

23. "*Bey ani*" quotation: Thompson 1929, p. 12.

23. Government purchase of Chichen Itza in 2010: www.art daily.org.

23–24. Chichen jades returned "as gesture to promote international understanding": Williams, p. vii.

25. Ramírez quotation criticizing Thompson's work at the Sacred Cenote: Ramírez, p. 4. The translation is mine.

25. Coggins quotation about Thompson: Personal interview.

25. Coe quotation about Thompson: Personal interview.

25. Thompson quotation defending his work: Thompson 1932, p. 299.

25–26. Thompson quotation that jade is the most romantic of all gems: Thompson 1932, p. 294.

26. Jade is "the green gold of the Maya": Elisabeth Wagner, quoted in Grube, p. 66.

26. Thompson quotation on durability of jade: Thompson 1932, p. 296.

27. Association of jade with wind and breath: Taube 2005.

27. J. Eric Thompson quotation: J. E. S. Thompson.

27. Cortés's meeting with Pitalpitoque: Díaz del Castillo, pp. 93–94. The translation is mine.

28. Thompson quotation about mystery of jade: Thompson 1932, p. 294.

28–29. Kunz quotation on the heartache of jade: Kunz.

29. Unconfirmed rumors of jade being discovered in Mexico: Proskouriakoff, p. 2.

CHAPTER TWO:
OLMEC BLUE

For general information on the Olmecs, I have relied most heavily on Richard A. Diehl's *The Olmecs*.

31. Stirling's excavation at Tres Zapotes: Stirling 1939.

31–32. Stirling's "Great American Sphinx" quotation: Stirling 1939.

32–33. Stirling biographical details: Coe 1981; Pugh.

33. Stirling encounter with small blue Olmec mask: Pugh.

34. Stirling quotations on the second journey to Tres Zapotes: Stirling 1939.

34. Stirling's observation that archaeologists made some of their best discoveries soon after arrival: As repeated by Michael D. Coe, personal interview.

34–35. Stirling quotations concerning the stone box and the discovery of Stela C: Stirling 1939.

35–37. Maya calendar and deciphering Stela C: Stirling 1939; Pugh; and Coe 1968, pp. 45 and 47.

35. Possible origins of the 260-day calendar: Stuart, pp. 156–58.

36. Schele and Freidel quotation on Maya and cycles of history: Schele and Freidel, p. 18.

37. Stirling's speculations on Stela C: Stirling 1939.

39. Stirling quotation on the Olmecs as basis of Maya and other cultures: Stirling 1940.

40. Physical description of the Olmecs: Diehl, p. 13.

40. Stirling excavations at La Venta: Stirling and Stirling; Stirling 1943.

41. La Venta pyramid may have been square: Diehl, pp. 63–64.

41–42. Stirling quotation on carving of seated woman: Stirling and Stirling.

42. La Venta seated woman one of the great masterpieces of Mexican art: Alfonso Caso, cited in Pugh, p. 8.

43. Perhaps the Olmec kings weren't considered dead: Charles C. Mann has made a similar speculation concerning the Inca; see Mann, p. 98.

43. Heyerdahl speculations: Heyerdahl.

43. Similarities between Olmec and Chinese cultures: Coe 1993, p. 45.

45. Size of La Venta: acreage, Diehl, p. 60; population, Robert Heizer, as reported in Coe and Koontz, p. 74.

45. Decline of La Venta: Diehl, pp. 81–82.

46. Quotation on Stirling's supposed illiteracy: Stirling 1939.

46. Stirling's appraisal of carved infant: Stirling 1941.

46. Diehl quotation on San Lorenzo real estate: Diehl, p. 29.

46. Population of San Lorenzo: Scarborough and Clark, p. 4.

47. Fall of San Lorenzo, Diehl, pp. 58–59.

47. Speculation on lack of jade at San Lorenzo: Stark, p. 54.

47–48. Coe speculation on lack of jade at San Lorenzo: Personal interview.

47. Stirling's unsuccessful 1964 search for source of Olmec jade: Pohorilenko.

48. Coe's reflections on Stirling: Personal interview; Coe 1981.

48. Stirling quotation on satisfactions of his career: Stirling 1947.

48. Marion Stirling quotation that Tres Zapotes was most exciting: Pugh.

48. Diehl quotation on the Olmec story: Diehl, p. 10.

48–49. Geographic extent of Olmecs: Coe and Koontz, p. 66.

49. Spread of Olmec culture: Robert Sharer, personal communication; Diehl, pp. 126–27.

49. The Olmecs may have used writing to identify the images on their monuments: Schele and Mathews, p. 18.

50. Stirling quotation that the Olmecs were among America's great artists: Stirling 1947.

50. Source of Olmecs' basalt: Diehl, p. 109.

50. Transportation of Olmecs' stone: Joseph Velson and Thomas Clark, as cited in Diehl, p. 118.

50. Stirling quotation on source of Olmec jade: Stirling 1941.

50. Coe's speculation on Olmecs' source of jade: Coe 1968, pp. 103, 110.

51. Stephens's speculation on source of jade: Coe 1993, p. 45.

52. Confucius quotation: www.about.com website, "Jade Culture."

52–53. Díaz del Castillo anecdote and quotation: Stirling 1940.

53. Raleigh quotation: Raleigh, p. 146.

55. Vaillant quotation: "A Pre-Columbian Jade." *Natural History,* November–December 1932. Quoted in Deuel.

55. Sahagún quotation: Sahagún. The translation is mine.

CHAPTER THREE:
MAYA GREEN

For general information on Maya history, society, and culture, I have relied most heavily on Robert Sharer's *The Ancient Maya.*

58. Square mileage of Maya's domain: Sharer, p. 22.

58. The Maya city-states were a "mosaic": Sharer, p. 63.

58. Number of Maya city-states: Schele and Freidel, p. 17.

58. Importance of trade in goods such as obsidian, hematite, and jade: Sharer, p. 232.

58. Some cities had a hundred thousand people: Sharer, p. 1.

59. To the Maya time was a living being: Rice.

59. Morley quotation: Morley, *The Ancient Maya,* cited in Rice.

60. Schele and Miller quotation on the king as the "manifestation of the divine": Schele and Miller, p. 103.

60. Maya invented their writing to broadcast kings' triumphs: Schele and Mathews, p. 18.

60. Grube quotation on kings' regalia: Grube, p. 96.

61. Taube quotation on inseparability of kings and jade: Taube 2005.

61. Schele and Freidel quotation: Schele and Freidel, p. 102.

62. Ruz biographical details: *El Reforma;* Coe 1999, p. 208.

63. Pyramids constructed one atop the other to concentrate supernatural energy: Schele and Mathews, p. 122.

63. Ruz's uncovering of the royal tomb of Palenque: Ruz 1970, pp. 105–20; Ruz 1996. Parts of my description paraphrase those of Ruz. Also, a few brief phrases are direct citations from him, though they do not appear with quotation marks in my text, so as not to hamper readability. All Ruz's thoughts and emotions are as he reported them or as they were reported by others who knew him; none are the result of speculation on my part.

65. Ruz's quotation on stucco heads: Ruz 1970, pp. 112–113.

65. Ruz's quotation about tomb lid: Fagan, p. 352.

66. Twenty-four "soul-shaking" hours: Fagan, p. 348.

68. Figurine thought to represent the corn god: Schele and Mathews, as cited in Taube 2005.

68. Ruz quotation that it was "the most extraordinary tomb so far discovered": Fagan, p. 349.

68. "One of the greatest historical legacies of the Americas": Schele and Mathews, p. 95.

69. Deciphering of Maya texts: Coe 1999; Sharer, pp. 135–46.

69. Thompson quotation: As quoted in Sharer, p. 140.

70. Interpretation of sarcophagus lid: Sharer, pp. 453 and 466.

70–71. Decline of Palenque: Sharer, p. 462ff.

71. Maya collapse: Sharer, p. 499ff; Schele and Freidel, p. 261.

72. Ruz's bitterness in later life: Personal interviews with Michael D. Coe, Clemency Coggins, and Ron Bishop; Coe 1999, p. 209 (including "fantasists" quotation).

74. The Maya today: Sharer, p. 22.

77, 79. Foshag biographical details: *New York Times* 1956; Schaller; Switzer, pp. 3–7; personal interview with Foshag's son, William F. Foshag III.

79–80. Foshag's mineralogical study for the Guatemalan government, including quotations: Foshag 1957.

81. Sapper's report and discovery of jade boulders at Quirigua: Taube, Sisson, et al., p. 204.

81–82. Leslie's discovery of the jade boulder: This story has been widely reported, but additional details have been provided to me by Gerald Leech, of Antigua, Guatemala, based on a conversation he had with Robert Leslie about 2007.

82–84. Foshag and Leslie's discoveries of jade, including quotations: Foshag and Leslie; Leslie; unpublished correspondence between Leslie and Foshag, July 3, 1952, to June 20, 1955, kindly provided by the Smithsonian Institution Archives.

84. 1967 discovery of a jade boulder along the Atlantic Highway, including quotation: McBirney, Aoki, and Bass.

CHAPTER FOUR:
SERPENTINE

89–90. History of San Miguel de Allende: Helm; Virtue.

90. Quotation from *Life* magazine: As recounted in Virtue, p. 120.

91. Quotation about San Miguel in the 1940s: Helm, p. 218.

91–92. Johnson family history: Personal interviews with Betty Kempe and Mary Lou Ridinger.

92. Mojica anecdote: Personal interview with Betty Kempe.

93–95. Ridinger family history: Personal interviews with Mary Lou Ridinger and Angela Ridinger; personal communication from Renée Ridinger Taylor.

95. Quotation that Lake Forest didn't have "sufficient oxygen for his spirit": Renée Ridinger Taylor.

98–99. Jay Ridinger's personality, response to Antigua, neighbors' reaction to him: Personal interviews with Mary Lou Ridinger and friends and employees John Mann, Thomas and Alma Olson, Jane Swezey, Gail Terzuola, and Maria Elena Streicher.

101. Discoveries of Hammond, et al.: Hammond, et al.

101–2. Ridinger's growing interest in jade: Personal interviews with Mary Lou Ridinger and David Sedat.

102–5. Ridinger's visit to the Library of Congress: This scene is based on personal interviews with Mary Lou Ridinger; some details, such as the exact content of conversations, have been invented.

106–7. Formation of jadeite: George Harlow, personal interview; Hannes Brueckner, personal interview and personal communication; Harlow 1993.

107. Jadeite is "nasty": Harlow 1993.

107. "As with baked Alaska" quotation: Seitz.

108–10. Ridinger's invitation to Mary Lou Johnson and her and her mother's reaction: Personal interviews with Mary Lou Ridinger and Betty Kempe.

Chapter Five:
Aventurine

111. History of Kaminaljuyu: Sharer, pp. 194–201 and 249–50.

111–25. Johnson's arrival in Antigua, relationship with Jean Deveaux, trip to Hong Kong, search for jade: Personal interviews with Mary Lou Ridinger; some details have been invented for dramatic effect.

113–14. Leech's background, arrival in Antigua: Personal interview with Gerald Leech.

114. Characterization of Deveaux: Personal interviews with Mary Lou Ridinger, Josh Rosenfeld, Bob Terzuola, and Gerald Leech.

114–15. Discovery of the Terzuola Site: Personal interviews with Gail Terzuola and Bob Terzuola.

116. Rosenfeld's assistance to Johnson and Ridinger: Personal interviews with Mary Lou Ridinger and Josh Rosenfeld.

118. Sedat quotation that "the story sells the stone": Personal interview.

120. History of Copan and Quirigua: Sharer, p. 482.

125–29. History of Guatemala, including the civil war: Woodward.

127–28. Eisenhower quotations: Eisenhower, pp. 421–26.

128–29. Assassination of John Gordon Mein, including quotations: *Time* 1968.

CHAPTER SIX:
JADEITE

Ridinger and Johnson's discoveries of jade and vicissitudes of their business, throughout this chapter, including all quotes not otherwise attributed: Mary Lou Ridinger, personal interviews.

134. Archaeologists' suspicion and resentment toward the Ridingers: Personal interviews with Mary Lou Ridinger, Ron Bishop, and David Sedat.

134. Coe's quotation that the mortal sin is not to publish: Personal interview.

135–37. Ancient jade working techniques: Bob Terzuola, personal interview; Foshag 1957.

137–39. Modern jade-working techniques: Personal interviews with Vinicio Jérez and Bob Terzuola.

139. Adage from Chinese jade carvers: Ward 1987.

141. Angela Ridinger reminiscences: Personal interview.

143–44. *New York Times* article: Treaster.

144–45. Guatemalan earthquake: *Time,* February 16 and 23, 1976; Olson and Olson.

147. Hammond, et al., research and quotations: Hammond, et al.

148–49. Mesoamerican Jade Project: Personal interviews with Mary Lou Ridinger, Ron Bishop, and Russell Seitz; Bishop, Sayre, and Mishara.

148. Bishop quotation that he had more questions than answers: Personal interview.

150–51. Takeover of Spanish embassy, including quotations: *Time,* February 11, 1980.

151. García crackdown: Willwerth and Russell.

151–52. Ríos Montt administration, including quotations: McGeary, Davidson, and Willwerth.

152–54. Civil war and violence in Antigua: Personal interviews with Mary Lou Ridinger, Jane Swezey, and Gail Terzuola.

154. Winding down of Guatemalan Civil War: Woodward, pp. 152–53.

156. *National Geographic* article: Ward 1987.

156–58. Denver Jade Conference: Personal interviews with Mary Lou Ridinger and Ron Bishop; Harlow 1993; Bishop, Sayre, and Mishara.

CHAPTER SEVEN:
JADE GUATEMALTECO

159. Difference in vegetation over serpentinite deposits: Taube, Sisson, et al.

161–62. Robin Ridinger's helicopter rescue: Mary Lou Ridinger, personal interviews; Miller. For dramatic effect, I moved the story out of chronological order: It actually took place in Fall 1985.

162–63. Gump's Chinese legends about jade magic: As retold in Steiber.

163. Terzuola anecdote: Personal interview.

163. Swezey anecdote: Personal interview.

163. Pérez anecdotes: Personal interview.

164. Ridinger pregnancy anecdote and quotations about jade: Personal interviews.

164. Rosenfeld opinions on jade: Personal interview.

164. Terzuola opinions on jade: Personal interview.

164. Jaime-Riverón anecdote: Personal interview.

166. Government agents turned to organized crime: Grann.

166. Conclusion of Guatemalan Civil War: Woodward, pp. 143–67.

166–67. Recovery of Guatemala National Police archives: Smith.

167–68. Discovery of lavender jade, including quotations: Mary Lou Ridinger, personal interview.

168–69. Ridingers' discoveries of additional jade sources: Mary Lou Ridinger, personal interview.

169–70. Ventana Mining activities: Personal interview with John Cleary.

170–71. Jake Ridinger discoveries: Personal interviews with Mary Lou Ridinger and Jake Ridinger.

171. Quotation on their mission and other information on Explorers Club: Explorers Club website, www.explorers.org.

171. Clinton anecdote: Raquel Pérez, personal interview.

172–73. Ridingers' problems with poachers: Mary Lou Ridinger, personal interview.

172. Reason for belated Chinese interest in Guatemalan jade: Gerald Leech, personal interview.

173–75. Theft from the Camino Real: Mary Lou Ridinger, personal interview.

176–77. Recovery of mask from La Democracia: Mary Lou Ridinger, personal interview.

178. Mary Lou Ridinger comments on preventing overexploitation of Guatemalan jade, including "non-invasive" quotation: Personal interview.

178. Burmese jade industry: Levy and Scott-Clark.

178. Observation that lack of salability is the key to the small size of Guatemalan jade industry: Personal interview with Virginia Sisson.

179. Mary Lou Ridinger's reflections on her life and quotations: Personal interview.

179. Visits of Robert Leslie: Mary Lou Ridinger, personal interview.

179. Mary Lou Ridinger quotation and other information on restoring national pride: Personal interview.

180. Anecdote of ambassador's wife and quotation: Mary Lou Ridinger, personal interview.

180. Ridingers had found just three small cobbles of imperial green: Angela Ridinger, personal interview.

CHAPTER EIGHT:
LOS JADEROS

The narrative of *Los Jaderos'* discovery is based on a number of published sources listed in the Bibliography—Sisson; Taube, Sisson, et al.; Seitz; Seitz, et al.; Associated Press; Broad; and Abrams—plus my interviews and personal communications with George Harlow, Russell Seitz, Virginia Sisson, and Karl Taube. I've listed below the sources of quotations and other specific information.

185. Seitz quotation on funny-looking jade: Associated Press.

185. Antigua jade "opaque," "oatmeal-colored," and "worthless": Russell Seitz, personal interview; "inexportably bad": Seitz.

185. Seitz quotation, "Lordy . . . where did it come from?": Broad.

186. Seitz was "thunderstruck": Associated Press.

186. Seitz quotation, "not just a bunch of boulders . . . competent vein of jadeite": Associated Press.

186. Seitz quotation that, though it was "not grade A . . .": Broad.

187. The consensus had been that jade would be discovered only north of the Motagua Fault and subsequent discoveries south of the fault: Taube, Sisson, et al.

187. Harlow quotation concerning "the big one": Broad.

187. The discovery expanded the size of jade deposits in Guatemala by at least sixfold: Seitz, et al.

187. Most of the jade was a "dull sea . . .": Seitz.

187. Harlow quotation that you couldn't make much jewelry of it: Associated Press.

187. Sisson quotation with comparison to Burmese jade: Broad.

187. "Bus-sized" boulders: Broad.

188. People were returning to the *campo*: Virginia Sisson, personal interview.

188. Hurricane Mitch damage figures: Inter-American Development Bank.

188. Hurricane Mitch "a perfect storm": Seitz.

188. *Antiquity* article: Seitz, et al.

188. *New York Times* article: Broad.

189. Associated Press article: Associated Press.

189. Sabloff quotation: Associated Press.

189. Escobedo quotation: Broad.

189. Reaction of Guillermo Díaz, Philip Juárez-Paz, and Guatemalan government: Elton.

190. Seitz quotation on "utter bilge": Personal communication.

190. Harlow's estimate of size of jade field: Personal communication.

190. Juárez-Paz quotation about wanting mining to grow: Horowitz.

190. Harlow's apology: Elton.

190. Harlow, et al. had never asked for a license in the past: Horowitz.

190. Seitz response and quotation on looking at rocks: Associated Press.

190. Seitz apology: Horowitz; Russell Seitz, personal communication.

191. Ridingers' reaction to *Jaderos'* discovery and "lightbulb" quotation: Mary Lou Ridinger, personal interview.

191. Mary Lou Ridinger comment in *Miami Herald*: Elton.

191. Seitz reaction to Ridingers' claim of priority and quotation "One thing's for sure": Associated Press.

191–92. Harlow observation on opportunity to connect geology and archaeology: Associated Press.

192–93. Research concerning different ages of north and south side of Motagua Fault: Personal interview, Hannes Brueckner. (A summary for the layperson appears as "Jade Sheds Light on Guatemala's Geologic History" on the American Museum of Natural History website, amnh.org.)

193. Speculation on north side surfacing later and shuffling of geologic cards metaphor: Virginia Sisson, personal interview.

193. Possibility of reheating event: Hannes Brueckner, personal communication.

194. *Jaderos'* discovery added evidence for Harlow's theory: Karl Taube, personal interview.

194. Landslides or volcanic eruptions could have buried the Olmec mines: Personal interviews with Russell Seitz and Virginia Sisson.

195. Seitz quotation that the jade deposits have been Pompeiied: Abrams.

195. Simple matter to date ash but the research might be hard to fund: Virginia Sisson, personal interview.

195. Maya would have preferred blue jade: Russell Seitz, personal interview.

195. Seitz quotation on Forty-niners: Personal communication.

195. Seitz's speculations on Maya jade shortage and quotation about "ugly outcrops": Seitz; also personal interview with him.

195. Seitz quotation that jade mining dwindled under the Maya: Seitz.

195. Some scholars find the idea of a jade shortage credible: Clemency Coggins and Michael Coe expressed this opinion in personal interviews.

195. Speculations on why Maya carved mosaic masks: Russell Seitz, personal interview.

195–96. Waste deposits at Cancuen and Tikal show abundance, and mosaics allowed a greater likeness: Chloé Andrieu, personal communication.

196. Olmecs may have made larger statues to show their jade to full advantage: Karl Taube, personal interview.

196. Terzuola observations on carving jadeite: Personal interview.

196. Color trumped all else: Chloé Andrieu, personal communication.

197. Jade shortage could have been caused by increase in demand: Bob Terzuola, personal interview.

196. Jade shortage could have been due to factors other than dearth of jade at the source: David Sedat, personal interview.

197. Sisson doubts on Olmec blue shortage: Personal interview.

197. Still millions of tons of jade in the Motagua: David Sedat, personal interview.

197. Quality is a cultural term with no objective meaning: Olaf Jaime-Riverón, personal interview.

197. Quality is an aesthetic judgment: Karl Taube, personal interview.

197. Quality is a value judgment, overlaying our cultural preferences on the past: Virginia Sisson, personal interview.

197. Bishop comment on jade quality: Personal interview.

198. Harlow comment on quality as an individual preference: Personal interview.

198. Mineralogical basis of jade quality: Virginia Sisson and Ron Bishop, personal interviews.

198. Harlow opinions on jade quality and comparison of Olmec and Maya jades: Personal interview.

198. Maya carvings are executed with more detail and movement: Olaf Jaime-Riverón, personal interview.

198–99. Terzuola observations on Maya versus Olmec craftsmanship: Personal interview.

199. Comments on the lack of an objective yardstick in judging jade: George Harlow, personal interview.

199. Sisson comment on "junk": Personal interview.

199. Terzuola observations on black jade: Personal interview.

200. Harlow quotation on "taste and commerce": Personal interview.

200. Taube, et al. research and quotation: Taube, Hruby, and Romero.

200–201. Taube on significance of celts: Taube; also personal interview with him.

201. Cancuen background: Schuster; Perlman.

201. Cancuen/Salamá Valley research: Chloé Andrieu, personal communication.

CHAPTER NINE:
"THE MOST MYSTERIOUS STONE OF THE WORLD"

208–9. Coe, Coggins, and Jaime-Riverón's belief in Mexican sources of jade: Personal interviews.

209. Discovery of jade in the Caribbean, including controversy between George Harlow and others: García-Casco, et al.

210. Caribbean sources show evidence of having been dug in pre-Hispanic times: George Harlow, personal interview.

210. Problems detecting ancient mining: Personal interviews with David Sedat, Chloé Andrieu, and Karl Taube.

210. When jade fractures it makes a noise like a gunshot: Karl Taube, personal interview.

211. Advantages of river stones for carving: Taube, Hruby, and Romero.

211. Bishop's comment that evidence would have to be found close to a jade source: Personal interview.

212. Researchers stumbled over a source of the Ridingers: Ron Bishop, personal interview.

212. Sedat quotation that it would be "conceited": Personal interview.

212. Seitz quotation that he would be "astonished": Personal interview.

212. Jaime-Riverón, Coe, and Coggins belief that *Los Jaderos* discovered the source of Olmec jade: Personal interviews.

212. The Olmecs may never have ventured into the mountains to collect jade: Olaf Jaime-Riverón, personal interview.

212–13. The roadway at El Ciprés may have been nineteenth century and most potsherds are from the Late Classic: Karl Taube, personal interview.

213. The mountain soil is unlikely to conceal artifacts: Karl Taube, personal interview.

213. Taube quotation that "there is no smoking axe": Personal interview.

213. Ancient prospectors would have collected loose jade from the valley below: Karl Taube, personal interview.

213. Coe speculations on armed expeditions and government control: Personal interview.

213. Taube speculations on lack of administrative centers, doubts that Olmecs collected jade themselves: Personal interview.

215. Olmec pottery research: Blomster, Neff, and Glascock.

216. Neff's doubts that there is a geological pattern to jade and difficulty of interpreting jade data: Personal interview.

217. Bishop quotation on "pseudoprobability analysis": Personal interview.

217–18. Research on Pakal's mask and Teotihuacan jade, methods of determining geographical patterns, and promise of isotope testing: Hector Neff, personal interview.

218. Isotope testing: Mostafa Fayek, personal interview.

219. Neff quotation that "sometimes the world isn't cut up the way we'd like": Personal interview.

219–20. Harlow's disappointment with chemical match and following observations: Personal interview.

220. Bishop's early doubts that the source of Olmec blue had been found: Elton.

220. Recent Bishop quotation that there is still no evidence: Personal interview.

220–21. Neff and Taube quotations on narrative in archaeology: Personal interviews.

221. Thompson quotation on High Priest's Temple: Thompson 1938.

221. Sabloff quotation on the role of hypotheses in archaeology: Personal interview.

221. Sedat quotation on multiple explanations from the same data: Personal interview.

222. Further analysis shows that the Olmecs may also have imported pottery: Robert Sharer, personal communication.

222. Bishop quotation on making up the best possible story you can: Personal interview.

222. Sedat quotation about stories being grounded in evidence: Personal interview.

223. Coe observation on trade route disruption: Personal interview.

223. Sedat quotation on competition for jade: Personal interview.

224. Bishop quotation on "huge mystery": Personal interview.

224. Sedat quotation on "magical mystery": Personal interview.

224. Thompson quotation: Thompson 1932, p. 294.

EPILOGUE

225. The family's wondering about the cause of Jay Ridinger's cancer: Personal interview, Mary Lou Ridinger.

BIBLIOGRAPHY

Abrams, Michael. "Rare-Jade Riddle Cracked." *Archaeology,* January 2003.

Aguilar, Manuel. "The Olmec Humboldt Axe and the Aztec Symbol Atl-Tlachinolli," in *U Mut Maya,* Volume VI. Tom and Carolyn Jones (eds.). Arcata, CA: Tom & Carolyn Jones, 1997.

Artdaily.org (no byline, no date). "Mexican State of Yucatan Buys Archaeological Site of Chichen Itza from Private Landowner."

Associated Press (no byline). "Scientists Solve Jade Mystery: Source of Olmec Treasure Discovered in Guatemala." June 6, 2002.

Benson, Elizabeth P. (ed.). *The Olmec and Their Neighbors: Essays in Memory of Matthew W. Stirling.* Washington: Dumbarton Oaks Research Library and Collections, 1981.

Bishop, Ronald L., Edward V. Sayre, and Joan Mishara. "Compositional and Structural Characterization of Maya and Costa Rican Jades," in Lange (1993), pp. 30–60.

Blake, Patricia. "Treasures from the Jungle." *Time,* July 15, 1985.

Blomster, Jeffrey P., Hector Neff, and Michael D. Glascock. "Olmec Pottery Production and Export in Ancient Mexico Determined through Elemental Analysis." *Science,* February 18, 2005.

Broad, William J. "In Guatemala, a Rhode Island-Size Jade Load." *New York Times,* May 22, 2002.

Brueckner, Hannes K., Hans G. Avé Lallemant, Virginia B. Sisson, George E. Harlow, Sidney R. Hemming, Uwe Martens, Tatsuki Tsujimori, and Sorena S. Sorensen. "Metamorphic Reworking of a High Pressure–Low Temperature Mélange along the Motagua Fault, Guatemala: A Record of Neocomian and Maastrichtian Transpressional Tectonics." *Earth and Planetary Science Letters,* June 2009, pp. 228–35.

Coe, Michael D. *America's First Civilization: Discovering the Olmec.* Eau Claire, WI: E. M. Hale & Company, 1968.

———. *Breaking the Maya Code.* Revised edition. New York: Thames & Hudson, 1999.

———. "Cycle 7 Monuments in Middle America: A Reconsideration." *American Anthropologist,* August 1957.

———. "Matthew Williams Stirling: 1896–1975," in Benson (1981).

———. *The Maya* (5th edition). New York: Thames & Hudson, 1993.

Coe, Michael D., and Richard A. Diehl. *In the Land of the Olmec* (Volume 1, *The Archaeology of San Lorenzo Tenochtitlán,* and Volume 2, *The People of the River*). Austin: University of Texas Press, 1980.

Coe, Michael D., and Rex Koontz. *Mexico: From the Olmecs to the Aztecs* (6th edition). New York: Thames & Hudson, 1994.

Coggins, Clemency Chase, and Orrin C. Shane III. *Cenote of Sacrifice: Maya Treasures from the Sacred Well at Chichen Itza.* Austin: University of Texas Press, 1984.

Desautels, Paul E. *The Jade Kingdom.* New York: Van Nostrand Rheinhold, 1986.

Deuel, Leo. *Conquistadors without Swords: Archaeologists in the Americas.* New York: Schocken Books, 1974.

Díaz del Castillo, Bernal. *Historia verdadera de la Conquista de la Nueva España* (2nd edition). Editores mexicanos unidos, S.A., 1992.

Diehl, Richard A. *The Olmecs: America's First Civilization.* New York: Thames & Hudson, 2004.

Digby, Adrian. *Maya Jades.* London: British Museum Publications Ltd., 1972.

Discovery Channel. Documentary film *The Mysteries of Jade,* 1999.

Earle, Timothy, and Jonathon Ericson. *Exchange Sources in Prehistory.* New York: Academic Press, 1977.

Eisenhower, Dwight D. *Mandate for Change, the White House Years, 1953–1956.* Garden City, NY: Doubleday and Co. Inc., 1963. (This excerpt available online at www.wadsworth.com.)

Elton, Catherine. "Controversy Mounts over Jade Find by U.S. Scientists in Guatemala." *Miami Herald,* July 22, 2002.

Fagan, Brian M. (ed.). *Eyewitness to Discovery.* New York: Oxford University Press, 1996.

Foshag, W. F. "Chalchihuitl: A Study in Jade." *American Mineralogist,* Volume 40, November–December 1955, pp. 1062–70.

————. *Mineralogical Studies on Guatemalan Jade.* Washington: Smithsonian Institution, 1957. Reprinted 1984.

Foshag, William F., and Robert Leslie. "Jadeite from Manzanal, Guatemala." *American Antiquity,* August 1955.

Freidel, David, Linda Schele, and Joy Parker. *Maya Cosmos: Three Thousand Years on the Shaman's Path.* New York: William Morrow & Company, 1993.

García-Casco, Antonio, A. Rodríguez Vega, J. Cárdenas Párraga, M. A. Iturralde-Vinent, C. Lázaro, I. Blanco Quintero, Y. Rojas Agramonte, A. Kröner, K. Nuñez Cambra, G. Millán, R. L. Torres-Roldán, and S. Carrasquilla. "A New Jadeite Locality (Sierra del Convento, Cuba): First Report and Some Petrological and Archaeological Implications." *Contributions to Mineral Petrology,* 158:1–16, 2009.

Grann, David. "A Murder Foretold." *The New Yorker,* April 4, 2011.

Grube, Nikolai (ed.). *Maya: Divine Kings of the Rainforest.* Cologne: Könemann Verlagsgesellschaft, 2001.

Hammond, Norman, Arnold Aspinall, Stuart Feather, John Hazleden, Trevor Gazard, and Stuart Agrell. "Maya Jade: Source Location and Analysis," in Earle (1977).

Hargett, David. "Jadeite of Guatemala: A Contemporary View." *Gems and Gemology,* Summer 1990.

Harlow, George E. "Hard Rock: A Mineralogist Explores the Origins of Mesoamerican Jade." *Natural History,* August 1991.

———. "Middle American Jade: Geologic and Petrologic Perspectives on Variability and Source," in Lange, pp. 9–29 (1993).

Helm, MacKinley. *Journeying through Mexico.* Boston: Little, Brown and Company, 1948.

Heyerdahl, Thor. *Early Man and the Ocean: A Search for the Beginnings of Navigation and Seaborne Civilization.* Garden City, NY: Doubleday & Company Inc., 1979.

Horowitz, Nathan. "Blue Jade Fever: Scientists and Shamans Romance a Mystical Stone," 2004. (www.mesoweb.com)

Humboldt, Alexander von. *Researches Concerning the Institutions and Monuments of the Ancient Inhabitants of America with Descriptions and Views of Some of the Most Striking Scenes in the Cordilleras* (Vol. II). Translated by Helen Maria Williams. London: Longman, Hurst, Rees, Orne & Brown, J. Murray, & H. Colburn, 1814. (Available online at http://books.google.com.)

Inter-American Development Bank (no byline). "Central America after Hurricane Mitch: The Challenge of Turning a Disaster into an Opportunity," 2004. (Available online at www.iadb.org)

Krebs, M., W. V. Maresch, H.-P. Schertl, C. Münker, A. Baumann, G. Draper, B. Idleman, E. Trapp. "The Dynamics of Intra-Oceanic Subduction Zones: A Direct Comparison between Fossil Petrological Evidence (Rio San Juan Complex, Dominican Republic) and Numerical Simulation." *Lithos* 103: 106–37, 2008.

Kunz, George. "A Gem Collector in America." *Saturday Evening Post,* December 10, 1927. Quoted in Thompson 1929.

Landa, Fray Diego de. *Relación de las cosas de Yucatán.* Mexico City: Consejo Nacional para la Cultura y las Artes, 1994.

Lange, Frederick W. (ed.). *Pre-Columbian Jade: New Geological and Cultural Interpretations.* Salt Lake City: University of Utah Press, 1993.

Leslie, Robert. "Archaeological Report on the Motagua 'Jade.'" Unpublished report submitted to William Foshag, July 1953. Smithsonian Institution Archives.

Levy, Adrian, and Cathy Scott-Clark. *The Stone of Heaven: Unearthing the Secret History of Imperial Green Jade.* New York: Little, Brown and Company, 2001.

Mann, Charles C. *1492: New Revelations of the Americas before Columbus.* New York: Random House, 2005.

McBirney, Alexander, Ken-ichiro Aoki, and Manuel N. Bass. "Eclogites and Jadeite from the Motagua Fault Zone, Guatemala." *American Mineralogy,* May–June 1967.

McGeary, Johanna, Spencer Davidson, and James Willwerth. "Guatemala: God's Man on Horseback." *Time,* June 21, 1982.

Miller, Anna M. "Mesoamerican Jade." *Lapidary Journal,* February 2001.

New York Times (no byline). "Great Maya Find of Relics Revealed." March 2, 1923.

———. "High-Priced Chewing Gum." August 11, 1901.

———. "Mexico Releases American Fishers." May 12, 1906.

———. "William F. Foshag, Geologist, Dead." May 22, 1956.

Olson, Robert A., and Stuart Olson. "The Guatemala Earthquake of 4 February, 1976: Social Science Observations and Research Suggestions." *Mass Emergencies* 2: 1977.

Perlman, David, "Falling into a Splendid Maya Ruin." *San Francisco Chronicle,* September 9, 2000.

Pohorilenko, Anatole. "The Olmec Style and Costa Rican Archaeology," in Benson (1981), p. 309.

Proskouriakoff, Tatiana. *Jades from the Cenote of Sacrifice, Chichen Itza, Yucatan.* Cambridge, MA: Peabody Museum of Archaeology and Ethnology, 1974.

Pugh, Marion Stirling. "An Intimate View of Archaeological Exploration" in Benson (1981), p. 3.

Raleigh, Sir Walter. *Discoverie of the Large, Rich, and Bewtiful Empyre of Guiana.* Manchester, England: Manchester University Press, 1998.

Ramírez, Luís Aznar. *El Saqueo del Cenote Sagrado.* Mexico City: Producción Editorial Dante, 1990.

La Real Academia de Historia, *Colección de documentos inéditos relativos al descubrimiento, conquista y organización de las antiguas posesiones de ultramar, serie 2.* Madrid: La Real Academia de Historia, 1900.

Reed, Nelson A. *Caste War of Yucatán.* Palo Alto, CA: Stanford University Press, 2001.

El Reforma (no byline). "Alberto Ruz Lhuillier: El 'Hitchcock de la archeología.'" June 15, 2002.

Rice, Prudence M. "Time, Power and the Maya." *Latin American Antiquity,* September 2008.

Ringle, William M., Tomás Gallareta Negrón, and George J. Bey III. "The Return of Quetzalcoatl: Evidence for the Spread of a World Religion during the Epiclassic Period." *Ancient Meso-america,* 9: 183–232, 1998.

Ruz Lhuillier, Alberto. *The Civilization of the Ancient Maya.* Mexico City: Instituto Nacional de Antropología e Historia, 1970.

————. "Pascal's Tomb at Palenque, Mexico," reprinted from the *London Daily News,* in Fagan (1996), pp. 345–52.

Sabloff, Jeremy A. *The New Archaeology and the Ancient Maya.* New York: Scientific American Library, 1994.

Sahagún, Bernardino de. *Historia general de las cosas de Nueva España* (4th edition). Mexico City: Editorial Porrúa, 1979.

Scarborough, Vernon L., and John E. Clark (eds.). *The Political Economy of Ancient Mesoamerica: Transformation during the Formative and Classic Periods.* Albuquerque: University of New Mexico Press, 2007.

Schaller, W. T. "Memorial of William Frederick Foshag." *American Mineralogist,* March–April 1957.

Schele, Linda, and David Freidel. *The Forest of Kings: The Untold Story of the Ancient Maya.* New York: William Morrow & Co. Inc., 1990.

Schele, Linda, and Peter Mathews. *The Code of Kings: The Language of Seven Sacred Maya Temples and Tombs.* New York: Simon & Schuster/Touchstone, 1999.

Schele, Linda, and Mary Ellen Miller. *The Blood of Kings: Dynasty and Ritual in Maya Art.* London: Thames & Hudson, 1992.

Schuster, Angela M. H. M. "Maya Palace Uncovered." *Archaeology,* September 8, 2000.

Seitz, Russell. "Feeling Jaded: The Hunt for a 300-Ton Jade Boulder." Adamant website (www.adamant.typepad.com), August 29, 2006.

Seitz, R., G. E. Harlow, V. B. Sisson, and K. A. Taube. "'Olmec Blue' and Formative Jade Sources: New Discoveries in Guatemala." *Antiquity,* December 2001.

Sharer, Robert J., with Loa P. Traxler. *The Ancient Maya* (6th edition). Palo Alto, CA: Stanford University Press, 2006.

Sisson, Virginia. "Rediscovery of Olmec Blue Jade." Website of the Houston Geological Society (www.hgs.org), October 1, 2002.

Smith, Julian. "Paper Trail." *Smithsonian,* October 2009.

Stark, Barbara L. Chapter Three, "Out of Olmec," in Scarborough and Clark (2007).

Steiber, Ellen. "The Lore of Gemstones." *Journal of Mythic Arts,* Spring 2005. (Available online at www.endicott-studio.com.)

Stirling, Matthew W. "Discovering the New World's Oldest Dated Work of Man." *National Geographic,* August 1939.

———. "Early History of the Olmec Problem," in Benson (1981), p. 3.

———. "Expedition Unearths Buried Masterpieces of Carved Jade." *National Geographic,* September 1941.

———. "Great Stone Faces of the Mexican Jungle." *National Geographic,* September 1940.

———. "La Venta's Green Stone Tigers." *National Geographic,* August 1943.

———. "On the Trail of La Venta Man." *National Geographic,* February 1947.

Stirling, Matthew W., and Marion Stirling. "Finding Jewels of Jade in a Mexican Swamp." *National Geographic,* November 1942.

Stuart, David. *The Order of Days: The Maya World and the Truth about 2012.* New York: Harmony Books, 2011.

Switzer, George S. (ed.). *Smithsonian Contributions to the Earth Sciences, Number 14: Mineralogical Investigations 1972–1973.* Washington: Smithsonian Institution Press, 1975.

Taube, Karl A. *Olmec Art at Dumbarton Oaks.* Washington: Dumbarton Oaks Research Library and Collection, 2004.

———. "The Symbolism of Jade in Classic Maya Religion." *Ancient Mesoamerica,* Spring 2005.

Taube, Karl, Zachary Hruby, and Luis Romero. "Jadeite Sources and Ancient Workshops: Archaeological Reconnaissance in the Upper Río Tambor, Guatemala." Foundation for the Advancement of Mesoamerican Studies, 2005. (Available online at www.famsi.org.)

Taube, Karl A., Virginia B. Sisson, Russell Seitz, and George E. Harlow. "The Sourcing of Mesoamerican Jade: Expanded Geological Reconnaissance in the Motagua Region, Guatemala," in Taube 2004.

Thompson, Edward Herbert. "Atlantis Not a Myth." *Popular Science Monthly,* October 1879. (Available online at www.wikisource.org.)

———. "Forty Years of Research and Exploration in Yucatan." *Proceedings of the American Antiquarian Society,* April 1929.

———. *The High Priest's Grave: Chichen Itza, Yucatan, Mexico.* Chicago: Field Museum of Natural History, 1938.

———. *People of the Serpent: Life and Adventures among the Maya.* Boston: Houghton Mifflin Company, 1932.

Thompson, J. E. S., "Maya Hieroglyphic Writing," in *Carnegie Institution of Washington Publication 589,* 1950; quoted in Hammond (1977).

Time magazine (no byline). "Death in the Tragic Triangle." February 23, 1976.

————. "Guatemala: Caught in the Crossfire." September 6, 1968.

————. "Guatemala: Outright Murder." February 11, 1980.

————. "Guatemala: The 39 Seconds: An Eternity of Terror." February 16, 1976.

Treaster, Joseph B. "Brilliant Traces of a Maya Civilization Are Newly Etched in Guatemalan Jade." *New York Times,* January 15, 1976.

Valentini, Ph. J. J. "Two Mexican Chalchihuites, the Humboldt Celt and the Leyden Plate." *Proceedings of the American Antiquarian Society,* April 27, 1881.

Virtue, John. *Leonard and Riva Brooks: Artists in Exile in San Miguel de Allende.* Montreal: McGill-Queen's University Press, 2001.

Ward, Fred. *Jade.* Bethesda, MD: Gem Books Publishers, 1996.

————. "Jade: Stone of Heaven." *National Geographic,* September 1987.

Willard, T. A. *The City of the Sacred Well.* New York: The Century Company, 1926.

Williams, Stephen. "Foreword" in Proskouriakoff (1974), p. vii.

Wills, Geoffrey. *Jade: A Collector's Guide.* South Brunswick, NJ: A. S. Barnes & Co., 1964.

Willwerth, James, and George Russell. "Guatemala: A New and Deadly Phase." *Time,* January 25, 1982.

Woodward, Ralph Lee Jr. *A Short History of Guatemala.* La Antigua Guatemala: Editorial Laura Lee, 2008.

INDEX

ABOUT THE AUTHOR

Gerard Helferich is the author of the widely praised *Humboldt's Cosmos: Alexander von Humboldt and the Latin American Journey That Changed the Way We See the World* and the award-winning *High Cotton: Four Seasons in the Mississippi Delta.* Before turning to writing in 2002, he was for twenty-five years an editor and publisher at several New York houses, including Doubleday, Simon & Schuster, and John Wiley & Sons. He lives in Yazoo City, Mississippi, and San Miguel de Allende, Mexico, with his wife, the writer Teresa Nicholas.